THE
POOL
IS
CLOSED

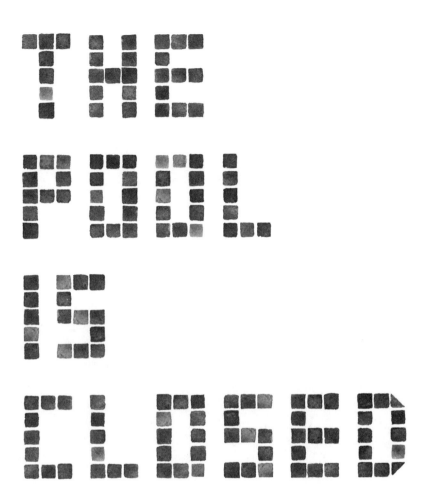

THE POOL IS CLOSED

Segregation, Summertime,
and the Search for a Place to Swim

HANNAH S. PALMER

Louisiana State University Press ||| Baton Rouge

Published with the assistance of the V. Ray Cardozier Fund and the Mike and Ayan Rubin Endowment for the Study of Civil Rights and Social Justice

Published by Louisiana State University Press
lsupress.org

Manufactured in the United States of America
First printing

DESIGNER: Michelle A. Neustrom
TYPEFACES: Calluna, text; Clockwise, display
PRINTER AND BINDER: Sheridan Books, Inc.

"The Lake and the Landfill" first appeared in *Southern Cultures* 27, no. 3 (Fall 2021).

Jacket illustration courtesy Adobe Stock / n.bird.

Cataloging-in-Publication Data are available from the Library of Congress.

ISBN 978-0-8071-8189-8 (cloth: alk. paper) — ISBN 978-0-8071-8319-9 (pdf) — ISBN 978-0-8071-8318-2 (epub)

CONTENTS

THE
POOL
IS
CLOSED

Metro Atlanta pools, parks, and swimming holes

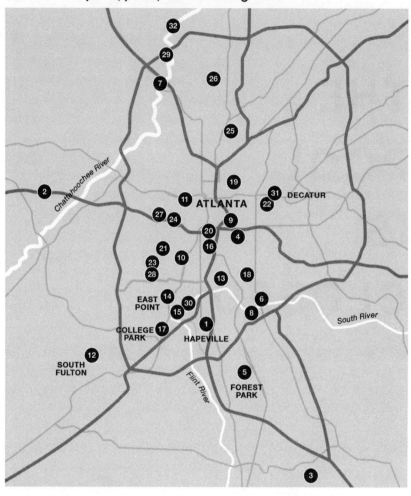

1. Site of Hapeville Municipal Pool
2. South Cobb Aquatic Center
3. Site of Lake Spivey Park
4. Grant Park Pool
5. Forest Park Recreation Center
6. Constitution Lakes Park
7. Chattahoochee River NRA: Paces Mill Unit
8. Lake Charlotte Nature Preserve
9. Martin Luther King Jr. Recreation and Aquatic Center
10. Reverend James Orange Park Pool
11. Maddox Park Pool
12. Welcome All Park & Multipurpose Facility
13. South Bend Pool
14. Site of Spring Avenue Pool
15. Site of Randall Street Pool
16. Pittman Park Pool
17. Hugh C. Conley Recreation Center Pool
18. Thomasville Heights Pool
19. Piedmont Park Aquatic Center
20. Rosa L. Burney Park Pool
21. John A. White Pool
22. Candler Park Pool
23. Adams Park Pool
24. Mozley Park Pool
25. Garden Hills Pool
26. Chastain Park Pool
27. Anderson Park Pool
28. Andrew & Walter Young Family YMCA
29. Site of Riverbend Apartments
30. River Park
31. Druid Hills Golf Club
32. Chattahoochee River NRA: Cochran Shoals Unit

INTRODUCTION

July 2017 WE NEED A POOL

I couldn't take my eyes off my kids. Guy, age six, and Bruno, nearly four, jumped into the pool with shouts of glee, as if they could swim, only to sink, still grinning, to the bottom. On our first visit to Forest Vale pool, their overconfidence frightened me.

Once I determined that they could tiptoe in the three-foot shallow end of this pool, where all the little kids were swirling around, I relaxed a little. There were a couple of dads ribcage deep, holding their red cups of beer over the splashing, ducking heads of their daughters. They would block any beach balls or toddlers from drifting into the deep water. Once I calculated that my children could safely bob around unassisted, I pulled myself out of the cold water, settled on a strappy lounge chair, and watched the driveway.

Minivans and SUVs crunched down the long, potholed driveway every half-hour or so, delivering more of my children's classmates and their parents. Towheaded Delia and her mother, red ponytail in her baseball cap. Georgia and Kelsey and their parents, all pink cheeked with blond ringlets. I was surprised to see that all these families were members of this pool that, an hour ago, I didn't even know existed.

Their faces were familiar, but I couldn't recall their names. They waved and smiled and forgave me for forgetting. They arranged their coolers and towels under the canvas umbrellas. The men started inflating the inflatables, while women pasted the kids' shoulders with sunblock.

So far, everyone here was white. I assumed some of the Black or Latino families from school would show up soon. Sonia and her grandma maybe. Theo and Cody live around here too. What about the Diaz kids?

Allison, a friend since our firstborns met in the infant room, had been inviting us for weeks. "You guys should come to the pool," she said, as we squeezed past one another in the hallway each afternoon.

What pool? Did Hapeville, the small town where our kids went to preschool, have a public swimming pool tucked away somewhere? We lived in neighboring East Point, a big city with no public pools. Like Hapeville, East Point was a railroad town that grew into an edge city on the Southside of Atlanta. East Point had sprawled to a population of thirty-four thousand, five times the size of Hapeville. If there's a city pool there, I thought, why don't we have one in East Point?

It was pointless to make small talk or plans during the afternoon shuffle of collecting our kids from their classrooms, during that fleeting window between the joyful reunion and car seat struggles in the parking lot. But Allison, transplanted from New Jersey, the PTA president, was ever inviting us to playdates and personally striving to overturn that myth that southerners are the friendly ones. Yes, I assured her. We would love to come swimming sometime.

I asked if the pool was public or what, and she was cagey. "Eh, you'll see."

Allison's husband was working on his MBA, studying nights and weekends all summer, and the pool was "saving her sanity." She took Kyle and Gracie, ages five and three, to swim every afternoon. "It wears them out," she said. "And I don't even have to give them a bath before bed. Just rinse them down and put on their PJs in the bathhouse." Perfect plan, I agreed. I heard another mom call this "chlorine clean."

I tried a couple times to meet up with Allison's crew, but pool trips with small children are a tricky proposition, and must be timed around naps, afternoon thunderstorms, and other spontaneous meltdowns.

Finally, one muggy Saturday afternoon in July, the clouds parted, and I managed to get my entire family into their swimsuits, into the car, and ready to join her at this pool, the exact location of which was still a secret.

My husband, Jason, asked for directions as he twisted the car's AC knob all the way to the right.

"I still don't know," I told him. "Head toward Hapeville." Hapeville was tiny. How hard could it be to find the pool?

I sent a message to Allison that we were ten minutes away. That's when she replied with an address.

We crossed the railroad tracks that stitched up the middle of Hapeville and into a neighborhood of midcentury ranch houses set deep in the lofty hardwoods. Between brick mailboxes and sloping front lawns, we found a thin driveway disappearing into the woods. A plaque hung from a rusty, wrought iron post: Forest Vale Club. And in all caps below: PRIVATE.

As our car lurched down the steep and crumbling asphalt driveway, into the dim forest, I felt a small wave of carsickness. I caught glimpses of the pool down below and tried to focus on the electric blue trapezoid flashing through the trees. Forest Vale Club was situated in a circular clearing formed by several backyard forests and the tall steel wall of the interstate. The steady drone of highway noise surrounded us like a force field.

"I already signed you in!" Allison called out from the pool deck.

The boys ran to the fence and screamed to the kids splashing in bright floaties and swim shirts.

We slipped past a bored teenager under an umbrella with a stack of text-books and a clipboard with our names on it. Allison even paid the five-dollar admission for each of us. The pool, the old-school concrete type with a diving board, was flanked by a generous patio scattered with lounge chairs and blue canvas umbrellas.

Jason stripped off his shirt and jumped in the water before I had even claimed a chair. No sunblock, no hesitation. Guy and Bruno clambered in after him, cheering to see Kyle and Gracie like they hadn't said goodbye just yesterday at school.

I circled the pool, staking out our territory.

This little resort was built on a series of descending terraces. Steps down from the parking lot, an American flag waved over a few picnic tables and grills on the first level. From there, a double flight of concrete stairs led down to the pool deck. The deck extended over the roof of a bathhouse, which was tucked into the side of the hill like a bunker. Below that, a little grassy area where some old metal playground equipment rusted by an overgrown chain-link fence. Mosquito valley, I presumed.

Everything looked a bit dated but solid and neat. In fact, it looked slightly over-constructed, like the same crew who had poured the asphalt for the interstate also created the Forest Vale Club.

Allison toweled off and joined me at a table. She was tan and glowing from many afternoons in this sunny clearing. I unfurled towels, unpacked peanut butter crackers and water bottles. We had time to chat about all the usual topics—kid check, husband check, work check—in that order, before I finally asked about the pool itself.

"This place is awesome," I gushed. "So can anyone just pay to swim here?"

She stabbed a juice box with a straw and laid out the details. "You have to be a member or a guest. We paid like seven hundred dollars to join, after that it's three hundred dollars per year," she said. I'm sure I looked wide-eyed.

"I can nominate you."

"Great," I said, thinking about money. "I might take you up on that."

It was so not southern of her to spill the actual cost of something out loud. Seven hundred bucks struck me as a huge amount. That was like a mortgage payment or a day care tuition check—an investment. But then, what did I know about the cost of private pools? Seven hundred dollars was probably a bargain compared to clubs in more affluent parts of Atlanta. I drove past the walled-off Lake Claire Pool and Venetian Pools in Decatur and heard stories about their years-long waiting lists but had never had the nerve to ask anyone what they cost.

I watched Guy, who was still careless around water, riding his father's back in the shallow end. Bruno darted after a water gun floating two inches out of reach. The depth was perfect for them. Shallow enough to touch the bottom and feel secure, deep enough to attempt swimming when they got impatient with their slow progress on tiptoes. They need this kind of pool, I thought. They need to experiment without floaties on, to be challenged by kids their own age who are also learning to swim.

As I eased into the surprisingly chilly water, I was already thinking about making the case to Jason. Was seven hundred dollars a reasonable price for a summer of swimming? After all, it was a survival skill, not a luxury like golf or tennis. They couldn't really learn to swim with random pool invitations, five dollars at a time.

We need this kind of place, I figured. Affordable, close, populated by preschool classmates. Forest Vale Club looked simple and sturdy with its freeway retaining wall and bathhouse bunker. I was trying on the story for size: My kids learned how to swim at this midcentury, working-class country club.

And then Allison added, somewhat casually, "I'm pretty sure this place was built during integration." Her Jersey accent reminded that she was a newcomer to the South, but me, a verifiable daughter of the Confederacy, I felt the weight of that comment. It was an ugly reminder of how whites resisted integration by building places like this.

She yelled to Kyle to put his floaties back on if he was going to jump in the deep end like that.

That's when I started watching the driveway, hopeful that some Black kids would show up.

■ ■ ■

It took me a while to notice that the pool was segregated. But so was most of my life.

Not officially, not by law. I grew up in public schools and libraries and parks, in Girl Scouts and debate teams and drama club, with kids who were Black and Latino, Vietnamese and Cambodian. My world was certainly more racially diverse than my parents' or their parents'.

I lived and shopped in an ethnically diverse neighborhood. I rode public transportation, frequented public libraries. And yet in the most intimate places—at dinner parties, church services, in meetings at the offices where I worked—I was almost always exclusively surrounded by white people.

I read about Atlanta's history of white flight and recognized how it had diluted any real social integration in the city. I understood that during the civil rights era, working-class white communities abandoned public spaces rather than share them with Black Americans. Instead of racial integration, we got a kind of wholesale transfer of neighborhoods and public facilities from white to Black. White people relocated and rebuilt private versions of those spaces.

By the time I was growing up in the 1980s, white flight looked more like a game of leapfrog, an accelerated cycle of development and migration. My white neighbors were always looking for the next "good" area down the road as soon as the strip malls started to show signs of age or signs in different languages.

Growing up, my working-class neighborhood didn't have country clubs and golf courses. Yet the public realm of my youth—freeways, suburban sprawl, shopping malls—was a landscape designed to shield white girls like me from the messy conflicts of integration. I absorbed the ideas that fenced backyards were preferable to public parks, that private cars were better than public transportation, and that my public school was inferior to the private—typically Christian—academies that the rich kids attended.

Did I ever swim in public pools? I remember at least one hated swim lesson at the Forest Park Recreation Center. Convinced that the instructor was trying to drown me, I searched for my father on the aluminum bleachers, hoping he would spot me through the chlorine fog and intervene.

Where I really learned to swim was in Meema and Papa's backyard pool. When I was nine, my grandparents moved into a subdivision of brick ranch houses in nearby Lake City, with big lawns, swimming pools, tennis courts, and no sidewalks. Their subdivision was developed in 1959, part of a national wave of suburbanization and residential pool building that anticipated the court-ordered desegregation of public facilities nationwide.

My cousins and siblings and I spent all day, every day, during the summers of the 1980s swimming in that pool, making sandwiches for lunch, then swimming until dinnertime. I learned without lessons during those long afternoons inventing underwater games. We swam so much we developed ear infections and our blond hair turned greenish and the skin under our toes cracked and bled. We never got tired of it.

Meema buried the pool after Papa died. On a visit from college, I saw the rows of tiger lilies she had planted in the rectangle of fresh dirt. I hated to see it, our childhood pool filled in, but I couldn't blame her. Maintaining a swimming pool required hours of work every day, and it was Papa's job. The grandkids had summer jobs, cars, boyfriends, and girlfriends. We were all good swimmers by then, confident in the water thanks to Meema and Papa's pool.

As I got older, the opportunity to swim became less and less frequent. Swimming happened occasionally at friends' apartments or lake houses, on beach vacations or weekend trips to see my in-laws in the suburbs, in ever more private, far-flung, and luxurious places. I wore my basic black one-piece bathing suit only a half-dozen times each year, so it lasted for a decade.

I never noticed the lack of pools in East Point until I had kids and I started to think about how they would learn to swim. We bought our home here, in an "inner-city" neighborhood, specifically for its decent public infrastructure—the MARTA train station in a quaint downtown within walking distance, with generous sidewalks to get there, shaded by giant old water oaks and pecan trees that felt like they belonged to everyone. The neighborhood itself had "good bones" but not a single swimming pool.

How did kids in East Point, without access to a community pool, learn to swim? Did they learn at all? In 2017, a study of swimming ability in American children by USA Swimming Foundation found that 64 percent of African American children had "low to no swimming ability." When you consider that 76 percent of East Point's population was Black, is it any wonder how such disparities compound over generations?

I lived here for a decade before I started to ask what happened to the pools. Did they shut down during the 1960s, the last battlefield of Jim Crow segregation? Did the city close the pools dramatically in protest? Or quietly, to keep the peace and avoid publicity?

From what I could tell, scenes of violence and protest were mostly avoided at the pools in Atlanta, "the city too busy to hate." That slogan, coined by Mayor William B. Hartsfield's administration in the 1950s, aimed to reassure the business community and to distinguish Atlanta from other southern capitals that struggled to desegregate public facilities. Opening day of the summer season, 1964, came and went, the public pools opened and were reported integrated.

But slogans are shallow. Slowly, over the following years, the public pools suffered a slow death by neglect. As white people evacuated the city, built private pools, or formed country clubs, attendance at the public pools plummeted, along with maintenance budgets. Eventually, these crumbling pools were seen as hazards, too expensive to be restored. That's the story I learned at the East Point Historical Society. The pools were closed due to maintenance issues. This is a story repeated all over the country.

The historical society is located a couple blocks from my house, in a historic home that was moved, poetically, to the site of the city's enormous public pool. Every time I drove past that building on a sweltering Saturday, I felt bitter that we couldn't walk over for a swim.

Instead, I was at the Forest Vale pool, looking for a place where my kids could splash around. I floated on my back for a while, appreciating the ring of treetops that framed our sunken oasis. I couldn't stop thinking about Allison's comment. *This was probably built during integration.*

It made sense—the era of architecture in the neighborhood, the bunker of a bathhouse with a yellow fallout shelter sign by the door, wrought iron railings everywhere, the steel playground equipment that you just don't see anymore. As the rest of the country battled over the right to shared public spaces, the white people of Hapeville sidestepped the unpleasantness and organized to build their own private pool.

As I thought about the secret pool in Hapeville, a stubborn question took shape in my mind. How many pools were still shrouded in secrecy or buried under tennis courts and parking lots? How many private lakes were drained to avoid integrating or the threat of lawsuits? How were even the beaches and rivers privatized and restricted? What if we knew the facts about what happened to our shared waters? What difference would it make?

The idea for this diary started with these questions. What if I took my kids to every public pool in Atlanta, just went down the list, the old ones and new ones, in Black neighborhoods and white neighborhoods and neighborhoods I'd never heard of? Pool hopping across Atlanta from Memorial Day to Labor Day—would they learn to swim?

And not just pools. There had to be creeks, lakes, and rivers where we could practice swimming. We would find the beaches and swimming holes of the South wherever they were. We could keep a bag of swimsuits and towels and sunblock in the trunk of the car for spontaneous swimming opportunities; I would keep a journal documenting all the places we went.

The boys were finally old enough for this kind of spontaneity. I wanted this to be a family adventure, and if I'm honest, I also wanted to escape the tight maze of our family routine. Maybe it was the calamitous presidential election that made me wary of all-white groups and spaces. In a city as diverse as Atlanta, racial segregation seemed artificial, but it was still the default. I noticed the comfortable and coded conversations that happened in all-white spaces, the way we reinforced each other's notions about good schools, sketchy neighborhoods, difficult people.

I reached the painful decision to leave the friendly, nondenominational church where we had been members for a decade, assuming for all those years that an all-white congregation was natural, inevitable, fine. That there was nothing anyone could do about it, nothing missing from our lives. We spent a few months floating. I hated the idea of shopping for a church, but I was certainly in the market for a pool.

Before I joined a Jim Crow era pool, I thought I should read the bylaws and the history. Not that I needed to expose old racism, which would scandalize no one, but to understand how sixty years after desegregation, this pool remained overwhelmingly white. Why did places desegregated by law remain segregated by habit? Would a Black family kick off their flip-flops and relax here? Or a Vietnamese family or a Mexican family—Hapeville was not just a Black and white town. Would families of color even feel safe here, in this time capsule of a private club?

I wandered down the stairs to the 1960s playground. I do this when I feel socially tired—I wander off, study the perimeter. Guy followed me. How sweet to have a six-year-old take my hand, no questions, no demands.

As I pushed Guy on the swing set, I scanned the crowd to see if the pool was still segregated. That day, at least, it was.

I rescued him halfway down the scorching sheet metal slide.

The lettering on an old sign on the fence caught my eye. ATLAS AWNING AND FENCE plus a five-digit phone number. As I walked closer, I heard the creek. Beneath the sound of the highway, behind the privet and poison ivy and barbed wire, was the unmistakable shush of tumbling water. I peered into the shade but couldn't see anything. It sounded like every creek I've ever heard. Every creek I've ever loved. It unlocked something in me. A brief flare on an imaginary MRI of my brain.

There was real water back there. I found the wet heart of the forest, invisible and primeval, winding under sixteen lanes of the interstate, making its way to the sea.

I had a lot of questions about this pool, but I already knew why it was located there, on this tiny scrap of land. The steep grade and the creek made the land hard to develop but perfect for a swimming pool. The pool was probably fed by a natural spring.

That summer, the summer of learning to swim, of trying to find a place to swim, I had just started on a couple freelance research and writing projects for conservation groups focused on restoring urban rivers. I was spending my days peering into storm drains, mucking under bridges, hiking through the kudzu and poison ivy behind strip malls and warehouses. I was starting to see repressed streams in all the weedy, forgotten margins of the city.

Studying neighborhoods plagued by pollution and flooding was opening my eyes to the ways racism was built into the structures of our city. My day job had me cataloging the sullied waters of the urban South, dreaming up ways to restore rivers and retrofit outdated infrastructure without gentrifying the neighborhood. It was becoming obvious that our water systems were designed to carry waste- and floodwater away from wealthier, white neighborhoods and dump them into poor, Black neighborhoods. In looking at sewers, it was clear that Jim Crow racism wasn't just a collection of laws and attitudes that were abolished in the 1960s but a system that was deeply embedded in the landscape. Segregation persisted because it was bricked into the pipes underground, not just the parks and pools.

The hidden creeks mapped out an X-ray of the city. Finally, a satisfying explanation of why our city—or any city—is shaped the way it is, from the first springs to the swimming holes, from the factories upstream to the housing projects in the floodplain. Lessons from stormwater engineers, hydrologists, ecologists, and activists filled my head. Part of me was constantly scanning the layers of concrete, even as I negotiated the mundane and urgent details of parenting.

To find a creek flowing freely behind this swimming pool, while I stood barefoot with my son, felt like an offering just out of reach. The site felt instinctive, like the swimming pool was an interpretation of a long-lost watering hole. Why was I pulled toward the creek? Was it love or gravity?

As we were leaving, a wiry old white man with a cooler and a boom box showed up. He introduced himself not to me but to my husband with a hearty handshake, like we were visitors at his church.

PART 1

LOST WATERS

I should start with the beach house we rented for New Year's Eve on Tybee Island. I'm afraid it was called "the Southern Cross."

A few years ago, we started going to the beach with two other families for that quiet week between Christmas and New Year's. Even before we had kids, I wanted to get out of town on New Year's Eve to escape the gunfire that erupted across our neighborhood. They called it celebratory, but I felt threatened by how close it sounded, how rapid. My neighbors were concerningly well armed.

Only now do I realize this annual beach trip was a way of seeking water. Even when it's too cold to swim, the sea has a pull on us.

How to explain the pleasant monotony of the Georgia coast in winter? Average highs in the sixties, more pelicans than tourists. In January, the Atlantic was steely blue and too cold to swim, but the kids didn't care. A deserted, blustery beach was still a beach. Endless sea and starry nights.

I liked the way the view flattened to blue-gray strips of marshland as we drove the thin, two-lane causeway toward the lighthouse. I liked that the ice cream shops and dive bars went dormant for the holidays. Once you were on the island, there was nothing to do but take naps, pilfer leftover Christmas cookies, walk on the beach, and speculate about the next meal. There would be fireworks from the pier at midnight on New Year's Eve, or we could sleep through it. We planned to cook collard greens and black-eyed peas on New Year's Day, and that was the extent of our plans. After the marathon of Christmas, Tybee was slow and kind and wonderfully dull.

Of Georgia's dozen barrier islands, you can only reach three by car—St. Simon's, Jekyll, and Tybee. The others are wild, protected seashores or ritzy, exclusive estates, accessible only by private boat, plane, or ferry. Jekyll and St. Simon's have the reputation of being resort communities, while Tybee, the shabbier but more welcoming cousin, offers public beaches to anyone willing to drive to the dead end of U.S. Highway 80. The easternmost point of Georgia feels like the edge of the earth.

At the turn of the century, the Central of Georgia railroad ran all the way out to "Savannah Beach," bringing loads of tourists to Tybee, a kind of Coney Island of the South. Layers of development, cycles of boom and bust, are still evident along the island's main strip. Tybee's modest cottages and tacky surf shops still have this mismatched, discount beach town vibe.

I first visited Tybee Island on a fifth-grade overnight field trip to the 4-H Science Center. I remembered the interminable bus ride down the piney plain, pretending to appreciate *Appetite for Destruction* as it was passed around on a Walkman. We squeezed wild sponges during Dock Ecology and tasted salty sea pickles in Marsh Ecology. At twilight, we dragged our toes through the sand at low tide and kindled trails of bioluminescent plankton. Had I ever been away from home without parents like that? On a beach in the dark? I remembered the cinder-block cabins, the rusty bunk beds where I slept with sand between my toes. Even writing this now, these ten-year-old encounters are surprisingly fresh in my mind.

I didn't go back to Tybee until the summer between high school and college. One night after our shifts waiting tables or whatever we were doing that summer, I studied a map with my two best friends and drew a line to the closest beach. We drove four hours to see the ocean, just because we could. The next morning, we dozed off in the sand near Tybee Pier. We wanted it to be this spontaneous escapade, but we drove home with the worst sunburn of our lives.

I was an adult before I experienced the beach in winter. New Year's on Tybee Island would be a thoughtfully planned, grown-up vacation, with comfortable beds and good food and a hot tub. The only thing I really wanted for Christmas.

A couple years ago, one of my friends forwarded a half-off "Winter Special" discount code for Tybee rental cottages. It was probably Meg Watson. She was so laid-back, it took me years to recognize that she was the planner of our group. She planned things like book clubs, demonstrations, and birthday parties way in advance. A flight attendant–turned–epidemiologist, Meg was a couple years older than me and always slightly more put together, more decisive. Meg reserved the four-bedroom, two-story "cottage" on the southern tip of the island: the Southern Cross.

Like every rental house on Tybee, this 1934 beach house had a goofy name. I hoped it was a reference to the constellation or that Crosby, Stills and Nash song. But when we arrived, a hand-painted sign bolted to the garage door featured the Rebel flag in a beachy palette. I cringed. Who would decorate the bedrooms of their beach getaway with framed portraits of Generals Sherman and Lee? The good news was the Southern Cross allowed small pets and featured a wide, second-story, wraparound porch with a hammock; a secluded patio with a firepit; and a deluxe in-ground hot tub.

Our first New Year's at the beach was warm enough to let the kids run around on the shore. Tripping in the tide pools, their bright rubber boots came up to their knees. This year, it was exceptionally cold. Right before Christmas, a freak snowfall had blanketed Savannah. The cold, gritty wind seemed to hit the island from every direction. Then the freezing rain started.

We spent the brief, gray days cooking, reading, redirecting the kids from video games to board games. I spent a considerable amount of time on my laptop noodling over old Atlanta maps for a project about the South River. I was trying to piece together a timeline of developments along this lost river, first labeled as Weelaunee, later treated like Atlanta's first sewer. Now and then, I would call out some trivia from my burrow on the sofa to a friend in the kitchen stirring soup or shuffling to the porch with a novel. "Hey, did you know Intrenchment Creek isn't named after a Civil War trench? It's on the 1822 survey, so it's actually some prewar reference." Or "Check this out: they called I-285 the 'Circumferential Expressway' in the 1950s." Nerdy conversations ensued.

During breaks in the rain, we dashed to the hot tub. The stinging cold air and nine-foot privacy fence made it feel even more extravagant. Except for the palm trees, we could be at a ski resort in Aspen.

Bruno practiced "swimming" the short diameter of the hot tub. Guy practiced reading the pool rules through the steam, sounding out bonus words like *capacity, beverages, responsible,* and *lightning.* The kids slipped around each other in the water, not exactly swimming but at least holding their breath underwater and approximating the basic moves. I set a timer for fifteen minutes or until they started to look limp and starry-eyed. When the chimes went off, I hustled them into towels as steam rose from their pink shoulders.

This hot tub was the chief selling point of the place, both for the grown-ups and our water-starved children. Maybe this is why we overlooked the Confederate tribute. We had a hot tub on an island and access to the sea. It felt like a bargain.

■ ■ ■

The year before, as we rang in 2017, I witnessed the Tybee Polar Plunge. I slipped away for a jog on New Year's Day; a flat island is the ideal place for making fitness resolutions. I heard the cheers of a crowd on the beach and zigzagged along Tybee's street grid toward the sound. I could hear the muffled voice of an announcer from the Tybee Pier and Pavilion, followed by thumping pop music, and expected to see maybe a CrossFit boot camp on the beach. Instead, there were thousands of cheering swimmers and revelers milling on the cold sand. Some were wearing wetsuits and bikinis, a few in polar bear suits and superhero costumes.

I slipped off my running shoes and walked down to the shore, past whole families with little kids and grandparents in matching T-shirts and custom bathrobes. It was the same swirl of people you would see on a summer day on Tybee's beaches, only instead of looking lazy and sunburned, everyone was bouncy and high on endorphins. There was cartwheeling and shrieks.

I stopped near a beaming young white woman as she toweled off her daughter's sandy hair. No, she chuckled, this fifty-six-degree water wasn't terribly cold to them. I think they were from Michigan or someplace Arctic.

"It's a tradition. It's like a baptism," she said. "It's a way to let go of the old year and start over."

She looked so cheery when she said that. This barefoot, sun-freckled, easygoing mom. She was in no hurry whatsoever as her children kicked at the winter waves.

I was struck with envy and inspiration. It was like the time I first laid eyes on a cluster of synchronized middle school cheerleaders prancing on the sidelines of a football field. Must have been the fall of sixth grade. I had never seen anything like it. *Next year,* I vowed, *that's going to be me.*

So, I registered for the Polar Plunge on New Year's Day 2018.

This year, however, the beach was slate gray and freezing. We waited until eleven thirty that morning to trudge over to Tybee Pier. Jason wore a black wool peacoat and a red toboggan with Hawaiian print swim trunks. Meg had a hoodie zipped over her hoodie. My loyal recruits. Our kids, bundled in fleece blankets, would watch with the others from the pier.

The crowd on the pier was looser than I remembered. There were maybe a couple hundred maniacs, when last year there had been a thousand. I saw a large, fuzzy Alf costume, a team wearing plunger hats, and a Prince tribute group, all shivering in purple lamé.

It was easy to make our way under the massive pavilion to sign a waiver and pick up our wristbands. The registration form said, "You do not need a wristband to swim in the Atlantic Ocean. Wristbands required to enter designated area of the beach."

It was funny to me that the vast Atlantic coast could be divided or restricted in any way. From fifth grade to college to now, Tybee was a place that represented freedom, escape, even silliness. It was hard for me to imagine that this beach, which always appeared to me so open and accessible, was once restricted to white swimmers only.

In 1960, eleven Black students were arrested for attempting to enter the ocean at a crowded all-white beach a few blocks north of here. Inspired by similar "wade-ins" in Biloxi, the Savannah NAACP Youth Council planned these protests. These young men and women, ages seventeen to twenty-one, were not arrested for swimming but charged with disrobing in public and disorderly conduct. One young man was charged for an improper license plate. The photos of the events are startling—barefoot Black teenagers shielding themselves with towels, exposed before the camera. Shirtless, angry white men surrounded them, stalking. "Take them back north," they shouted, and worse. The students were from Savannah.

These ugly scenes made national news, and ultimately, the protests worked. The beaches and all of Savannah's public places were desegregated in 1963, months ahead of the Civil Rights Act that forced other southern cities to end Jim Crow segregation.

Today's crowd, intent on "disrobing in public," knew none of this history. The beach seemed always free, even on a frigid New Year's Day.

My face, the only part of my skin that was exposed, was already sore. I slid off a glove to check the weather on my phone: thirty-three degrees with an icon for "windy." We posed for a photo with the Tybee polar bear, all of our noses pink.

At a quarter until noon, Jason, Meg, and I descended the stairs from the pier to the sand. More than half of the crowd stayed up there by the DJ booth, either changed their minds or congratulated themselves on sitting this year out.

The plungers hopped in place on the beach. The gray waves churned, whipped by wind that sent icy gusts into our faces. I spotted a team of EMTs in ski masks stationed beneath the pier. Was this even safe?

At the three-minute countdown, people started stripping off their clothes, hooting in pain and glee.

"Why are we doing this?" I screamed.

"Free T-shirt!" yelled Meg.

"Live a little!" shouted Jason.

Meg was like me, stubborn. Never backed away from a challenge. My husband, I wasn't so sure. Here was that reckless streak that both turned me on and made me nervous.

It'll be worth it, I thought, just to say we did it. To say we jumped into the Atlantic Ocean on New Year's Day.

As the DJ counted down, I fumbled out of my sweatpants and galoshes. Startled by my numb, lavender legs in the weak sunlight. My feet were on fire. The crowd surged toward the water, and I ran to keep up.

January 8 BIG-BOX POOL

School was canceled due to a winter weather advisory. The mere suggestion of black ice was enough to stall fleets of school buses, but by noon, it was cloudy and damp, a non-snowy snow day. Meetings canceled; I was stuck at home with the boys.

They were wearing their swimsuits, just like they did all weekend. Slippery shirts and shorts, bright orange with pineapple print and teal sharks. My sister, Myra, stopped by yesterday and said, Why are they wearing swimsuits? I had no answer. Just dreaming of July? In memory of that hot tub at the beach? Bruno insisted the silky polyester shorts make him "fast."

They jumped barefoot on the furniture, wrestling, zinging around the house like tropical birds. Stacks of brand-new Christmas toys still in their boxes, plus a new puppy, an adorable Aussie mix, tumbling through the wrapping paper, and Bruno said, "I want to do something really fun now."

Was this not fun? I was hunched over my laptop "working from home," which meant scooting little colored cells around on my calendar, rescheduling everything, as our new puppy peed on the carpet, again.

It felt like this happened every year, the never-ending holiday break. We lurched through nearly six overstuffed weeks of feasts and formalities, somehow too busy and too lazy at the same time. By January, some discipline sounded appealing. I stealthily disposed of the kid-decorated sugar cookies, gave away the leftover beer from our Christmas party. But we sputtered to reboot every single year, even before we had kids. There was always a sobering early-January ice day or two before the AmEx bill arrived.

I gave up on my laptop. A wise mom once told me, *You can have it all, just not all at once.* I decided to take the boys to a pool.

This was a snow day for Fulton County but not all of Metro Atlanta. Maybe one of those big suburban indoor pools was open. I remembered a photo posted by my friend Karyn, maybe a year ago, on social media. Where was that pool? It showed her son and husband grinning and splashing in a limitless, light-filled chamber surrounded by toddlers, while a coiled blue waterslide filled the entire background. *Great place for a birthday party,* said the caption. This was when they lived in Smyrna, in Cobb County. With a little internet sleuthing, I identified the pool: the South Cobb Aquatic Center.

On the drive from East Point, I pointed out the muddy Chattahoochee River and then a pair of roller coasters, bright skeletons glowing in the winter forest. Cobb County was home to two major amusement parks—Six Flags over Georgia and a water park called White Water. It was only twenty minutes from our house, but the subdivision gates, the virgin curbs, the young pines, thin and skinny, all suggested we had entered another, more fortunate world: suburbia.

We found the aquatic center at the end of a complex of brick-and-glass public facilities hidden in the woods off Six Flags Drive, along with a recreation center and the Boys and Girls Club. The South Cobb Aquatic Center was built in 2002 and, like everything around here, looked fresh and new compared to East Point.

An hour later, Bruno, Guy, and I waded into the warm, chloramine-scented waters of the nearly empty, zero-entry pool. Inside the belly of this sheet metal barn, the boys' whoops were drowned out by the shush of spraying water and exhaust fans. It was uniquely satisfying to paddle around in the warm water as icy mizzle collected on the wall of windows overlooking the parking lot. I congratulated myself. For $17.25—the total nonresident fee—we had the whole place to ourselves.

The kids' "spray area" was like a playground up to its knees in water, with a tubular waterslide and a series of spray features the children could control with big black valve wheels. Bruno twisted right, and a set of hoses stood straight up, shooting water in a high arc towards the rafters. He twisted left, and the hoses slumped down. Squeeze and release. The boys fought over the controls. The lifeguard watched from her elevated seat just out of range of the spray guns.

On the other side of the children's area was a lap pool with a diving board, an enormous waterslide that my kids weren't quite tall enough to ride, and a feature called a "lazy river." I pulled two little red flotation vests from a bin by the waterslide and strapped them onto the boys. We dashed around the lazy river loop, for a while, not exactly swimming or floating but singing and giggling. I wished for more kids to show up, but apparently, Cobb County schools were still open.

How did this place compare to old, outdoor, neighborhood pools like the ones buried in East Point or hidden in Hapeville? Besides the fact that we could visit on a so-called snow day. Out here in the suburbs, where backyard pools were standard, public swimming pools had to offer something new, something over-the-top, a new model for the shared swimming experience.

This concept of replacing traditional public pools with multimillion-dollar municipal water parks started in the early nineties in the landlocked Midwest, in the suburbs of St. Louis. The city of St. Charles, Missouri, opened the Wapelhorst Aquatic Facility, the first of three grand aquatic centers that resembled a major amusement park more than what you'd think of as a swimming pool. These facilities offered what private pools could not: a maze of colorful waterslides spanning lazy rivers and tiered play structures. They were designed to be a regional destination for families to mix and play together.

The South Cobb Aquatic Center was a product of this national trend, a climate-controlled, city-owned mini-water park. It was clearly beloved and well used, and we were happy to travel outside of our neighborhood, OTP, or "outside the perimeter," to visit. This new experience of sharing water in public was born in the nineties, after the wade-ins and swimming pool riots, with none of the ugly baggage of the Works Progress Administration era municipal pools and Jim Crow public beaches. It should be, theoretically, integrated, reflective of the diversity of Cobb County. But on this day in January, the boys and I were kind of lonely and bored in the cavernous facility. What good is a water park without other kids to splash?

■ ■ ■

We went back two weeks later, and Jason came with us. It actually snowed a couple inches, but those inches froze and stubbornly clung to the streets for days. All of Atlanta was shut down, stir-crazy. This trip to the pool wasn't spontaneous; it was drawn on the fridge calendar as a reward. I sketched a waterslide on the white square of Saturday, praying the roads would be clear by then.

This time, the aquatic center was busy with a multicultural mix of kids and parents, some toting pink gift bags to a birthday party in a small room overlooking the pool. I took a spin down the giant waterslide, while Jason cruised around with the boys in the lazy river. I was too old for spiral waterslides, apparently. It made me dizzy and claustrophobic.

The suburbs were never quite as white and homogeneous as I imagined them to be. Children of every age and complexion, Black, white, Latino, Asian, flipped off the diving board, tumbled with the current, spilled and splashed all around me.

But unlike a sunny outdoor pool, the aquatic center was neither relaxing nor sexy. It stressed me out to watch all the different families in action.

I couldn't stop staring at other parents' bodies. I noted the creative engineering of ladies' swimwear on display. The swim skirt that clings to matronly butt cheeks and had to be picked and fluffed each time one emerges from the surf. A grandmother's breasts threatened to spill out of her ruched halter. The boy shorts, the frills, the strategically placed color blocks and black stripes; there was no optical illusion that could reverse the aging bodies of us parents.

I, too, was tugging at my navy-blue swimsuit, the ultimate mom getup with all of the above: halter, ruching, boy shorts, etc., yet still falling down when the boys climb on me in the deep water.

After an hour of wading, splashing, whirling around the lazy river (which was inaccurate; the current was swift enough to scrape me along one concrete turn and take the top layer off my elbow), I was done. I draped my arms over the wall of the shallow end, examined my skinned elbow, the surface of my pickled fingers. The warm water lapped at my waist. I had a view of the entire pool, could spot the boys darting around the waterslides. With red life jackets on and their father nearby, not to mention a team of professional lifeguards, I wasn't too worried about my children drowning in two feet of water. It's possible that I relaxed a little.

I watched the boys scamper up the play structure and down the slide repeatedly, pausing to crank the spray valves and yell about it. I watched a boy about their age run the same circuit, get admonished for running by the lifeguard, but continue unfazed. A large, bearded white man trailed the boy, his father, likely. He spoke to the boy, then to the lifeguard. The kid never stopped running; the lifeguard returned to her post. Something in the boy's hyper focus and jagged movements suggested a neurological diagnosis. As a mother of a child with special needs, I recognized this exchange and watched with interest.

I assume the father was explaining that his son was autistic, but I heard nothing over the fans and fountains and shrieking swimmers. Something was certainly different about the child, his lack of self-consciousness. Not like the young Black man with Down syndrome moving cautiously along the tiled wall. More like my quirky son, flapping at that very moment in gleeful anticipation as his brother filled the huge water bucket that would overturn on their heads.

I watched the father reach for the child and miss, call to him unsuccessfully, position his body to block his path. I recognized that harried but intent expression, some faraway flow. Like any good parent, he was beyond caring about what me or anyone thought of them.

After a while, my contact lenses were burning, and it was hard to see.

And here was where my little census fell apart. My observations from the shallow end, silently matching, diagnosing, playing anthropologist, imagining myself some distance from the parenting bullshit, when I was no different from the other moms with their dimpled thighs, parents of the weird kid with snot trapped in a nostril. I expected to see racial diversity, delighted in the range of skin tones, but seeing disability disarmed me. Until then, I had not really thought about pools as a place where different bodies, aging bodies, injured and obese bodies, were on display. All of us needed a place to swim on a Saturday, to be together but not talking. Just grateful, bored, overcome by the fumes.

January 24 GATED BEACH

Daybreak. The low sunrise baked the edges of a crisp row of McMansions. The blankness beyond the clubhouse, I presumed, was Lake Spivey.

As I walked across the dark parking lot, I pulled a scarf up to my chin. A man spotted me and halted by a row of golf carts. I introduced myself.

"So, you're our speaker for the day," he said, skipping right past the part where he tells me his name. "I have a question for you."

Here we go, I thought. Pop quiz. He looked about my father's age, silver mane, big glasses, bomber jacket, slacks. Obviously headed to the Rotary Club meeting with me.

"You can follow the Flint River all the way from Atlanta to Griffin without crossing any railroad tracks," he said. "Now why is that?"

I mustered up a general answer about Atlanta's founding as the convergence of several railroads built on high ridgelines. The railroads generally followed the boundaries of the river basins. All the creeks and rivers flowed downhill from the ridges and away from the railroads. But he already knew all that. He was testing me.

I was there at the monthly meeting of the Clayton County Rotary Club to talk about restoring the Flint River where it begins on the Southside of Atlanta. This was part of my job, working for two conservation nonprofits, raising awareness and support from institutions, elected officials, and residents to help rescue the caged headwaters.

At every speaking engagement, I would meet a man, typically a white man, an expert in his field, who would quiz me about history, development, infrastructure, rivers, and stormwater, testing for weaknesses, until he found an opportunity to educate me. Once a man complimented my presentation with, "Great job, kiddo."

"That's right," he congratulated me. "They said you were coming to talk about the Flint River, but I thought, 'We're not in the Flint watershed right now.'"

"Yes, we're on the other side of the tracks," I joked, glad I had done my homework. "But half of Clayton County is in the Flint watershed, so I guess that's why they invited me."

As we walked up to the clubhouse drive together, I looked for Lake Spivey. The six-hundred-acre private lake was the nucleus of this whole golf course and country club development, so it must be around here somewhere. It was the brainchild of Walter Spivey, a wealthy dentist who had converted his swampy peach orchard into premium waterfront property in the 1950s by damming Rum Creek. Lake Spivey was now home to a curious set of South-side Atlanta notables, including TV news anchors, fast-food barons, and hip-hop stars.

In Clayton County, the name Spivey accrued an air of wealth and prestige in an otherwise working-class county. I drove next to the dam every time I visited my parents in Jonesboro, but I don't remember ever swimming in the lake. There's no public access to Lake Spivey. You have to know someone with a dock or a boat or a lake house. Someone rich.

From the clubhouse parking lot, all I could see were some ponds in the golf course.

"If you like history, you should read about the making of Lake Spivey," the Rotarian continued as he held open the door. A large table was set up in the foyer; a breakfast buffet was arranged in the next room. I filled out a name tag and stuck it to my sweater.

"The guy who wrote it came and spoke to us a couple years ago," he went on. "They had a beach and an amusement park here for years. Roller coasters, big concerts, a Wild West show, skiing competitions. It was really something."

I was impatient to finish this conversation and set up my presentation. A reporter was supposed to meet me here. I scanned the room, looking for the podium, the projector, and the coffee.

But then this man did something that made me trail him over to the breakfast buffet, where a stainless-steel vat of oatmeal steamed, same color as the gravy. He glanced around to make sure the kitchen staff was out of earshot, then he dropped his voice.

"They had the park up until 1970 when they told Mrs. Spivey she'd have to integrate." He reached for a plate and uncovered the biscuits.

"Oh really?" He found the gap in my knowledge.

"She wouldn't do it. Shut the whole thing down instead."

Late that night, while my family was sleeping, I sat at the dark kitchen table watching glitchy old films about Lake Spivey, "Atlanta's Fabulous Playground," on YouTube. They were digitized and posted by someone who received the reels after Emilie Spivey's death.

These ten-minute promotional films captured Lake Spivey Park at the height of its popularity—beach antics, barefoot shag contests, ski stunts, beauty pageants, pleasure cruises on a pontoon boat called the *Spivey Queen*. There was even a miniature steam engine winding past the golf course and the in-ground trampolines. I concluded the promos were produced, at no small cost, around 1966, when the new "Fort Spivey" western village attraction opened.

The first film was narrated by a fictional tour guide named Beauregard B. Bills, a windbag with a phony Deep South accent. The running joke was that he kept getting distracted by all the pretty girls in bikinis. The second film detailed the park's attractions from the perspective of a precocious young narrator, including commentary on her daddy's preferred amusements—"He helps the lifeguards watch these girls."

Both films relied heavily on footage of the "aqua ballerinas" and girls frolicking in chaste sixties swimwear. Both scripts were peppered with corny sexual innuendo and casual advertising to upgrade to an annual membership card, book a corporate picnic, or invest in your own "beautiful plot of ground in Lake Spivey Estates." Everyone, from the matching ski show performers to the throngs of families on the beach, looked remarkably thin and tan. Everyone was white. The southern ideals of youth, beauty, wealth, and health could all be yours at Lake Spivey.

As Lake Spivey's attractions flashed by one by one—skiing clowns in drag with sandbags for breasts, a faux Indian chief in a headdress driving the tiny locomotive, the gunfight at Fort Spivey, teens lined up to be crowned Miss Lake Spivey, blonde, brunette, redhead—I cringed at all the offensive caricatures and the sleazy humor. I recognized these tropes from my own suburban childhood. I'm old enough to remember the "good old days" when grown men engaging in racist and homophobic mockery, explicitly rating girls' bodies, then pretending to gun each other down in the street, was considered good, clean family fun.

On a second viewing, I noticed all the risky practices I've been drilled to avoid as a mom. Sunbathers oiled up for maximum sun exposure. Babies rode in their mothers' laps on roller coasters. Ski students tied dinky white flotation belts around their waists. Toddlers flocked to the shallows, no lifeguards in sight. Everyone was eating fried chicken and cotton candy but still skinny as hell. On and on. I felt too old and cynical for what they were selling. All I could think about was drowning, skin cancer, and flesh-eating bacteria in the lake.

I felt a little loopy and unfair about all this. It was a marketing spot, after all. Today's equivalent might be an ad for a beachfront timeshare or a Disney resort. As a cultural artifact, the Lake Spivey films had not aged well, but they were entertaining from a grainy, three-inch screen on my laptop at 2:00 a.m.

All that aside, the most stunning anachronism was the beach itself. It was miles long, with sand like sugar. The voice-over girl told me, "This spring-fed water is so clean, you can walk up to your head and still see your feet." I tried to imagine it. A freshwater beach in Clayton County, Georgia, was a mirage, an aberration. They were swimming in a brand-new lake, a landscape recently flooded, with virgin sand trucked in for the occasion. I have never walked into a clear lake in Georgia or anywhere else, but I recognize the sensation of rinsing pine straw mixed with sand off my feet. The pine straw floats; the sand sinks.

When Dr. Walter Spivey and his investors in the Jonesboro Development Company built a dam on Rum Creek, they did more than delay the water's eastern flow to the South River, the Ocmulgee, the Altamaha, and ultimately the Atlantic Ocean. They flooded Spivey's money-losing farmland and transformed it into valuable lakefront property.

In 1959, there was nothing quite like Lake Spivey Park on the Southside. Pristine water as far as you could see, white sand beaches, and an amusement park. The park grew rapidly through the sixties, adding new attractions each year. It was a suburban escape twenty miles away from the sit-ins, protests, and choreographed scenes of desegregation happening in public pools in Atlanta. Then it closed abruptly at the height of its success.

The Spiveys sold the park property after the summer season ended in 1969. The Spivey Foundation's account explained that they never intended to close the park, but neither did they have a plan for sustaining its continued growth. Dr. Spivey was a dentist with a side hustle as a real estate developer, and Mrs. Spivey was a trained concert organist who suddenly found herself the CEO of a massive amusement park. At one point, they hosted meetings with Walt Disney Enterprises about selling the park.

The Spiveys claimed that park attendance fell and "profits evaporated" due to "the resistance of patrons to the integration of Lake Spivey in compliance with the Civil Rights Act of 1964." According to the family, it was the customers who refused to integrate, not the operators. The 1966 films portrayed a state of de facto segregation that lingered after it was illegal for the

Spiveys to deny entry to nonwhite customers. This lag was common all over the South. As a teenager, I studied my father's 1969 yearbook from Forest Park High School, baffled that the faces in his senior class were still all white.

In the same statement, the Spiveys complained that competition from new Atlanta amusement parks like Stone Mountain Park, which officially opened in 1965, and Six Flags Over Georgia, which opened in 1967, had an impact on attendance at Lake Spivey Park. I visited both parks many times as a child. Both featured Confederate battle flags everywhere and a Wild West Action show with cowboys shooting blanks.

I read the Spiveys' explanation a few times before I spotted the contradiction. Technically, Six Flags and Stone Mountain Park were integrated on opening day. White patrons couldn't resist integration by boycotting Lake Spivey and, at the same time, take their amusement park dollars to any other park. They were all integrated, at least by law.

The truth was probably closer to what the Rotarian had muttered over the breakfast buffet. Instead of complying with the Civil Rights Act, the Spiveys changed their business model to restrict access to the lake. They weren't alone. Lots of private park operators got out of the beach business when it became a political act to sell access to the water.

Until the 1980s, there were dozens of private lakes around my neighborhood—small-scale, family-owned operations, where the owner erected a couple picnic pavilions or fishing docks and charged an admission fee to the public. As Atlanta grew and rural areas transformed into neighborhoods, highways, shopping malls, warehouses, these reservoirs vanished—drained, redeveloped, or too polluted with urban runoff for recreational use.

The lakes were always optional. No one had to mention integration or "mixed bathing" to quietly withdraw from the business of private recreation. How many owners simply found a higher, better use for the land? In one sitting, I found a string of lakes that we collectively lost, through no coordinated plan but along the same timeline.

In Forest Park, Lake Mirror Road still cut across a forbidding industrial area. The lake disappeared around 1968. The only trace of water was a detention pond between Georgia Power's compound and a factory producing Clorox wipes.

In Riverdale, Crystal Lake Road dead-ends at a rock quarry. Milky pools collect in the base of the quarries, Google Maps mislabeled them "Crystal Lake."

In Morrow, Joy Lake Food Mart still sold bait and tackle even though the lake is contaminated. The U.S. Army admitted burying industrial solvents upstream at Fort Gillem. The swimming docks fell into ruin in the late 1960s; swimmers reported skin irritation and rashes.

In Jonesboro, Tara Beach was replaced by a subdivision called Tara Beach Estates. Swimmers with happy memories of the place could buy a 3/2 ranch on Sunny Way or Sand Court.

And Lake Spivey Park was carved into large lakefront lots, each with a private dock. The palaces on Lake Park Drive were listed for up to a million dollars.

As usual, I stayed up too late getting sucked in by old maps and Facebook memorials, endless threads of commenters correcting each other's faulty memories but never challenging each other to reconsider that the good old days were profoundly unjust. These mythical swimming holes where they once learned to swim, ski, play hooky, and French kiss had disappeared, along with their youth, along with everything golden.

February 9 SINK OR SWIM

How do kids learn how to swim?

When Guy was four years old—Bruno was still in diapers—I signed him up for group swimming lessons at a public pool. It seemed like all the other moms were doing it, along with soccer, piano, ballet, and Spanish lessons. As with so many things with my firstborn, I feared we were way behind.

We met on a balmy Tuesday evening at the Grant Park Pool, a big, active public pool overlooked by stately Victorians in Easter egg colors. The pool had an austere 1970s design, but it had been upgraded with murals and a splash pad. Lessons were held in the northwest corner of the giant rectangular pool, while a high school swim team practiced in the lap lanes. I knew Grant Park well, but this was our first visit to any public pool in Atlanta.

Despite my reassurances, Guy was frightened and weeping when I left him with the other "tadpoles" and instructors. This is normal, I told myself. This is tough love.

I crossed to the other end of the pool and plopped baby Bruno in the splash pad. Almost immediately, I heard the lifeguards' whistles. Suddenly, dozens of swimmers swarmed the deck for their towels and phones.

It took me a minute to gather what had happened. Everyone had to get out for thirty minutes while the lifeguards shocked the pool with chemicals. Someone had vomited in the pool. I found the culprit, my skinny little boy, shivering blue, inquiring about the lollipop he was promised for finishing the lesson.

I felt wretched, both betrayer and betrayed. I knew swim lessons would be scary, but how much fear was okay? All the basic developmental milestones were an ordeal for Guy—walking, talking, even eating, required therapists and specialists and evaluations. In addition to physical therapy, his neurologist recommended group sports. Group sports! We laughed, then cried a little, daunted. How was I supposed to challenge this child without traumatizing him?

The next week was rainy, so lessons were moved to the enormous indoor pool at Washington Park, our introduction to another historic Atlanta swimming pool. I don't remember much except that by the time I hauled Bruno up to the bleachers to watch the lesson, Guy did it again. Cried until he barfed. Everyone out of the pool.

I put off swimming lessons for another summer.

■ ■ ■

I started asking everyone how they had learned to swim. My colleagues and cousins, people at church, at conferences, at coffee shops. The question is an innocent icebreaker. But this wasn't just a parenting question. When we talk about water, we're talking about race and class. How we swim—and whether we have access to water at all—is tied up in the landscapes that shape our identity. I was surprised at first, then less surprised, at how many people shared that they had never learned to swim at all. All of them were Black.

These stories were full of trauma. Memories of being thrown in the deep end, held underwater, overpower the stories about swimming success. Did "sink-or-swim" methods work? Could you startle someone into swimming the same way you circumcise an infant or pierce the ears of a toddler, just get it over with while they're too young to remember?

Lots of people over a certain age were subjected to the sink-or-swim approach.

Once, at Rosie's Coffee Cafe in East Point, I leaned over to ask the man next to me, a trim Black man in a suit also gazing at a laptop, for the Wi-Fi password. Dr. Darryl Jones introduced himself, and we started comparing notes about which coffee shops were well suited for writing.

When I said I was researching swimming pools, he volunteered a story about how he got the sink-or-swim treatment at age nine when someone tossed him in the deep end of the Joyland Pool. He nearly drowned.

He explained that swimming courses were required at Morris Brown College, just like ballroom dancing. Morris Brown was one of the historically Black colleges of the Atlanta University Center. Like many HBCUs, the swimming program and aquatic facility at Morris Brown have vanished as funding dried up.

He had no fear of water now. In fact, he lived on Niskey Lake.

Later I had to look up these places—Joyland, Niskey Lake. They were beyond the limited geography of Atlanta in my mind, the network of public places inhabited by white people. Joyland, a community in Southeast Atlanta, was developed on the site of the city's first "colored Amusement Park." Niskey Lake was a suburb on the western outskirts of the city.

My husband believed that bad swimming lessons were the source of his anxiety in large bodies of water. He had patchy memories of attending a church summer camp at Camp Calvin when he was very young, maybe Guy's age. He was paired with another camper for swimming lessons. The boys were instructed to hold their partner's ankles, wheelbarrow style. Jason was supposed to keep his head above water by paddling. I'm not sure how the exercise was supposed to work. Jason paddled furiously as he sank and choked, until he kicked the kid holding him down, left the pool, and asked the camp director to call his mother to come pick him up. He thought they were trying to kill him.

He must have learned to swim somewhere between occasional visits to the rock quarry in Griffin, the base pool at Fort Gillem, the hotel pools of Panama City Beach, and the swimming holes in Conley Creek. Jason still can't float on his back, but he can swim well enough.

There's what they try to teach you, then there's how you actually learn.

I remember the thrill I felt the first time I swam by myself. I was maybe seven years old, and it wasn't at the local recreation center where I took lessons but at a crowded backyard pool party. Dozens of kids and teenagers from church waited in line for the waterslide, the diving board, running with half-eaten hot dogs and Supersoakers.

My pruny fingertips were scraped raw from hanging onto the brick coping of the pool. So, I let go. I held my breath and darted around underwater, then came up triumphant. Did anyone see what I did? Kids everywhere, hollering, splashing. No one saw. I practiced a bit more that day, and then I was swimming.

Were lessons necessary? Did parents always torture their kids this way? A hundred years ago, how did people learn how to swim? I called my ninety-year-old grandparents to ask. They lived in the same small town where they grew up, in the mountains of western North Carolina.

"I never was a strong swimmer," said Granny. "Mama taught us girls in the creek. I guess everyone had their particular swimming holes."

I have never seen my grandparents in water. The immodesty of a swimsuit, their pale knees. I'd never seen her ankle deep in a creek or even in a photo by the seashore.

She passed the phone to Granddaddy. He had learned to swim in the same clear mountain creeks, the Cartoogechaye and the Wayah, that wound through the rural community where their families owned and farmed the land.

"My cousin Tom and I would swim as we worked. We'd hoe a line of corn and jump in the creek at the end of the row," he remembered. "One day we did that seventeen times."

I knew the place he was talking about, a field on the Cartoogechaye. It was once pastureland or a cornfield seventeen rows deep. My family camped there in the summers. I loved that creek.

Granddaddy explained why they didn't swim with girls. "I never had a stitch on! I would just run my arm under my galluses and drop my overhauls."

My grandparents never had lessons, but they had creeks, several of them, flowing through their clans' remote hillside terrain. For half the year, the creeks were theirs to explore for free, no swimsuits required.

"In the navy, of course, we had to swim," he continued. "They taught us how to tie off the cuffs of our trousers. Had to swing them over our heads to fill them up with air and make a life preserver that you wore around your neck."

During World War II, my grandfather enlisted at age seventeen and served on a ship in the South Pacific. In black-and-white photos, he looked so skinny in his navy uniform. I never thought about why the legs were so wide in those pants.

"Once we were traveling through the Panama Canal and had to stop to take on fresh water. It was a fine place to swim. Several of us got permission to jump overboard."

I tried and failed to picture my teenaged granddad leaping off a battleship into the Panama Canal.

"Before I knew it, one fellow was climbing on top of my head," he said. "We went under two or three times, and I couldn't shake him off. He would've killed me, but another fellow saw just what was happening, and he pulled this man off of me and swam back with him. Later we asked him, what were you thinking jumping in like that if you knew you couldn't swim?"

How could a young man join the navy and get stationed on a warship without knowing how to swim? But then, how qualified was a teenager like my grandfather, a "hillbilly" who had never seen the ocean before he enlisted?

"He said he figured it was the kind of thing where if you had to do it, you would. Sink or swim."

■ ■ ■

I forgot all about Guy's disastrous swim lessons for a while. Forgot, or didn't want to remember. A year or two went by. Then one blazing hot summer day, I took the boys back to the Grant Park Pool.

I expected them to frolic in the kiddie pool, but both boys leaped into the deep end. I watched their heads sink through the blue water in slow motion, thinking clearly, *This is terrible.*

Even when I yanked them up sputtering to the surface, they were laughing at each other. They had become fearless little boys, competing to see who could jump the farthest and sink the fastest. They saw swimmers swimming and assumed they could do it. They were not even afraid of drowning. Why didn't I bring floaties?

The stakes felt immense. This was not like learning to ride a bike or tie shoelaces, cute childhood milestones that make parents brag or sigh. Swimming was not a luxury, something we could get around to later, when we had time.

When I compared how rarely my city kids encountered water with how Jason and I and even my grandparents had learned to swim, I realized I would have to be intentional, even tenacious, about providing them with lessons and practice and access to water. Some magical combination of all three.

And so, I found Miss Michelle. Today I booked fourteen private, one-on-one swim lessons with a local swim school, five months in advance. Seven weeks of lessons, seven lessons per kid. Unless it rained and lessons were canceled, that would be $350.

I had no idea finding lessons would be this expensive and complicated process that happened in February. If I had waited until June, when my friends started boasting about their little swimmers on social media, it would already be too late. Swimming lessons book up fast.

I had heard about this backyard swim school through neighborhood parent chatter for a while. Michelle Rawlings was a neighborhood celebrity. She couldn't walk through a public place in the Tri-Cities without being stopped by a grateful parent. The kids, on the other hand, didn't recognize her with dry hair.

Every summer, Miss Michelle gave swimming lessons all day long, one kid at a time for twenty minutes each, back to back. She taught babies how to put their face in the water and blow bubbles. She urged them to kick, kick, kick. The beginners learned to float on their backs; the older kids learned how to dive or do backstroke. She stashed toys around the pool, tricked reluctant swimmers into racing her. They always won. Twenty minutes was enough, somehow, to make progress with each child without too much frustration or fatigue. She was in the pool all day, the water as warm as the air.

This would be our second summer with Miss Michelle. Last year, there were tears and protests on her patio. Bruno was shy. Guy was terrified that he could slip down the drain. I tried to dissociate myself from the drama. It's only twenty minutes, I thought. They are safe; this is important. Still, my chest was tight. I had to focus on breathing.

While the boys took their turns in the pool, I sat at the table on the patio and scanned the clipboard holding the day's schedule. It was like an inventory of children from our preschool—the Hanson girls, the Overton boys, Eboni and Sienna, Khloe and Chloe, Caden and Aiden. It was a racially integrated list, but we all represented the socioeconomic class that could afford private lessons. In a chronically impoverished area, we were the privileged families buying access to water. Some families returned year after year.

The true cost of learning to swim was so much more than the price of private lessons. The sink-or-swim folks acted like it's no big deal to learn, but they forgot that it takes time, access, intention, and consistency to find lessons and then practice them somewhere, another overlooked example of the unpaid labor of moms. I would take at least two hours off work on these Wednesdays. How does one begin to calculate the time and value of this kind of omnipresent research, strategizing, the career sacrificed in favor of the required flexibility? How did I get sucked into this hustle? Was it worth it?

I checked her website patiently, persistently, all through January, waiting for her to post the schedule. I wanted to be the first in line for lessons. February arrived dark and cold, longest month of the year. The puppy, who was probably not getting enough walks or attention, was still chewing everything, then snarling, biting, her antics the trigger of many household arguments. Both kids had some kind of virus that involved barfing. Jason was depressed and short-tempered. I made a note for next February that seasonal depression was real, that we should prepare for it somehow.

I booked swimming lessons and marked the calendar for June, banking on warmer, sunnier days ahead.

March 2 BLANK RIVER

It's not every day you get to meet a river, to discover one in your own city for the first time.

Today I hiked with a small film crew to see the South River. I have lived near this river for most of my life, must have driven over it a thousand times. I spent months researching its history and sketching out a concept for restoring Southeast Atlanta's postindustrial riverfront, but this was the first time I ever saw the South River. Today was one of those days my job seemed like a high school field trip.

The river looked lovely but dead.

We met at the Kroger on Moreland Avenue—not the one with an olive bar and a Starbucks inside but the south Moreland location, the one flanked by Laundromats and pawnshops.

The morning was clear and cold enough for puffy jackets. The four of us— Ryan Gravel, an urban planner; Adam, the filmmaker; and Jessie, assisting with sound; and me, the historian—all white people with advanced degrees, prepared to explore the urban landscape. We stacked tripods and camera gear into the trunk of Ryan's Honda. Locking our own cars, we carpooled one mile south to the confluence of Intrenchment Creek and the South River.

It was early enough that mist still settled on the power line easement that cut behind the old Donzi landfill. As if on cue, a large buck moved beyond a chain-link fence.

"Did you get that?" I asked Adam. He tried.

Footage of wildlife was worth a thousand words. It meant the place wasn't completely toxic.

I waited in the car while Adam shot video of an old television, one of those heavy wooden sets, dumped on the side of Key Road. A few dump trucks passed. Cherry blossoms and Bradford pears, always the first to bloom, filled the roadside with pale petals and the fragrance of sweet garbage. Squint, and it was a dreamy scene.

On our way south to Constitution Lakes, we stopped to get footage of a passing freight train that blocked the road. Landfills, now closed, rose like grassy mountains to the north and south.

We were making this video for the same reason we were making this plan—so Atlanta could see the potential for preserving the remaining greenspace, degraded though it was, along the South River. The area was changing fast. The south end of Moreland Avenue, near I-285, had been an industrial wasteland for most of my life; the north end was already gentrified or about to be. This patchwork of gritty industrial properties and majority Black, low-income neighborhoods in Southeast Atlanta were at a tipping point, and the South River, Atlanta's dirty secret, connected them all.

The city of Atlanta's Planning Department and some environmental groups recognized this as a moment to secure the undeveloped land and finally clean up the river. By investing in public greenspace—we were calling it the South River Forest—we hoped to restore not only the river but the long-suffering neighborhoods that had lived with chronic environmental racism for decades. But would a big park make the area unaffordable? Would cleaning up the river ignite more gentrification?

It was already happening, slowly, in pieces, stalled by the recession. By 2004, all the landfills were closed and capped, converted to solar or methane farms. When the Atlanta Housing Authority demolished the last of its housing projects in 2008, they forced thousands of residents, almost entirely Black families, to seek affordable housing beyond Atlanta's city limits. Leila Valley, Gilbert Gardens, Thomasville Heights, and Jonesboro North, once home to thousands of people, had not been redeveloped. It was strange to see vast, barricaded meadows marked with overgrown driveways where apartments once stood.

Meanwhile, large film studios were moving into the industrial sites; artists were moving to the area, looking for cheap studio rent. New parks and trails along the river meant that people—mostly white newcomers—were already out birding and biking and trespassing, "discovering" the overgrown beauty of this postindustrial landscape. Meanwhile, despite these dreams of reclaiming this green corner of Atlanta from decades of industrial degradation, the Atlanta Police Foundation was quietly developing plans to build a massive police and fire training facility on the site. Once revealed, the city's plans to clear-cut the forest would ignite a local battle to "defend the Atlanta forest" and a worldwide movement to "Stop Cop City."

Ryan knew a shortcut that led directly to the river and seemed a lot like trespassing. I felt a little nervous as we hiked the gravel path along the railroad tracks. As the green light of the forest held us, we could still hear the steady hum of speeding cars on Moreland Avenue and airplanes carving overhead, the distant beeping of trucks rolling into formation.

I had been to Constitution Lakes Park, a newish DeKalb County nature preserve, a couple times before. The park felt big and isolated, which is the point, I guess, if you want to be fully immersed in nature and forget about the city. Growing up in Forest Park, I sped past Moreland Avenue's truck stops, strip clubs, junkyards, housing projects, and rancid landfills. It's an area I avoided my whole life, now enshrined as a park. My friend Shawn, who occasionally hiked around Constitution Lakes with his dachshunds, told me to be careful. "It's like the woods have eyes, you know?" Those of us who grew up on the Southside couldn't shake the feeling that we weren't allowed to be there even though the sign out front said it was a park.

In a windowless meeting room at Atlanta City Hall, the city councilwoman for this district told us that spending money on these urban forests would be a tough sell with her Black constituents. "I was raised in the country and in the creeks," she said, "so I get it." But given the history of crime and dumping in the area, residents didn't want strangers traveling on trails through isolated areas on the backside of their property. The messaging around the South River Forest would have to focus on "raising our children to enjoy the outdoors without fear."

Last spring, when my friend Christa was on maternity leave, we met for a midday walk at Constitution Lakes. The place was deserted. We hesitated in the gravel parking lot, waiting for someone else to arrive. Did the newborn strapped to her chest make us safer or more vulnerable? Then a car pulled up, and a skinny white guy took a skateboard and a fishing pole from the trunk of his car. Without acknowledging us, he hopped on his board and skated out of sight. Lunch break, skate break, fishing break. We laughed about it, forged ahead into the woods.

I heard her whole birth story in gory detail as we hiked the winding Doll's Head Trail. By the time we strolled the boardwalk loop around the lakes, past sunning turtles and flocks of Canada geese, we were discussing day care tuition and pumping at work. The view of open water had a cathartic, relaxing effect. It brought us closer, somehow. We never saw the fisherman skater or another soul in the woods.

The "lakes" were formed by pits quarried by the South River Brick Company, established in 1892, which excavated clay to produce millions of bricks a year. In my digging, I read that these bricks were used to construct Atlanta's first municipal sewer lines, which is poetic, since those early trunk lines conveyed sewage from downtown into Intrenchment Creek. The South River became Atlanta's first sewer. South River Brick closed after fifteen years of production, but the cluster of pits, rapidly filled by the polluted river, remained.

I started this historical research back at the Southern Cross in January, layering maps to trace the source of the river and the origins of its trouble. It started as a spring in industrial East Point, in the segregated East Washington section of town, downstream from the fertilizer plants. Multiplied by creeks from Southeast Atlanta neighborhoods, the river flowed eastward under I-85 and I-75, around Polar Rock, then Lakewood, through the golf course at Brown's Mill Park, down to South River Gardens. It flowed past three former landfills, two prisons, hundreds of acres of asphalt truck lots, and into suburban DeKalb County.

As Dr. Jackie Echols, the board president of the South River Watershed Alliance, put it, "The South River was Atlanta's first sewer, and it has never recovered." It continued to be a dumping ground for generations because "this river has always been on the wrong side of town."

In Southeast Atlanta, there were vast, undeveloped edgelands along the river but no access to the river itself. Except here, if you followed the railroad tracks from Constitution Lakes back to a tall and skeletal railroad trestle, circa 1881, tagged with graffiti. Underneath this rusty steel monument, I met the South River. It was shallow enough that I could see the naked, sandy bed beneath the cloudy stream. No stones or vegetation in this wide bend, just a couple tires, half-buried in sandy sediment. Banks clawed out by flash floods, limp plastic tangled in the green fuzz of new privet. Engineers and ecologists called this "reading" the stream, this act of looking for signs of life, erosion, and contamination. I was becoming literate, and this river looked devastated.

While Adam and Jessie set up to record B-roll footage, I wandered downstream to get out of the shot. I followed a sewer line easement alongside the creek. Climbed the concrete pedestal of a manhole to get a few photos. Framing the shot, searching for some loveliness, making my way downstream even as steady pops of gunfire from a police firing range echoed in the distance. One part of me was wary about romanticizing marginal landscapes. Another part yielded to the current.

Here the sandy banks were crossed with the track of ATVs and pricked by raccoon claws. Not wilderness but wild. People were certainly drawn here to play and hide out from the world and, I suspect, to swim and fish. It was already a destination, an unofficial park, unread and untranslated by planners and storytellers like us.

March 7 RIVER THERAPY

Guy's speech therapist, Ms. Linda, called me this morning as I drove him to the dentist in six lanes of rush hour traffic. I put her on speakerphone and continued lurching northward on I-285.

She said the school year was almost over and it was time to review Guy's IEP. The Individualized Education Plan is the formal document that explains what special-education services our county is legally required to provide to my "exceptional student." She listed Guy's current goals, the ones he had mastered and a few that were still very difficult for him.

We called it speech therapy, or ST, but really it was communication-speech-language therapy. In first grade, Guy didn't need help like I did, at that age, to overcome a mild lisp. His "annual goal" was much more fundamental. "Increase overall receptive/expressive language skills" meant following multi-step instructions, recalling details from readings, answering complex who, what, when, where, why, and how questions, and initiating conversations. Put simply, Guy was learning how to talk.

Ms. Linda and I communicated beautifully. She told me Guy was making good progress, that his lovable nature and surprising statements made working together easy and fun. But that most days, when she poked her head in the classroom to collect Guy, he was gazing off into space, deep in his own little world. Content but alone.

I watched him in the rearview mirror, buckled into the back seat, sporting his little gray PE uniform with long johns underneath, squinting in the sunlight, happy to be skipping school. How much of this conversation did he hear and understand? What was going through his mind?

I loved Ms. Linda. Always pretty and cheerful, earrings matching her cardigans, she was free with hugs and advice. My fears for my son made her nostalgic. She told me about her three children who were now in college; one had overcome learning challenges. She had helped hundreds, thousands, of kids with a long list of developmental delays and counseled their parents along the way. She was confident about God's big plans for Guy.

She said things like, "God smiles on the moms of boys. You just have to feed 'em and love 'em. Girls are a whole-nother level of drama."

Today she delivered another reassuring seed that landed softly in my brain, burying its way deep. It was something along the lines of why I shouldn't worry too much. She told me that Guy had many advantages and one of them was "being exposed to a variety of experiences."

Maybe she meant that our lives were full of concerts, museums, and camping trips. I took that as encouragement to keep throwing him in the water. I heard permission to take him all over the city to swim in different pools. To lead him under bridges, to dead-end roads, to investigate storm drains and culverts to find the hidden creeks. I heard that it was okay, beneficial even, to send him to a Title I school where he was the only white kid in his class, where I had serious doubts that the "services" he was receiving could help him catch up with his peers academically or socially. As long as his education was also happening on these car rides or on the MARTA train on a school night, sitting next to a sleeping man. Ms. Linda said this "variety of experiences" would somehow help him communicate, not confuse and destabilize him even more.

Guy announced that we were about to cross the Chattahoochee River. I shifted lanes to the right so he could get a glimpse of it over the beige blur of the bridge. Once, on this same drive to the dentist in Vinings, I glanced over to my right and saw a driver huffing nail polish remover. Just as casual as sipping coffee from a travel mug on the way to work.

After the call, the drive, and the long dentist appointment with laughing gas, drilling and fillings, Guy whimpering and struggling against the nurses that held him in the chair, so I had to leave the room to keep from crying, then crying in the hall anyway, it was only ten thirty in the morning, and I was already exhausted. Years of this already, early appointments and doctors' offices and praying in hallways before work. This is how, I figured, parenting ages you.

Instead of driving Guy back to first grade, then myself back to the land of emails and Doodle polls, I made a detour to the Paces Mill Unit of the Chattahoochee River National Recreation Area. As I dropped the five-dollar parking fee in a wooden National Park Service brown box, Guy skipped along the trail that followed the river.

Neither one of us wore coats, and we were unprepared for the refrigerated wind down by the river. The high Chattahoochee rolled behind the gray hardwoods, featureless and cold, big enough to block out the sound of Atlanta traffic. We didn't stay long, but it was enough. I wanted to give this to him, to both of us.

March 17 LAST DAYS OF THE NATURE CENTER

Another overcast Saturday morning leading a tour of the Flint River head-waters around the Atlanta airport. This was a busload of planners, landscape architects, parks and recreation department directors, and assorted nature lovers. I was averaging a couple of these tours a month; this one was part of a conference on urban parks.

I directed the bus driver to an empty parking lot between a Courtyard Marriott and the airport, where the headwaters were channeled into a concrete box culvert. In the middle of the parking lot, you could look down a steel grate and see water flowing.

People were excited. They took turns shooting photos down the storm drain. I cringed as one guy clambered over the low guardrails and down to the bushy creek bank. He had signed a liability waiver, but I still cautioned him to stay away from the water.

I wandered over to Michael Halicki, the conference organizer, an expert on parks and greenspace in Atlanta. In his tucked-in khaki shirt and cargo pants, he looked like a forest ranger.

"My boys love this kind of thing," I told him. "They're so easily entertained, we don't need Chuck E. Cheese." We commenced bragging about our whole-some little explorers.

"All they want is a creek to play in, some rocks to climb on," he agreed. "We do birthday parties at parks—Morningside Nature Preserve, Cascade Springs. My son is sixteen now. He forgets how cool it is, then other kids show up and they absolutely love getting outside."

I told him my son's birthday was in one month and I'd been mulling over party plans. What should I do with twenty-five sugared-up seven-year-olds? They were getting too big for inflatable bouncy houses.

He thought about it for a minute, then declared he knew the perfect place—Cochran Mill Nature Center.

Michael knew more about parks than almost anyone in Atlanta, so I agreed and thanked him. The park was only twenty minutes away, near Newnan. But silently, I hesitated. Didn't a child recently drown there?

Subsequent research confirmed my dread. The nature center was com-pletely shut down recently when a five-year-old boy died at the summer camp.

This nightmare story was the kind of clickbait you read in the local news and—if you're the mom of small children—instantly regret reading. The information becomes part of the subliminal ticker tape of worst-case scenarios, always running at the bottom of the screen as you supervise your children.

The news articles online all showed the same portrait of the lost child, smiling at the camera, light-brown skinned and adorable. In the photo, he was backing onto a playground swing, tiptoes in black slip-on water shoes. It looked like one of those smartphone shots that camp counselors post on Facebook so that parents can relax.

According to the reports, one summer Friday last year, this little boy wandered away from the twelve other Camp Cricket campers after lunch. They had hiked to a waterfall for a picnic, and the children were allowed to splash in a shallow creek. After lunch, the four supervising adults came up short in their headcount. He was found submerged in a nearby pool.

I skimmed the surface of this news story as lightly as possible, already knowing how it ended, only testing for the moment when the tragedy could've been averted. It's easy to imagine a five-year-old rambling toward water on a hot summer day, following the shady contours of the creek, throwing rocks and watching them splash. Why didn't they anticipate it, these adults who were paid to protect him?

Georgia's state day care licensing agency shut down the nature center that sponsored the camp. The center's director was indicted on a felony charge of involuntary manslaughter.

I had a dozen different tabs open, still trying to determine if the place that *Atlanta Magazine* called "perfect for birthday parties" was still an option for my first grader when a funny thing happened. I felt a spark of sympathy and outrage for the indicted director. I read about her in a feel-good interview piece from January, before the tragedy. She was pictured feeding a chocolate-colored llama at the nature center. Wasn't she just a nice lady managing a nonprofit who happened to lose track of a wild kindergartner? How many times have my boys vanished on me? How many times have I let it happen? Negligence maybe. But manslaughter?

Just like that, I slipped into the white woman's shoes.

Easier to relate to the white director than the Black parents, whose shattering grief was like a knife in the gut. There it was—that self-protective bias. And what is that but racism?

That afternoon, when I picked up my own wild pre-kindergartner from school, I stopped to visit with Ms. Tia in the nursery. When my boys were infants, I trusted Ms. Tia with their every need. I'm pretty sure she saw Bruno take his first steps before I did. She had deep roots in Newnan's African American community, and I wasn't wrong to guess that she had been following the story too. I asked if the indictments worried her, as a caregiver, that she might be held accountable for an accident someday.

"It never would have happened if they had been doing what they were supposed to be doing," she said, swishing her long braids behind her shoulder. "Listen, I never relax when kids are around water. Even a sprinkler. It can happen so fast."

I sighed. Kids are drawn to water—it's like a law of nature. That precious boy didn't do anything wrong.

Cochran Mill Park, the public, eight hundred–acre nature preserve, was still open. Somewhere in there was the pool where the child was found unconscious, the shoals where these campers enjoyed the last boring picnic of their old life. The camp administrators were held responsible, the camp was shut down, but the waterfall went on falling, day and night, innocent as gravity.

April 4 TYBEE PEOPLE

"Any plans for spring break?"

This was the small talk of every parent I encountered last week; everyone was counting down to a week off school. I told one colleague we were going to Tybee Island for the week, that we love Savannah and try to go every year. He said he'd never been.

"We're more Charleston people."

I repeated that term in my head—*Charleston people.* He claimed the place as a part of his identity.

I had only visited Charleston once, as a tourist, and it seemed a lot like Savannah. Both were picturesque southern capitals, lots of astonishing old graveyards, frilly architecture, and oversized, smothering flora. Both cities' streets were imposed on riverfronts in an orderly grid, scaled for life before cars, with ample parks and plazas to park your horse.

In both cities, I observed the Black and white divide in the historic district, old-money townhomes alongside housing projects. In both cities, I overheard a blend of languages on the streets. International traders, new-money investors, and a wandering scrum of tourists filled the curbside cafés and farmers' markets, sweating in their big white sneakers, tucked-in polos, and bright floral blouses.

Who were Savannah people? Savannah College of Art and Design, Jason's alma mater, mixed up the demographics by annually importing a community of young misfits from diverse backgrounds, all united by the quality of their portfolios and ability to pay the hefty annual tuition. We started dating during his senior year at SCAD, when he lived in a junky, west-facing apartment in Drayton Towers.

We fell in love during those brief weekends together, biking at night when the temperature dropped to eighty, picking up a plate from Rib Castle Lounge to share, back when there was a schizophrenic man holding court in every square, down to River Street to watch the tugboats wrestle an enormous cargo ship while we ate free samples of pralines. Even the smell of the paper mill and carriage horse manure seemed romantic.

Twenty years later, we were still paying off student loans, and there was an Urban Outfitters on Broughton Street. As much as we adored Savannah, felt forged by it, we wouldn't claim to be Savannah people. It was too old and spooky, haunted by generations of slavers and the enslaved, tourists and traders, artists and soldiers passing through, like the container ships on River Street.

On one New Year's trip, we booked a boat tour through the marshes to go shelling on Little Tybee Island. Captain Howard introduced himself as a fifth-generation Savannah native. His accent was so broad he pronounced it "Little Tabby." He didn't strike me as wealthy, but he owned boats, plural, and in his retirement, was involved in restoring a lighthouse, that kind of thing. That's Savannah people.

Where we spend our time on vacation is the label we choose for ourselves. Where we choose to swim is a kind of identity, branded into the backsides of our SUVs. SALT LIFE. LAKE LIFE. I wasn't ready for a bumper sticker. What did it mean to be Tybee people?

■ ■ ■

On Monday, Eve flew down to Savannah for the day with her two young children, two-year-old Jacque and four-year-old Tripp. Bruno and Tripp were born a week apart and had been together in school since the nursery. They looked like brothers with their chubby pink cheeks and shaggy blond hair.

At first, the boys were the only thing that Eve and I had in common, but it turns out, that's enough. We logged a lot of hours on playdates talking about our bosses and mothers, soccer and dance class, finding babysitters and house cleaners, managing screen time and bedtime, planning birthday parties and playdates. It added up to a practical sort of alliance that was more intimate than most of my closest friendships. The joy of our bright little boys was the equalizer hinging us together.

I didn't know four-year-olds could have intense, best friend relationships, but Bruno did. Tripp and Malcolm, Malcolm and Tripp. Bruno talked about his best friends constantly, listed them in his bedtime prayers, pestered me to call their moms and arrange playdates. Bruno casually said we were "beige" like Tripp, while Malcolm was "brown."

In August, the three boys would attend different schools for the first time in their life. Bruno and Malcolm at different charter schools, Tripp at a private school. If they were going to remain friends, it would be my job to facilitate.

When Eve texted, *Any plans for spring break?* I told her about Tybee. She asked if she and the kids could fly down for a day trip.

Flying somewhere for the day sounded like a splurge to me, but Eve worked for an airline, so it was free to fly standby. Plus, she knew how to sail through all the stressful parts of air travel—parking, reservations, security lines. She brought one backpack, containing bathing suits, flip-flops, phone chargers, and granola bars. Renting a car took longer than the thirty-five-minute ATL-to-SAV flight.

They had never been to Tybee Island, and I wanted it to be worth the trip.

"We've been to St. Simon's Island the last few years. Before that we went to Seaside. Back when it was quiet and not too crowded. Where *The Truman Show* was filmed."

I had never been to either place. For years, I saw people driving around Atlanta with turquoise oval-shaped bumper stickers that said "30A" and had no clue what that meant. Only very recently, after working with landscape architects and urban planners, did I catch on that this was a highway in Florida with its own brand. Highway 30A linked a string of master planned beach towns on the white sands of the Gulf Coast—Seaside, Rosemary Beach, Alys Beach, Celebration—all flavors of New Urbanist utopia. The blue sticker was a nod to other savvy vacationers.

It wasn't warm enough to swim in the Atlantic in April, but lots of people were out pretending it was July, visitors and retirees, all races and ages. Runners and beach cruisers weaved around the pop-up tents, skim boards, and girls sunning in bikinis, despite the cool temperature. Snatches of Reggaeton carried in the sandy breeze. Everyone making the most of their spring break vacation. No one was out in the water.

Eve and I kept our sweaters on. The kids didn't notice the cold. They skipped in and out of the low tide.

Even at the beach, a public pool would be nice. From 2012 to 2015, a nonprofit made up of Tybee residents developed plans to build and manage "a multi-use, heated, year-round, swimming pool for the residents of Tybee Island and visitors." Over those years, I remembered campaign signs for the Tybee Island Community Pool, their yellow rubber duck mascot was all over the island, and it seemed like an easy win to me. Being near the ocean in January and April was delightful but not actually good for swimming. I looked online for this promised swimming pool and found out that voters defeated a referendum to build it. What happened?

The community pool effort became surprisingly controversial once the issue was on the ballot. At least in the press, public debate about the pool focused on the cost and whether the pool would be sustainable for the city to manage long term. Folks also seemed particularly hung up on the fact that a saltwater pool was being proposed. One article summed up the defeat with: "Opponents said the ocean is a perfectly suitable source of salt water and other areas of Tybee Island need funding more than a pool."

I talked to Chris Garbett, a longtime Tybee resident who published an editorial in the *Savannah Morning News* in favor of the community pool. I asked her if the referendum failed because of the budget.

"It failed because of racism," she told me. Tybee's nearly all-white residents were uneasy about attracting "day-trippers" and outsiders to the community.

"Unfortunately, those of us who worked on it for four years, we didn't see it coming. We were aware of Tybee's history. I know Edna Jackson, the mayor of Savannah who was arrested during the wade-ins on Tybee. We knew the history, but I thought we'd gotten over it. We were so naive."

Garbett, who is white, has lived on the island since 1995 and has been involved in community planning and politics for years. In 2000, final plans for the first Tybee Polar Bear Plunge were made in her living room. In this same spirit of community building on this small island of about thirty-one hundred full-time residents, she got involved with plans to create a community swimming pool.

"I desperately wanted a pool for the children. We did all our research. We held parties and information sessions for four years, saturating the island. We raised twenty thousand dollars. We had a location, did a survey, developed a price structure. We knew we could do it. At first, the feedback was all positive."

"But when we went door-to-door soliciting support, half of the people told me to my face, 'That's fine, but we don't want *them* coming here.'" She confirmed what I assumed, that *them* was code for people of color. "We were staggered. We were caught off guard by the force of the racism."

At the same time, Tybee was making headlines for its over-policing of Orange Crush, an annual spring break weekend for HBCU students that brought thousands of Black college students to the island. The city's police welcomed them with roadblocks, police checkpoints, and special ordinances forbidding drinking on the beach and playing loud music for that one weekend. Attendees complained of "dismissive treatment by local merchants and residents; and racism and general hostility towards the idea of large groups of black people on an entirely public beach." Eventually, the U.S. Justice Department got involved.

From Orange Crush to the defeat of the pool referendum, Garbett has seen this underlying racism influence many decisions over public transportation and public space on the island.

"Tybee is very open on the surface," she said. "But if you scratch the surface, too many people don't like the idea of Black or 'other' people living here."

As a tourist, I liked how democratic the beach felt. Anyone could drive twenty minutes from Savannah, park by the pier for six dollars, and enjoy the beach all day. I had done that as a teenager in college, just ran away to the beach with my best friend and no money. The crowds looked diverse, but then there was the Southern Cross, our Confederate home away from home.

Sharing the afternoon with Eve and her kids, I felt a little self-conscious about the unprettiness of the beach. A giant dredging rig parked on the horizon. Colossal shipping fleets in the haze. Waves churning with seashells and jellyfish, murky brown into gray blue.

There were dozens of other beaches I wanted my kids to fall in love with, as soon as they were old enough. Old enough to ferry over to Cumberland Island and Sapelo Island and camp or to road trip seven hours to Wilmington or Cape San Blas. Jason thought they should play mini golf in Myrtle Beach and Panama City Beach like he did as a kid. I wanted to see alligators in the Okefenokee and Everglades. Honestly, I'm not much of a beach person. My heart is in the Cartoogechaye Creek.

The kids brought us seashells and daisies leftover from a beach wedding. In the distance, we could see the greenish fuzz of Hilton Head Island where they must have trucked in the sand, it was so white.

That evening, after Bruno and Tripp's tearful goodbyes, we had one of those vacation restaurant experiences where the service was disorganized, the food was late, overcooked, and over-seasoned, and it was still okay because we were sitting next to the shore watching gulls hover on the breeze.

Biking back from the pub, Jason slid a speaker in the water bottle holder and blasted Sun Ra. I loved the gauzy purple sunset behind the lighthouse. I loved the muscles in Jason's back as he pedaled. The boys still fit in the little bike trailer behind him. I loved their cartoonish helmets bonking as they chanted along to the music.

We passed a group of teenagers playing volleyball in the park. We turned on Second Avenue, where there were no cars, just occasional bikes, golf carts, tiny headlights winking like lightning bugs. Through the tunnel of oaks, we spotted an old man walking two terriers. It was Captain Howard, who waved hello. Turns out he lived around the corner; he was Tybee People too.

Tybee felt like home to me, from its small cottages to familiar locals. And it was the easiest drive to any beach from Atlanta. But as much as I was charmed by the island, I felt wary of my own attachment to it. Part of me wanted to remain a tourist on vacation, unbothered by currents of racism and discord under the surface. The other part knew that ignoring was a luxury and a privilege, one that not everyone who visited Tybee could afford.

April 15   URBAN BAPTISM

Today we attended the baptism of our friends' baby girl in Decatur. As we rolled into the church parking lot, it occurred to me that the last baptism I witnessed was also in a strip mall.

My brother-in-law got baptized last Easter, or Resurrection Sunday, as they called it. We all drove down to Griffin for the occasion.

It must have been April, but I remember the heat of the parking lot, my summer dress clinging to the back of my thighs. Open Range Church, a cowboy-themed nondenominational church, filled the corner of an aging strip mall anchored by Davita Dialysis and K Beauty Supply. Most of the other storefronts looked empty, until I spotted a few Black churchgoers in their Easter finery heading into a storefront a couple doors down. We shared a cordial wave. He is risen, indeed!

After hymns and tithing, prayers and scripture, the congregation funneled out the back door into the blank backside of the strip. Someone had hauled a water hose to a big aluminum horse trough and moved some planters full of pansies around it. Beyond the asphalt, a strip of trees shielded us from traffic noise on the Dixie Highway.

After a few words of blessing, the pastor leaned Jason's brother, barefoot in a T-shirt and shorts, into a backbend toward the water. We sweated and cheered. It felt like a party.

Today little Lena Mae would be given to Christ in a building adjacent to the Dollar Tree.

We had been to this church once before to see their older son get baptized. An urban satellite of a big Anglican church, Trinity had tastefully transformed the 1960s supermarket that likely occupied this space before. The A&P or Big Star had been updated with classrooms and offices, a coffee bar and lounge carved out where the checkout lines used to be.

First thing I noticed was the number of children. The little ones had multiplied in the two years since the last baptism we witnessed. Waist-high bandits swarmed around a platter of bagels, twirled in the hallways, circled their mothers' skirts. Bruno eyed the mob of preschoolers and declined to join them. Guy spotted Play-Doh and ditched us for the first-grade cohort.

Second, as we entered the spacious, putty gray sanctuary, I saw the bellies. There were so many pregnant women scooting through the rows of chairs.

Nothing brings you closer to God, or regular church attendance, like the looming prospect of parenthood.

Third, the black, nonslip floor mats secured with black duct tape leading up to the temporary baptismal font. Picture a rectangular hot tub. Try not to picture a burial vault. Was it made of fiberglass? Did it have wheels? Could you order one online, or did you find them in specialty Christian supply stores? How did they fill it with water? Was the water warm enough for the babies?

I was raised Methodist, where this sacrament was accomplished with a handful of water from a fancy bowl, so I was inexperienced with the ritual of "full immersion." My Baptist friends cited the Greek word for a sunken ship: *baptizo.* Jesus was transformed by his dip in the River Jordan, and what would Jesus do?

The few times I found myself in the inner sanctum of a Baptist church, I wanted to study the spooky bathtub behind the altar, behind the curtain, a pastoral creekside scene painted on the wall. Stripped of ornamentation and context, today's utilitarian baptismal font seemed even more abstract. Wouldn't it be less clumsy to take the church out to the water than to bring the water into the church? I figured the Holy Spirit could work through a sprinkle just as well as a lake, but it struck me that that full immersion sets a higher environmental standard: water clean enough to stick your face in it.

Fourth, I noticed the babies. The front row was full of mothers and fathers holding infants dressed in fluffy white gowns. I forgot that they always baptize the Sunday after Easter, and a year's worth of youngsters were waiting for this day.

Fifth, the grief. During the first act of the service, the maximum volume praise-and-worship set before the baptizing began, I noticed women weeping modestly while the band wailed. I saw them mouthing prayers and giving each other knowing squeezes. I would've bet my bagel they were praying over miscarriages or missed periods, ultrasounds and HCG levels, amniocentesis, and rounds of IVF. I had forgotten, as quickly as possible actually, the all-consuming predicament of fertility, the desperate prayers of hope and longing. The sight of all these baby bumps and infants was painful for them; the sight of these women was triggering for me.

Finally, the sweet moment arrived. Our friends joined the parade of husbands and wives and babies at the holy bathtub. Each child was baptized with a brief but personal dedication, a handful of water smoothed over their fuzzy heads—in the name of the Father, the Son, and the Holy Spirit—a photo, a blessing, and a towel. No dunking, no tears, no mess.

Lena Mae glowed with reflected light as her mom held her over the water. She gazed at the rippled surface with wonder or tolerance, I'm not sure. Who can say what babies remember about water?

Later, I was thinking about how Atlantans used to worship on rivers and creeks. Researching for urban river restoration projects, I've heard many stories of baptism in Proctor Creek and Peachtree Creek—but they're always set in the distant past, accompanied by black-and-white photos. The whole choir, fully robed, going down to the river to pray. When my teenaged cousins were baptized in the Cartoogechaye Creek, I was almost tempted to join them. The pastor, my uncle, waded out waist deep with the candidates. Us cousins, in bathing suits and flip-flops, waded in for a better view. We are mostly a head-sprinkling tribe, but when you own a creek in the mountains, clear and bracing cold year-round, full immersion is a luxury.

It's no wonder city Baptists built their own tidy tubs into the wall. Baptizing in an urban creek, taking chances with fecal coliform bacteria, parking lot runoff, even flash floods, would be an act of faith crazier than snake handling.

What if those dozen babies in Decatur were doused in Trinity's closest creek, Sugar Creek? Would their parents tell them stories about hacking kudzu to clear a path, pulling out tires and clearing litter for the special occasion? How many of these children might develop, over time, a sense of connection to this corner of East Atlanta? Would some learn, eventually, that Sugar Creek flows to the South River and trace on a map, with blessed assurance, the water's progress to the Altamaha River and the Atlantic Ocean? Would they feel obligated to take care of their creek? Someday, when they grew into homeowners, parents, and activists, would they support a lawsuit against DeKalb County for allowing decades of spilled sewage to pollute their creek?

In the forest downstream, Sugar Creek's floodplain widens, forcing I-20 into sharp angles. Down on the wild banks of the creek, evidence of life and destruction all around, would the new mothers, the would-be mothers, the thwarted mothers, find a green and quiet place to pray?

Thinking of these hidden creeks, I remembered the strip mall church in Griffin. What swimming hole did the horse trough replace? The city of Griffin had no public swimming pool. In 1965, after twenty-two Black students were arrested for blocking a sidewalk in front of the still-segregated white pool, the city of Griffin closed its public pools "in the interest of public safety and for the good of the people of the community." In 1969 the city filled and graded the pool.

No pool, but Expressway Village Shopping Center was built next to a blue line on the map. A creek was right there in the trees hugging the backside of the property. Shoal Creek, making its way to the Flint River, was only twenty-five yards from where we stood. The proximity surprised me, but it shouldn't have. I felt it in the parking lot together—the journey to the water, all of us pulled there and bathed in sunlight.

April 20 THE LAKE AND THE LANDFILL

Lake Charlotte started to bother me one summer while I was working on a freelance project with a nonprofit called Trees Atlanta. Somewhere in the organization's sunny building, I saw a poster illustrating Atlanta's tree canopy— a kind of heat map of forests around the city. Red-orange blocks downtown sprawled into yellow-green neighborhoods and green parks. I studied it while waiting for my meeting to begin, amused to see the typical city map in reverse, defined by its undeveloped pockets instead of highways. The deepest green was in the southeast corner of the city, an emerald parcel bounded by a landfill and I-285. I knew what it was—Lake Charlotte Nature Preserve—but I had never been there.

According to this map, the forest was larger and greener than Piedmont Park and Grant Park combined. I tried to picture it and came up blank. All I remembered was the forbidding landfills and barren truck lots clustered in the elbow of the interstate. Old junkyards, strip clubs, and public housing projects scattered along Moreland Avenue. Long before I knew about zoning, I recognized the land-use pattern that sited poor Black neighborhoods alongside industrial districts. For most of my life, I had avoided this area—home, apparently, to the single largest concentration of intact tree canopy left inside the city limits.

As a Southside native and a generally outdoorsy mom, I was embarrassed by this gap in my mental map of Atlanta. I would rectify this immediately. Take the kids for a sweaty ramble around the lake and document it on Instagram. This weekend. But as I mapped out our first trip to Lake Charlotte, only eight miles from home, I couldn't find any information on the City Office of Parks website. No photos or trail reviews, only curious explorers sharing rumors on message boards. There were places where you could sneak through the fence, they said, but no public access.

All the maps were wrong. They showed Lake Charlotte Nature Preserve as a green rectangle with a thin, whale-shaped lake in the center. The blunt face of the whale must have been a dam once, its body a flooded valley. But the satellite image showed a meadow, no lake. Stymied by these findings, I let summer turn to fall, then the holidays arrived without an expedition to Lake Charlotte. A couple more summers went by. Every time I saw it labeled falsely on a map, it bothered me more. Was it ever a public park? Who was Charlotte, and what happened to her lake? And just what was behind that fence?

■ ■ ■

The recent history of the land was easy to find online in property records and local news sites. Fulton County listed Lake Charlotte's owner as Waste Management, Inc., same owner of the adjacent parcel in DeKalb County, the monumental Live Oak landfill. Live Oak opened in 1986, and it bought the forest next door in 1989, anticipating future expansion.

Live Oak always struck me as a comical name for a dump, devoid, as it was, of trees and living things. As a teen in the 1990s, commuting between my dad's and mom's houses, I learned to crank up my car window as soon as I spotted the grassy ziggurat that loomed on the horizon and punctured the dark with spooky blue flares. But even with the window up, the sour milk stink of the dumps lingered in the car well past businesses like Hub Cap Daddy and The Foxy Lady.

I remember reading about the controversy surrounding the landfill. It was located in DeKalb County, but the smell traveled for miles, into neighboring Atlanta and Clayton County neighborhoods, where residents gradually stopped hosting backyard cookouts, stopped leaving their windows open at night. In 1993, when Waste Management applied for a permit to expand into the Lake Charlotte property, Atlanta residents—most of them Black working-class homeowners—organized in protest. Live Oak was one of several enormous "solid waste handling facilities" already dominating Southeast Atlanta and southwest DeKalb County. The city denied the permit, and residents celebrated.

Instead of expanding outward, the landfill rose like a loaf of bread—a rotten rectangle squeezed straight by the county line and the interstate. The Lake Charlotte property was the only buffer between the reeking dump and backyards in South River Gardens, a predominantly Black neighborhood. By 2000, Live Oak started accepting "sludge," a by-product of sewage treatment plants that is typically converted to fertilizer, and the smell became unbearable. Live Oak's waste handling was both sloppy and illegal, which ignited further protests.

Southwest DeKalb residents appealed to their legislators and rallied at the state capitol, framing their burden as a case of environmental racism. In 2003, when Georgia's Environmental Protection Division (EPD) finally ordered Live Oak to shut down operations, the landfill was already full to capacity and over a decade past its original life expectancy. In 2007, Waste Management started harvesting methane from the capped landfill but held onto Lake Charlotte. For decades, the two hundred–acre Lake Charlotte property remained undisturbed and mislabeled on maps, a forgotten forest with a padlock on the fence.

■ ■ ■

I had to dig into the city's planning documents from the late seventies, comprehensive plans and land-use plans and annual reports from the Bureau of Parks and Rec with sexy typography and optimistic sketches, to find proof that once upon a time, briefly, Lake Charlotte Nature Preserve was exactly what it sounded like: a public park with a lake in the center.

This inner-city campground was the brainchild of Ted Mastroianni, Mayor Maynard Jackson's "fast moving and aggressive" director of parks and recreation. Recruited from New York City's parks department, he joined Mayor Jackson's team in 1975 and declared they would be "balancing the park system" by acquiring and protecting a half-dozen wooded tracts across the Southside. "What seems to excite Mastroianni the most," according to the *Atlanta Constitution,* "is the acquisition of natural open spaces." In the 1975 annual report, he appears with bushy hair and a double chin over his wide necktie and lapels, captured mid-laugh so you can see his molars. He was only thirty-six years old.

"We want areas where you can walk and lose yourself, rather than having to drive two hours to the North Georgia mountains," Mastroianni told the reporter. "If we develop good parks and campsites inside the cities, maybe people will stop hating the cities." I could picture this young New Yorker flying into Atlanta, gazing down upon the Southside with that big grin. From a planner's eye view, it seemed like a great idea to preserve these forests before they were swallowed by development. In 1977, Mastroianni marshaled federal and state grants to purchase the placid ten-acre Lake Charlotte and forty acres surrounding it. He told reporters that the park would be "open as soon as the paperwork is completed." When Mastroianni said, "Practically no improvements are required. It just becomes a park," he underestimated what it would take to make an inner-city wilderness feel appealing and safe.

Despite these visionary investments in the city's park system, by the 1980s,

the area was at a tipping point. Growing landfills and declining public housing projects surrounded Lake Charlotte. There's a term for infrastructure and
industrial sites like landfills that nobody wants in their backyard: LULU, or
locally undesirable land use. DeKalb County was committed to expanding industrial land uses here, near I-285 and the new interstate bypass I-675, a development trend that eventually eclipsed Mastroianni's idea of a fun family
getaway.

In 1986, the city scrapped the entire project, saying that "the unattended
nature of the park attracts illicit acts." They sold the land at a loss to a private
developer named Herman Lischkoff. I struggled to imagine the context—the
crisis, really—in which such a disposal of public lands could be done without
scandal. But the more I read about Atlanta's creeks and forests in the 1980s,
the more I learned about the infamous Atlanta Child Murders. For a night-
marish period between 1979 and 1981, a Black child went missing in Atlanta
nearly every month. Twenty-nine cases were linked to one killer, and many
of the victims' bodies turned up on the riverbanks and vacant wooded lots of
Southside Atlanta.

On November 1, 1980, the tiny body of Aaron Jackson Jr., age nine, was
spotted by a passerby from the South River bridge, one block north of Lake
Charlotte Nature Preserve. I was shocked to come across a photo of the crime
scene on an amateur true crime website that revealed brown ankles in black
sneakers laid out on stone riprap. "I wish I hadn't seen the body," Jackson's father told the newspaper after identifying the child at the city morgue. "That's
what I see every time I close my eyes."

The ongoing horror of those killings profoundly affected Atlantans' perception of urban waterways and wilderness for years. The murders deepened
whites' fears about the dangers of the inner city, accelerating white flight
into the suburbs. And an entire generation of Black residents learned to fear
and avoid Atlanta's forests and rivers. In 1981, Lake Charlotte made headlines
when a body was found in the lake. A twenty-seven-year-old lawyer named
William Brown was beaten and dumped by muggers from the Cabbagetown
neighborhood. Officially, the city breached Lake Charlotte's earthen dam and
drained the lake in 1982 in compliance with the U.S. Safe Dams Act. Unoffi-
cially, it was haunted.

Lischkoff combined the Lake Charlotte parcel with 163 more acres, citing
vague plans to create an industrial park. After a long and losing battle to get

the parcel rezoned, it was he, not the city, who sold what was once a public nature preserve to Waste Management, Inc.

■ ■ ■

I finally explored Lake Charlotte Nature Preserve when my colleague Ryan Gravel got a key to the padlock. He was still working on the South River Forest project, a very Mastroianni kind of plan to preserve the remaining forests of Atlanta. Using the heat map from Trees Atlanta and penalty funds paid by developers who had cut down trees, the city was looking to buy forested land and make it publicly accessible. Forty years after the first attempt, this nature preserve seemed like a viable project again.

I drove to Lake Charlotte one warm afternoon with all these stories in my head, bubbling over with internet research and rumors about a place I had never actually seen. Stacy Funderburke, an attorney with the Conservation Fund who had been working on behalf of the city to buy the property from Waste Management, met Ryan and me on the corner of Forrest Circle. This was one of the Black neighborhoods that had fought the landfill and won. I parked in front of a modest, brick split-level and felt conspicuously white piling into Stacy's Subaru. Would these residents benefit from a nature preserve across the street? Or would it mean a different kind of unwelcome traffic?

We pulled into the gate near the South River bridge and startled a trio of deer crossing Forrest Park Road. Once inside, we stepped over giant truck tires and a scrum of fresh litter. Hunters snuck in, Stacy told us. They cut the lock off a few times a year, and the tire dumpers followed.

With the gate locked behind us, we walked into the trees, following the rutted remains of "Woodsey Way," once a residential street leading to Lake Charlotte's lakefront estates. Up ahead, a pile of tires blackened the forest floor, as if children had made a game of rolling downhill tucked inside them. The sounds of the outside world blurred with each step. Beech leaves cast corrugated shadows, blocking out the sky. Stacy pointed out a shagbark hickory, a tree that appears as the shaggy Gandalf of the forest. My contribution was the name of this ghost road, last paved in the 1960s.

Eyeing the diameter of the beech trunks, Stacy guessed some of them were 175 years old. He took photos of Ryan and me gazing up, dwarfed by poplars as we ventured down the trail. At a moss-covered DEAD END sign, we continued south on Lake Drive. Ryan and I peeked inside the ruins of a two-story brick lodge. No sign of squatters in the rain-collapsed rooms. We speculated about who had lived here and when. By the front porch, I toed a leather roller skate, also covered in moss. Based on the pop-tops on the beer cans and typeface for Diet Pepsi, the litter here was late-1980s vintage. Postapocalyptic scenes like these are why *The Walking Dead* is filmed in Atlanta. Humid overgrowth devours a house in no time.

Farther down the road, Stacy spotted a great horned owl moving from tree to tree and quietly screwed a telephoto lens onto his camera. I wandered over to the stone gate of a once grand lake house, testing the ground for hidden wells. Right there among the ruins, I pulled up a historic topographical map on my phone. Structures dotted the road here in 1928, overlooking "Mount Manor Lake."

Later I would spend countless hours sifting through newspaper archives and old maps, trying to learn who had developed Mount Manor Lake in the 1920s. Dr. R. F. Ingram came up several times. He was a prominent Atlanta dentist, businessman, politician, "convicted bootlegger," and president of the Mount Manor Estates Fishing Club. At some point, Woodsey Way became Ingram Drive.

Eventually, reading obituaries and society pages, I found a Charlotte in the Ingram family. Miss Charlotte Sage, a wealthy, well-documented Ansley Park debutante of the 1936 season, was Dr. R. F. Ingram's only granddaughter. For years, her outfits and social "gaieties" were breathlessly chronicled in the Atlanta society pages. Even after Miss Charlotte's wedding to a naval officer in 1948, the papers continued to cover the celebrity couple.

The notice of Charlotte's funeral in 1956 surprised me. She was only thirty-seven years old, without a husband or heirs. It said nothing about how she died, and my imagination filled the blank space with a tragic scandal. Her name vanished from the newspapers, but by 1960, Lake Charlotte appeared on Atlanta maps, a watery tribute that outlasted the lake itself.

As a girl, did Charlotte love this place? I wondered about this as I balanced on a log to cross the creek. I could hear Ryan's and Stacy's voices moving up the hill toward the landfill. My T-shirt clung to my back as I hiked up the shady hillside, past holly bushes and boulders scarred with mossy divots. Thousands of years before Muscogee people settled here, between 1500 and 600 BCE, people sat on this hillside carving bowls out of the dark-green stone. Geologists called it Soapstone Ridge, and archaeologists in the late 1970s made a heroic effort to document the ancient quarry sites and recover priceless stone artifacts before they vanished under landfills and truck lots.

At the top of the hill, the sound of whirring machinery broke the spell. Ryan and Stacy were taking photos of the landfill's blank backside, a grassy expanse pocked with shiny, expensive-looking machinery. No doubt, a surveillance camera somewhere was watching us. I held my breath until I was hidden by the trees again. I spotted at least three strange devices before I Googled the name for them—piezometer, an instrument that measures the pressure of groundwater. It reminded me that Waste Management's greenspace served a purpose, filtering and buffering contaminants from Live Oak. We joked, uneasily, about the chemical odor of the landfill and what might be in the water.

The afternoon shadows grew long, but we refused to leave until we reached the lake, or what was left of it. We tromped down the hill toward the creek bed. The sky opened up in the clearing where the lake used to be. The plush, sun-dappled floodplain was dotted with lowland sycamores, patches of cattails shifted in the breeze. The shadows of turkey vultures and hawks crossed the swaying lake bottom like fish used to do.

What we found was probably more like what was here before the Ingram family. It was what Indigenous people might have seen—a clearing with a thin creek snaking through it. I tried to memorize this fleeting, wild, in-between state—after the lake and before the park. Like Charlotte Sage greeting a friend at the airport in 1940, matching furs and dark lipstick, after her debut but before her wedding. In the busy non-silence of the forest, I imagined the river cane filtering whatever was leaching from the landfill.

When I got home later that night, still high from forest bathing, grainy ringlets plastered to my neck and perfumed with DEET, I found Jason reading in a corner armchair, the kids already in bed. I practically twirled in the door, wanting to tell him about this mysterious place. I tried to pull him away from his reading, suggesting that he come upstairs and check me for ticks. The forest can do that to you—remind you of your animal flesh, your short life span—even in the middle of Atlanta.

Within a couple years, Black Atlantans who were promised a park in the 1970s and fought the landfill in the 1990s will finally be able to walk past the chain-link fence, owners of a place that was off limits for generations. Their grandchildren's inheritance is not just the land but the chance to "lose themselves" in a carefully managed wilderness in a way that their parents never could. Soon, too, white families like mine who have never ventured to this corner of Atlanta will discover those woods on afternoon picnics, marveling at the beech trees and soapstone boulders.

Enshrined as a nature preserve, what will we name the place? Should we erase Charlotte Sage, ill-fated princess of Mount Manor Lake? Or honor Ted Mastroianni, Aaron Jackson Jr., or Herman Lischkoff—all of the figures whose fates entwined with the place and made it so difficult to bulldoze? Whatever we call it, I hope it will honor the countless Southside neighbors who organized to prevent Lake Charlotte from becoming a dumping ground. This is their victory and their park.

April 22 HOTEL POOL

My brother, Lowell, planned a surprise marriage proposal to his longtime love, and he invited us to witness the surprise at her parents' house near Columbia, South Carolina. It would be a long drive for just one night, but I figured the proposal would be a joyful moment worth the trip and the kind of family story that grows into a legend with every retelling. No way I was going to miss being part of the conspiracy.

Jason and I used to love road trips, and the boys were finally getting old enough to enjoy them too. We taught them to play cow poker, to look for BBQ and boiled-peanut stands. Downtown Columbia was cool, I told them; we could see a new state capitol, find the bookstores and donut shops near the University of South Carolina campus. Unlimited iPad screen time on the drive helped sweeten the deal.

Plus, we could splurge on a hotel with a swimming pool. That sold it. I packed the boys' tiny swim trunks.

Saturday afternoon, we checked into the Hilton Garden Inn in Columbia and found my parents, excited and waiting in their double queen room. The plan was to pile into their minivan, carpool to the house, and gather with Lindsey's extended family in the garage while my brother led his unsuspecting sweetheart to the backyard swing for a heart-to-heart.

Right on schedule, we crept into the living room and watched through the blinds as Lowell took Lindsey's hands. Relaxed from a day lounging by the pool, she had no idea what was coming. As he sank to one knee, she screamed with delight and embraced him.

Inside the house, we cheered. Lindsey's mom pulled lasagnas from the oven. Her dad popped the cork on some champagne. My future sister was further shocked to find us all hugging and laughing in her parents' kitchen.

Unbelievably, we had pulled off the surprise. My baby brother was getting married to the love of his life. We celebrated with dinner in the backyard. The adults told and retold the story of the proposal that had just happened. We replayed the video of Lindsey's reaction. My kids kicked a soccer ball around with Lindsey's niece and nephew. The dogs sniffed the paper plates forgotten on the brick patio.

The next morning at 6:00 a.m., I texted my parents from the hotel elevator. *We are going downstairs to the pool, want to come?* They were early risers; I knew they had been up for an hour.

The ground-floor hotel pool was shallow and steamy. Something about the lukewarm water and fluffy white towels reminded me of a giant bathtub. My father came down in his overalls and sat with me and my paper cup of bad coffee. We watched my boys take turns leaping into the water, slippery in Jason's waiting arms.

I thought about sneaking into the pool at the Hilton Garden Inn in our neighborhood. There must be thirty hotels within five miles of our house. Did any of them sell pool memberships to local residents? Or what about Atlanta's downtown luxury hotels, with their rooftop pools? I could call the Four Seasons, the W, the Ritz, to inquire about day passes. Or what about the Georgian Terrace, where Jason and I swam in the rooftop pool early the morning after our wedding? We could see the sunrise over Stone Mountain, the whole city spread out in mauve and green. Could I take the boys there?

This is what kids do, I guess—fill your days with mayhem and anticipation, nonstop scheming and dreaming. There at the hotel pool, I tried to practice what my father did so well—soaking up the present. It was almost painful, my heart swelling with love for them all.

I added this tiny pool to my diary, not sure how hotels would fit into the puzzle of water access. Would they remember this?

Only later, when I rewatched the video of Lowell's proposal—recorded through the screen door, blurry, no audio—did I notice that my brother chose to create this moment next to Lindsey's family's swimming pool. Just standing near the rippling water made you feel light and hopeful.

May 16 STORMWATER

I heard about the drowning three times before it started to seem real.

The first time was at the Historic College Park Neighbors Association, held in a warm little chapel on a private school campus. I was there to talk about restoring the Flint River's withered headwaters and how it could benefit residents on the Southside of Atlanta. The chapel was full of folks who owned the large, historic homes with the highest property values for miles, a bubble of wealth and whiteness in an otherwise Black community, lower-income working people, not wealthy ones.

Before I even made it through the lobby, a middle-aged white woman approached me and said, somewhat cheerfully, "You're here to talk about the Flint River? I remember someone drowned in the Flint River."

No surprise, I thought. The river is vast. I needed to deliver my slides to the podium.

"I can't remember her name. She drowned right here in College Park and got washed into a drainpipe."

I frowned, tried not to say something incredulous. The perennial trickle in those streams was only about three inches deep. How could someone drown in College Park? I took an interest in the tray of brownies.

"When was that?"

I had toured the headwaters streams in College Park—labeled the "West Fork" on old maps—and they looked like a series of narrow ditches carved along the backside of backyards and apartment buildings.

"Honey, do you remember when that lady drowned in the Flint River?" She called out to her husband, who was already seated in a pew.

This is not the news you want to hear before you step to a microphone and pitch the idea of uncovering lost waterways. Where was the meeting organizer to rescue me?

The husband did not recall. It was time to find our seats for the Pledge of Allegiance.

She had to be mistaken, but later that night, I searched the internet for anything about a drowning in the Flint River in College Park. This sounded like something I should know about, but without more details on the incident, it remained a mystery.

The second notice, months later, was also cryptic but harder to ignore. I was standing in a boardroom in front of a group of forty people, talking about urban runoff, when the slide on the screen behind me showed a triple box culvert bulging with stormwater the color of chocolate milk.

I shot this photo one afternoon in the rain. I took Guy with me, straight from school in his little school uniform, to the spot where Harvard Avenue dead-ends at a wall that seems to hold up the freeway. The culvert would be unremarkable except for the tall, barbed wire cage surrounding it and no less than four security cameras trained on the opening.

We stood there in the rain for a long time, transfixed by the churning water whipping branches and litter into the lightless pipe. Guy's bright-red polo shirt the only color in my photos. There is no limit to how long he will watch water in motion.

Gesturing to this photo, I was interrupted by a voice in the audience, an engineer in a necktie. He wagged his finger at the culvert.

"We lost one down there once," he said, sounding like a funeral director.

"Ah, yes." I rolled with it, a real serious look on my face. "Someone mentioned that at a neighborhood meeting."

Next slide, please.

If I believed the story of the drowning, if I dared imagine it featured this particular dead-end culvert, I wouldn't have taken my child to that site in the rain. Now it seemed both dangerous and haunted.

The meeting was the usual rush of PowerPoints, handshakes, and business cards. I left with leads to research and emails to return. As for the engineer's dark comment, I filed it away as river lore. Ancient history.

The third time, I was admonished by the mayor at the kind of mahogany board meeting where there's a gavel, an invocation, and nameplates at each seat. Again, I was there to talk about the forgotten Flint headwaters and their potential to revitalize the neighborhood.

My presentation went five minutes over, and I was sweating through my cardigan, but the questions and applause seemed sincere. Next up on the agenda was the unveiling of a big office park development where a neighborhood used to be.

I quietly exited to find a water fountain. The mayor of College Park was right behind me. He said, gruffly, "You know we had a drowning in the Flint River."

He answered his phone then, striding toward the exit. He'd been the mayor for decades, a tall, white-haired fixture with the kind of drawl that belies the political intelligence and ferocity that has resulted in multiple reelections.

Again, no one was offering details, just the comment, like a warning. Be careful what you wish for.

■ ■ ■

I had to leave College Park, leave the watershed entirely, to finally learn her name.

I visited the Northwest Community Alliance, a small but often-quoted group of active Northside citizens, as a guest speaker one night.

They met in a small brick church in a leafy old neighborhood. No steeple, no stained glass, same modest dimensions of the 1950s houses on the block. Again, the passing of cookies and bottled water in lieu of communion. Announcements, followed by a couple speakers, a friendly exchange of questions and comments.

After my talk, an elegant Black woman in a bright dress waited to be the last to speak to me.

"I love what you are trying to do," she said, "your daylighting the river and all, but you should also point out that it's very dangerous. I had a cousin who drowned in the Flint River in College Park."

I'm sure my face fell, jaw dropped. That sinking feeling must show on the outside somehow.

"Your cousin?"

"She drowned in a storm," she nodded. "So, you have to be careful over there."

I believe that's all she wanted to say, just a polite footnote. She started to move away. Even though my composure was disintegrating, I could not let her go.

"I've been hearing about this," I said. "When did it happen?"

"It was a long time ago. And I was living out of state at the time." She paused. Eyes calculating behind her glasses. "Her sons were young back then. Now they are grown men."

This was the moment the drowning became real for me. Became a person. I realized I had been reluctant to believe it was true.

"I remember her as a sweet kid. I was her babysitter one summer."

I asked if we could talk more, stay in touch.

She handed me her business card. Beneath the Georgia Tech seal: Dr. Jacqueline Jones Royster, Dean, Ivan Allen College of Liberal Arts.

"And what was your cousin's name?" I asked cautiously.

She spelled it as I scribbled on the back of her business card: Carolyn Harmon. The rumor, the warning, the mystery. It was her.

■ ■ ■

Her name unlocked the whole story. The next day, camped out in a busy coffee shop, I downloaded a handful of newspaper articles from Labor Day weekend 1992 covering the freak accident and the following rescue and recovery effort. I found myself wound into a ball, shivering and caffeinated, pulling my eyes occasionally away from my laptop to jealously observe the flow of normal life in the café.

The *Atlanta Constitution* reported that late Friday night, September 4, Carol Harmon and her boyfriend started the holiday weekend at a friend's place in College Park—the Villa Nieves Apartments on Harvard Avenue. When they arrived, it had been raining heavily all day, and the parking area was flooding. Apparently, there was a creek next to the parking lot that had overtopped the concrete footbridge connecting the parking lot to the apartments. That creek was the Flint River, but only an engineer would know that.

At one in the morning, Harmon decided to leave. She tried the back door, not realizing the path led into the floodwaters.

In one article, the water was waist-deep, in another, shin-high. Either way, it was high enough to obscure her path, dark enough to hide her proximity to the culvert, swift enough to make her lose her footing, and powerful enough to drag her under. Harmon was swept into a drainage pipe.

I didn't let myself think about what happened next. Surely, I told myself, she lost consciousness before she had time to be afraid.

The accident didn't make the news until Monday, Labor Day, in an article titled "College Park Flood Victim Still Missing" in the local section.

"What bothers me most," said Mattie Harmon, Carolyn's mother, the voice of reason, "is a creek like that didn't have a fence or wall around it."

The biographical details included in these articles read like cards stacked against her: a Black woman, a teen mom, a cleaning lady at the airport. There was no reference in the articles, as her mother points out, to her being more than "a cleaning lady." She was an independent entrepreneur who had a cleaning business. Her thumbnail portrait showed traces of a smiling face, but the image was so dark and saturated, it became a black rectangle in the digital archives.

Search crews, including members from her church, spread out along the banks of the Flint River in Clayton County, on the other side of the airport. As police conceded that they may never find her, Mattie Harmon remained hopeful. She told a reporter, "I believe that she is holding on down in that place, somewhere."

That place. In future nightmares, I conjured the shock and struggle of her last moments, the crushing darkness and the tangle of branches that would become her grave. The media danced around the horror and violence of her death. The tragedy was part of a roundup of weather-related mishaps from the weekend, four inches of rain, widespread flooding, car accidents, residents evacuated to hotels.

A week later, volunteers found her jacket downstream, over seven miles away from where she disappeared. The search narrowed; trained dogs were brought in to recover a body. They searched in vain for another two weeks, but Harmon was never found.

Later Dr. Royster told me that her cousin has a grave but there's no body in it.

A follow-up story, "Tenants Feared Hard Rains," ran later that month in the Southside Extra section. Witnesses vented about recurrent flash flooding. Who was responsible for installing a protective railing or fence? The landlord believed it was the city's job. The city argued that it couldn't erect a fence on private property, nor could it force the owner to do anything.

On the same newspaper page, a column about "residents riled" over muddy runoff from the construction site of a ten thousand–seat megachurch ran next to a story about dump trucks hauling earth to build a new runway at the airport. Seeing this juxtaposition decades later, the relationship between these issues was glaring, but at the time, there was only a common anxiety running through these stories. Readers sensed the ground shifting beneath them.

Flooding always presents as local news, breaking news. Just an act of God, with no history or context. No one in the Southside Extra section was getting into technical stuff about increased impervious surfaces and stormwater volumes, connecting streamflow shifts to urban development. One piece called the site of the tragedy a "drainage system," but before it was constrained to pipes and parking lot channels, it was a natural stream with a name. Did we think we could repress the Flint River forever?

The next article came from October 1994. "Ruling: Woman's Death Her Own Fault: Judge Throws Out Family's Lawsuit." A Fulton superior court judge ruled that Harmon was, "by her conduct, the proximate cause of her own drowning" and refused to let the case go to trial.

Reading this, my stomach turned. I tried and failed to imagine a fictional universe in which this headline might apply to a middle-class white mother violently flushed into an open sewer and never recovered. But we don't treat rivers this way in white neighborhoods.

The Harmon family's attorney vowed to appeal. "We think the judge was wrong. The conditions at that apartment complex were atrocious, the city of College Park and the apartment owners knew about those conditions and they ought to be held responsible."

A few months later, they would lose the appeal too.

■ ■ ■

I stewed over all of this and drafted a wordy and earnest email to Dr. Royster. I thanked her for introducing herself and telling me about her cousin. I told her I was piecing together what had happened.

"I would like to understand the conditions that led to this tragedy and what changes followed. I would like to be able to accurately tell Carol's story as part of why we need to rethink these headwaters and their impact. Certainly, her story—and the larger story of environmental justice—is at the heart of any restoration work or new greenspace in the area."

She responded promptly with a note of agreement, reminding me that her cousin's name was Carolyn, not Carol.

I fumbled for my notes. Then apologized. The *Atlanta Constitution* had it wrong, which seemed like yet another indignity. I said there should be a memorial for Carolyn, so people would know her name.

A few minutes later, another note. She asked me to send links to the articles. She explained that at the time of the tragedy, she was living out of state and knew very little about what really happened. Dr. Royster and I traded a number of emails that afternoon. We agreed to keep researching and sharing.

What I didn't say is that I was troubled by my own desire to ignore this story. It was sad and inconvenient to think about it. It didn't fit into my pitch about river restoration. The news hardly covered it, the courts wouldn't hear the case, and the city and landlord were too busy pointing fingers to acknowledge a family's pain.

I stood in a long line of well-educated, well-meaning white people looking away from the truth. How could I even talk about saving the river without finding Carolyn and bringing her, finally, to light?

■ ■ ■

The next day, by chance, I had lunch with a friend who works as a paralegal. Over fancy salads, I blurted out what I had learned, that I wanted to write about it.

"Am I going to get sued?" I sputtered. "I mean, I'm not trying to reopen the case, or old wounds, but this is unbelievable."

Later that afternoon, he emailed me a PDF fished out of the depths of one of those pricey legal research services: "Court of Appeals of Georgia. *Harmon et al. v. City of College Park et al.* Reconsideration Denied, July 26, 1995."

The decision was only four pages long but offered a detailed analysis of the accident, most of it scrutinizing Harmon's final footsteps. I found the focus not only wrong, filled with unfair assumptions, but cruel, even decades later.

The only voice of reason was P. J. McMurray, who wrote in his dissent:

> I do not think that it can be said (as a matter of law) that Ms. Harmon was aware of just how precariously close the submerged drainage ditch was to the sidewalk she was traversing moments before her death. Most persuasively, however, is the absence of proof that Carolyn Harmon was aware of the powerful suction at the narrow drainpipes which ultimately dragged the victim underwater and jettisoned her body to some obscure location within the City's sewer system. Under these circumstances, I cannot go along with the majority in saying that the evidence demands a finding that Carolyn Harmon had a full appreciation of the specific danger which caused her death.

Exactly, I thought. Could I interview him? It took me a little while to figure out the judge's name wasn't P.J.; he was the presiding judge. Unfortunately, I gleaned this from his 2017 obituary, which read, "He took a special interest in slip-and-fall cases, standing firm in his belief of the jury system being one of the greatest systems ever devised by man. Valuing the right to trial by jury, Judge McMurray left a legacy to the people of Georgia by writing many dissents and believing that the public should have their day in court by a jury of peers."

Reading this remembrance, I felt a twinge of loss for the honorable Judge William Leroy McMurray Jr. and aspired to write a dissent of my own.

I reread these documents a few times before I understood that Harmon's death was considered a "slip-and-fall" case. Like an accident caused by an over-waxed floor or a busted sidewalk. That explains the narrow focus on her final footsteps, her decision to go out the back door instead of the front, her failure to hold on to the fence as she waded into the floodwaters. On the boyfriend's final words to her, how much alcohol he had consumed that night, his inability to rescue Carolyn from the whirlpool. All of the things she did or didn't do to deserve death.

The argument was insane. Where was the analysis of the thing that actually stole her from us, the flash flood? How had a common parking lot transformed into an inescapable drain? Why was an apartment complex built on top of a creek anyway? And given all this, I shared her mother's commonsense question—why was the culvert unsecured? How could Harmon ever imagine where the water came from or where it led? At one point, Dr. Royster mentioned that her cousin was a strong swimmer, but how would she know she was crossing a river?

I didn't want to reconstruct Carolyn's story as a true crime puzzle to be solved. Instead, I craved the historical context that didn't make it into the grim news stories or the aborted court case, the bigger picture of urban development that had led to the flood.

I looked up the historic aerial images and topographical maps to see how the stormwater problem had been compounded over time on the block at the center of this story, 1555 Harvard Avenue. When the property owner sued College Park for damages, the city manager denied that they had done any work upstream that would "adversely affect" the property. Yet anyone could tell you the landscape had changed completely since the 1960s, when the apartments were built with a stream flowing through a neat little channel in the parking lot.

In the earliest aerial photo from 1938, College Park's residential street grid unfolded from the central railroad tracks, the streets named for universities—Princeton, Columbia, Cambridge, Oxford. Our block on Harvard Ave. stands at the rural east edge of a booming town, between the College Park Cemetery and a patchwork of marbled fields where the Atlanta airport will soon stretch out its runways.

After World War II, College Park quadrupled in size. The crisp 1955 aerial photo was somehow much more detailed than any satellite image to come later. The rural edges of the city filled in with blocks studded with new houses. The Flint River's West Fork cut a straight path from northwest to southeast, a wooly seam slicing through the city blocks. Low-lying areas remained undeveloped, allowing the creek to meander down to three small lakes clustered south of our block.

In 1960, some clever developers found a way to design small garden-style apartments into the previously undeveloped floodplain lots. At 1611 Harvard Avenue, a horseshoe-shaped complex was built practically on top of a stream, with decorative footbridges and floating staircases leading to the central courtyard. The stylish Villa Nieves Apartments at 1555 Harvard Avenue debuted in 1962, all thin white brick and Havana breeze-block. I counted eight of these creekside apartment complexes still standing today, each containing a dozen units or less.

In 1968, the lakes disappeared. Where did they go? I might have cussed, toggling back and forth between the maps, before and after. They were drained to make way for interstate I-85, which amputated Harvard Avenue to the west of our block. That extra water would have to go somewhere. A decade later, I-85 was rerouted to make way for the new airport terminal, pulled northwestward even closer to our block. Another chunk of the neighborhood was wiped out; the noose tightened around 1555 Harvard Ave.

As the airport expanded in the 1970s, the Federal Aviation Administration began a program of residential buyouts in this area, relocating all the single-family houses that were impacted by airport noise. The apartment buildings were left standing, however, because this program didn't cover multifamily units. The apartments where Carolyn drowned were left surrounded by empty lots, dead-end streets, and driveways to nowhere, a kind of postapoca-lyptic ghetto in the elbow of the freeway.

In less than four years, this corner of College Park was transformed from populated and forested blocks to vacant bottomland, designed for no one but populated, nonetheless. Who always settled in the Bottom, downhill from the mill, the factory, the city on a hill? The people who were less powerful, who have fewer financial resources—in this case, Black people who were ordinary laborers, factory workers, cleaning ladies, restaurant workers, delivery people.

Add to the 1988 map a sprawling College Park MARTA train station and the headquarters campus for the FAA, both constructed upstream of our site, paving over twelve, then sixteen more, acres that once absorbed rainfall. A tangle of interstate ramps connecting to the airport terminal appeared, com-pleting the transformation.

By 1995, the topographical map had fundamentally changed. The contour lines that followed the urban stream now drew a bullseye around 1555 Harvard Avenue. It was a dangerous place, an accident years in the making.

Eventually, after Carolyn's drowning, the city of College Park engineered a solution for these flooding problems. In 2005, it rerouted the stream around the Villa Nieves, through a series of huge new retention areas that looked like grassy bowls carved out of a city block, surrounded by eight-foot-tall fences. Industrial-sized upgrades, forbidding and expensive. The parking lot chan-nels were capped near the apartment building, erasing the scene of the crime.

Maybe the city finally made this investment because it took thirteen years to assemble the funds and the land to overhaul the storm sewer sys-tem. Maybe it waited until the lawsuits and media around the drowning faded away before starting in on the fixes that would prevent further tragedy. But if all of this had been done in the 1970s, around the time I-85 replaced the lakes, Carolyn wouldn't have drowned, and countless residents wouldn't have suf-fered through flooding.

Who is responsible for racism written into the landscape over a hundred years of development? I have implicated agencies at all levels of government here, from the Georgia Department of Transportation for plowing an inter-state highway through a neighborhood and filling in a lake in the process, to the Atlanta airport for forcing a river underground. I can blame the FAA for funding the buyouts of houses but not the apartments, along with MARTA for underestimating the impacts of runoff from its new train stations and parking lots. I would blame the developers who engineered these apartments into floodplain lots, but their plans relied on 1960s hydrology, when this creek stayed in its tidy channels.

From my seat, they all look complicit, but only the lowest on the totem pole paid a price. The city of College Park lost a ten thousand–dollar judgment to the landlord in 1995. The landlord let the property go into foreclosure in 1996.

Carolyn came last in the hierarchy.

In *Harmon v. College Park,* the judge points out that in her final moments, Carolyn Harmon failed to hold onto a chain-link fence on the left side of the walkway. This was supposed to be proof that "the victim failed to exercise ordinary care for her own safety."

Harmon's family disagreed with this report. The family re-walked Carolyn's pathway and found there was no fence or anything else to hold onto. This tragic death was not due to negligence of any kind on Carolyn's part.

What was this fence, this evidence that sank the Harmons' case before it ever began? Years after the drowning, I visited 1555 Harvard Avenue one breezy, blue morning after I dropped off the kids at school. I waited in the parking lot as a woman left an apartment, drove off to work, leaving the street empty. The old creek path left a grassy scar curving around the front doors of the apartments.

The little concrete footbridge was still there, though it crossed nothing more than a storm drain. My shoes squelched in the grass as I followed the indentation upstream from the parking lot to the engineered meadow of clover and cattails behind a tall security fence. The river, just a creek today, had been trained into right angles around the apartment building. I couldn't see any water down there.

I took a few photos, waved at passing neighbors. Forgive us our trespasses, I thought. I must look suspicious back here.

Finally, I walked along the back of the building, ducking under kitchen windows, along the footpath that Carolyn followed. I was looking for what I couldn't find in the maps and aerial photos.

To my left, up a berm and behind a security fence, lay the retention pond, the caged river, but this wasn't there in 1992. Once upon a time, there were houses on that side of the block. Their backyards backed up to the Villa Nieves.

If there had been a fence on the left to mark the edge of their property, all of that was demolished in the early 1990s. The fence wasn't there to protect Carolyn from the stream. It was there to protect the homeowners from the apartment dwellers and the bad things that they thought happened on the other side of the fence.

May 20 PFDs

I bought two little teal life vests for the boys today. "PFDs," they're called—personal flotation devices.

The weather forecast leading up to our annual Memorial Day weekend camping trip showed thunderstorms all weekend. It was another week of rain on top of a month of rain and reports of mudslides in the mountains. Knowing how hard it would be to keep the kids out of the creek, I added life preservers to my list of camping supplies.

The Cartoogechaye Creek was not just a pretty backdrop for camping; it was the focal point. The creek flowed through our family campsite, a forty-acre meadow where we've been hosting camping trips and family reunions my whole life. Every year, the Memorial Day itinerary was simple: spend the mornings and evenings chatting around the campfire and every minute of warm daylight wading, tubing, fishing, garnet mining, and skipping rocks in the creek. All day, we were drawn to the Cartoogechaye. All night, we heard voices in the rushing water.

My parents drove up to Franklin a few times a month to check on Granny and Granddaddy and to tend the family property. They reported that the creek was high and rising, its banks badly eroded. We should not pitch our tents too close to the edge.

If you saw me squinting in the white light of the Target sporting goods aisle, poring over the ratings on the children's Speedo swim vests, that's what I was preparing for. Summer fun and drowning. The Cartoogechaye surged through my nightmares, pulling my pale children from my arms.

But it wasn't just the rain that made me anxious; it was all these deaths and lawsuits. It was only May, and my diary already had a body count. When I mentioned that I was writing about swimming, so many people told me about the drownings they had witnessed—a child trapped by a broken swimming pool pump, ocean swimmers dashed on rocks. And every time I researched a lost lake or creek, there would be fishermen surprised by a flash flood, teenagers swept into deep water. To look at water was to turn up bodies. And so many of those bodies were Black.

For example, when I was reading about Ted Mastroianni, Atlanta's maverick parks director in the late 1970s, I loved that he brought paddleboat rentals to Piedmont Park. They were already popular in Stone Mountain Park and

Callaway Gardens, so it matched Mastroianni's goal to make the city parks more competitive with the suburbs.

The paddleboats had been available for one month when twenty-seven-year-old J. C. Foster drowned in Lake Clara Meer. When his three-year-old son tumbled into the green water, Foster jumped in to save him. The father managed to rescue the child, but he couldn't swim, and he wasn't wearing the "white ski belt" they had given him. After he went under, neither the lifeguards nor the bystanders that Sunday afternoon could find him. How did a healthy young man drown in a calm, shallow lake, in broad daylight, in front of his family and everyone else at Atlanta's premier park?

The newspaper didn't say if Foster was Black, just that he lived in the Old Fourth Ward and didn't know how to swim. This all sounded like a vaguely familiar refrain, a pattern repeated in the news.

It reminded me of the shocking death of a teenaged classmate from Forest Park High who drowned at a local water park called Dancing Waters. How we cried over this boy, those of us in the marching band and the drama club. He was handsome and talented, a star. He was only nineteen years old.

Perhaps because there was no explanation for the drowning, we white girls consoled ourselves with the vague assurance that the accident couldn't have been prevented. Our classmate was Black, so he probably couldn't swim. It was like a heart condition, just something unfortunate he was born with. Nobody talked about it, so we found ways to comfort ourselves. Such a thing would never happen to us, we figured, because we were white.

When, the following summer, two more children, ages five and seven, drowned at Dancing Waters, officials were mystified. "I honestly do not know what could've been done to prevent these," said a park consultant. "And that is bothersome." The newspaper omitted the victims' race and, like the consultant, didn't consider it relevant, didn't see a pattern reaching back generations.

My classmate's mother sued Dancing Waters for two million dollars in damages. The suit alleged that lifeguards had failed to respond to her son in distress and did not apply the appropriate lifesaving procedures once they found him. Did she ever get justice? After all, in the words of Ms. Tia, "it never would've have happened if they had been doing what they were supposed to be doing."

Fighting lawsuits and bad publicity, the park operators rebranded Dancing Waters as "Atlanta Beach" before selling the property to Clayton County Parks and Recreation as a venue for the 1996 Olympic Games.

Looking back, I see how we, who wept over the young man's death, did not take an interest in the case or consider his death an injustice. The lawsuit got a three-sentence mention in the "Police Blotter." On the local news, we saw another grieving Black family and changed the channel.

■ ■ ■

The whispered notion that Black people can't swim wasn't a stereotype; it was an epidemic.

The CDC found that "the fatal unintentional drowning rate for African Americans was significantly higher than that of whites across all ages," but the disparity is "most pronounced" among children in pools. African American children drowned in swimming pools at rates 5.5 times higher than whites. For eleven- and twelve-year-old Black children it was ten times the rate of that of white kids the same age. The CDC did not suggest why it happens, just the numbers.

A few days after J. C. Foster's drowning in Piedmont Park, Atlanta's favorite columnist, Lewis Grizzard, wrote a preachy opinion piece titled "No Excuses." In his view, a series of weekend drownings were the result of irresponsible people unwilling to spend a couple hours and twenty-seven dollars at the YMCA to learn how to swim. "It takes little effort to learn," he admonished. "Now what's your excuse?"

Maybe Foster was like that fellow who climbed on top of my granddad in the Panama Canal. He had so little experience in water, he thought that if he really needed to, he would be able to swim.

Again, there is no mention of race, but from Grizzard's condescending tone, it was clear to me that he was talking about Black victims. This slant way of blaming them, insinuating that their own laziness and fear were the problem— it was all too familiar to my white ears. It was always the "home training," as one white board member of the East Point Historical Society told me, that led to such personal failings. Not the long history of racial discrimination in swimming facilities. Not the tragic outcome of a racist system.

Never mind that African Americans were denied access to public parks and pools and lakes and beaches up until the 1960s. "Were denied access" sounds too passive. White people got really creative to keep Black people out of the water. They unceremoniously filled thousands of public swimming pools with dirt, converted them to tennis courts or ball fields or historical societies. In news footage that shocked the nation, Jimmy Brock, manager of the Monson Motor Lodge in St. Augustine, Florida, poured cleaning acid into the swimming pool while shouting at protesters hosting a swim-in at the segregated motel.

In 1963, rather than comply with court-ordered integration, officials in Greenville, South Carolina, put three sea lions in the city pool and renamed it "Marineland." Atlanta did the same thing in Grant Park. In 1960, the city of Atlanta filled in Lake Abana, a "swimming pool of Roman magnificence," and built Zoo Atlanta in its place. Some of Greenville's seals ended up in Atlanta, photographed with the caption "Latest addition cavorts in Grant Park Pool."

Meanwhile, whites who could afford it built their own country clubs and backyard pools. Forest Vale Club was built in 1964; Meema's house was built in 1960. And they drained the lakes on their way out the door. My diary was becoming a catalog of lost southern waters. The Flint River, the South River, Lake Charlotte, Lake Spivey, and all those little private lakes in Clayton County where white families once played—all were now drained, polluted, or fenced off to the public.

I resented Grizzard's suggestion that "it takes little effort to learn" as not only ignorant and racist but sexist. I could already tell that teaching my sons to swim was going to be this gradual, multiyear project, made expensive and challenging by our lack of access to water. So far in 2018, I had managed to get my kids into a swimming situation four times—a hot tub on Tybee Island, two trips to the South Cobb Aquatic Center, and an hour in a pool at the Hilton Garden Inn. It was lot of driving and research and unpaid labor, all of it falling on me, the mom, to coordinate. Which was not to bash Jason, who was working, always working, whose steady paycheck made my flexible work arrangement possible. But I was the freelancer who adapted my schedule to juggle kid demands. My ability to be this kind of ever-available mom was both a luxury and sacrifice. I worried about my lack of retirement savings; I worried about my financial dependence on my husband, about the traditional gender roles we were modeling for my kids. Then I worried about worrying too much. It was no "little effort."

People warned me that swim floaties, like training wheels, were counter-productive because kids learned to rely on them for support instead of truly learning to swim. False confidence, they said. I bought the PFDs anyway. I bought them knowing that we would probably cancel the Memorial Day camping trip to the creek. I was determined to take the boys swimming in every public pool in Atlanta. Pool season was about to begin.

PART 2

POOL HOPPING

May 26 SHINY NEW NATATORIUM

At the last possible minute, we canceled the Palmer family Memorial Day camping trip. The forecast was stormy, and no one wanted to camp in the mud. Saturday morning was opening day for most outdoor public pools, but it was gray and raining. I was left with two disappointed little boys and a long, free weekend.

It was chiefly parental desperation that reminded me of the brand-new Martin Luther King Jr. Aquatic Center and motivated me to look up its hours of operation. Every reviewer gushed over the new facility with its open, light-filled, modern design, pristine equipment, easy parking, and reasonable fees.

I announced to Jason that I was taking the boys to an indoor pool, tossed some towels and the new swim vests in the trunk, and we headed downtown. Our first pool of the summer!

I had seen coverage of the pool's grand opening on the local news. What kind of swimming pool merited a ribbon cutting with speeches from Martin Luther King Jr's children and performances by the Morehouse Glee Club? Behind the podium where mayors and dignitaries delivered their remarks, a soaring steel cutout of Dr. King's face loomed over the entrance to the sleek facility.

Mayor Reed said, "We don't lose assets with the name Martin Luther King on them. We actually come back and build them better. And we build them stronger."

This was something I would hear over and over about Atlanta's pools, many named after civil rights leaders and community heroes. Each facility was expected to do and be much more than just a pool.

Driving from Edgewood Avenue to Tanner Street to Hilliard Street, past a series of crumbly brick storefronts as old as anything in Atlanta, I found myself weaving through a congregation of homeless men. The downpour broke just long enough for them to emerge from their under-bridge tents, and dozens of men fanned out across the street. Lord help my callous heart, hammering with panic. What would happen if I accidentally hit one of them with my Volkswagen?

Bruno asked me once if all the men who lived in tents were brown skinned. No, no, I lied. But it certainly looked that way downtown.

On the next block stood the recreation center, a jarring, two-story black steel-and-glass-paneled vault, surrounded by creamy sidewalks and young shrubs. I once worked for the architecture firm that designed this facility, and I recognized their style of municipal modernism—clean lines, natural light. They were quite evangelical about the power of design to uplift and heal the masses. It was a stark-looking cathedral, surrounded by some desperate-looking citizens.

We arrived at a freshly painted parking lot. The boys ran up the stairs, and I made them pause for a photo under the stainless-steel letters forty feet high: "I have a dream . . . that one day this nation will rise up and live out the true meaning of its creed, 'We hold these truths to be self-evident, that all men are created equal.'"

They sprinted through the soaring central lobby, two matching fluorescent yellow swim shirts in a gray hallway, bounding from the windows of a basketball court where some teens were shooting hoops to a conference room full of red and black balloons. I ran my eyes over the concrete floors, buffed to a shine, the big empty gray walls leading up to a skylight. A pair of large abstract paintings and beige leather sofas seemed dwarfed by the space. Sober, rainy-day light from above made it feel like a museum or a hospital.

The kids didn't stop running until they saw the pool, which stopped our steps and our breath. I can only describe it as a warehouse full of water. Fully one-third of the building footprint was pool; a glass wall in the lobby overlooked the blue water. The reception desk felt like it was on the edge of a lake.

Fees paid, we raced through the locker rooms and out to the water. Bruno flopped on his back three steps into the zero-entry pool. Guy squealed and flapped his way over to a tall spray structure, a cluster of umbrellas that created their own rain. It looked sedate compared to the South Cobb Aquatic Center, but I was grateful for the kid features. The original MLK pool was strictly for competitive swimming.

I had never been to the old natatorium. It opened in 1978 in the Old Fourth Ward, the neighborhood where King grew up. It was the first indoor public pool in Atlanta. While King loved swimming, his wife, Coretta Scott King, never learned how to swim. After his death, she worked to create the natatorium alongside the national historic district. Her dream was to create a place where the urban youth of Atlanta could learn not only how to swim but to compete in swimming.

For a generation of Atlantans, the pool was a legendary proving ground. Olympic swimmers trained there; it hosted one of the few minority programs in the country.

As a suburban white kid, I never visited the MLK natatorium or any of Atlanta's pools. I also never visited the King Center for Nonviolent Social Change or King's boyhood home or Ebenezer Baptist Church. I confused the MLK natatorium with the tiered water fountains surrounding his tomb next door. I thought of these as monuments for Black people, not for me.

I was a senior in college before I ventured over to the Martin Luther King Jr. National Historic District. I was surprised to see National Park Service rangers in starched green uniforms and dimpled Stetsons leading tours down Auburn Avenue like it was the Grand Canyon. I joined the tour alongside tourists from Spain, Japan, and Canada, feeling alternately proud to be from the same city as their hero and ashamed that it had taken me so long to go visit.

■ ■ ■

I trailed the boys into the water, trying to decide if it was warmer to stay dry or be submerged. Once my swimsuit was wet, I had to commit.

As the clouds shifted, the square skylights created square spotlights on the surface of the water. I swam into those blocks of white light, trying to find warmth.

The boys' voices lifted to the soaring skylights. For a while, it was just us and a young white dad and his toddler. An Asian woman, I assume the mom in this family, was waving from the lobby, hugely pregnant in a striped summer dress. A few solo lap swimmers were working their way across the south side of the building. Unlike the old natatorium, there were only four diving platforms, four lanes for lap swimming, and no seating for spectators. My kids were rapidly losing interest. What makes a pool fun is not the architecture but the people inside of it.

Thankfully, another white dad showed up with two dark-haired little boys. Then an Asian grandma with a young grandchild in arm floaties. The boys wanted me to play with them, and I wished for more kids their age to show up. The lifeguards looked bored too. They tuned a boombox on one of those little wooden fold-out side tables that might normally hold up a TV dinner.

From the pool, you could see Atlanta through the huge floor-to-ceiling windows, and Atlanta could peek in and see us too. Look past the young maple trees, the four-story gated apartments where Grady Homes used to be, and there were two icons of south downtown—the Corey Tower, a smokestack with a giant, vertical LED display, and the neon script of a Coca-Cola billboard.

Later I posted a photo of the boys splashing in one of those squares of light. A friend commented, "We're there every Sunday morning." He lived in Old Fourth Ward with his wife and daughter. I puzzled over the fact that he was Asian like half of the pool users today. I was expecting a pool full of Black kids from the neighborhood, but clearly, the neighborhood had changed.

Councilman Kwanza Hall, who grew up swimming at the original natatorium, talked about the need for a public pool to serve the needs of the poor. "You've got folks not making a whole lot who deserve to have a place to go, just like everyone else does," he said. But where were the neighborhood kids?

By rebuilding the pool, did they rebuild the users? They made a place that was welcoming to people like me, white people, people from outside of the neighborhood, people with options.

I felt like one of those online reviewers, offering my judgment of a place based on one visit. But it was our first pool on the first day of summer, and our snapshot of the place was striking. It made me question how the surrounding neighborhood had changed so much that there were no Black families there on a Saturday morning the first weekend of summer. The public housing project Grady Homes was replaced with the Veranda at Auburn Pointe, affordable housing for seniors. Historic Old Fourth Ward, with its million-dollar homes on the Atlanta BeltLine, had become the poster child for gentrification.

Who was left besides the homeless men and the O4W newcomers? Was there anything in between? Was a high-end aquatic center what they need? Who feels welcome here? For first-time visitors like me, it was lovely but curious. How would this modern fitness temple, so sterile and new, evolve over time?

As we shuffled into the ladies' locker room, we passed one of the lifeguards pulling a hose on his way out. I made the boys cover their eyes and hustled them through the shower area, nodding apologetically to a grandma and her squalling grandchild.

I bolted my little ones in a family restroom stall before I realized that every surface was dripping wet, the walls and floors, the lockers and benches, the toilet and the sink. I looked around in vain for a place to stash our towels and dry clothes so I could use both hands to untangle the shivering boys from their swimsuits. There were no ledges or hooks to hang up a towel or a bag.

The lack of fixtures made no sense. It's like the designers didn't want to clutter the new walls, or maybe they ran out of money for final details. I squeezed our dry clothes between my knees while I helped the boys step into their shorts and shoes.

Before we left, I could see that the entire space was designed that way, waterproof and seamless. This room had just been hosed down. It was meant to be easy to clean.

May 27 ORANGE PARK

The next day, I looked up another pool that was just a couple miles from our house—the Rev. James Orange Park. Michael Halicki, the parks guru, told me that he had worked with Oakland City residents to redesign the pool before the city began renovations. My mom rode along with the boys and me to find another new public pool close to East Point.

We drove north along the railroad tracks, Atlanta's skyline in the distance, a MARTA train racing along beside us. I knew Oakland City not as a city, or even a neighborhood, but just a stop on the MARTA line, between East Point and downtown. The park, with its granite walls and massive oak trees, was one of Atlanta's oldest parks, established not long after this area incorporated as Oakland City in 1894. At the center of the park was a spring-fed swimming lake.

Mom pointed out that someone had smashed a little sign that marked the neighborhood on our left. Blue placards with gold lettering hanging from a wrought iron pole.

"Now why would someone do that?" she asked, more of a mom judgment than a question. I tried explaining that the start of summer in East Point always brought a rash of petty vandalism and car break-ins as bored teenagers tested their freedom. Still, it was a bummer. The Colonial Hills Neighborhood Association had probably raised funds for these little markers to add "character" and improve real estate values. They looked brand-new.

I hoped it was innocent. Kids being kids.

Last week, I watched Bruno grab a big bar of soap in the bathtub and break it in half just to see if he could do it.

I blurted, "Why did you do that?"

"I don't know what to tell you," he said, not even sorry. It was such a cute response to a mom question.

"Don't break my things," I said, laughing. "Break your own things."

I turned near Big Daddy's Meats, onto an old street that was new to me. On our left, a series of boarded-up bungalows; on our right, long rows of gray brick, two-story apartments. We cruised past a girl on a pink bicycle, a woman standing in a screen door, three men tending a fragrant grill—everyone was Black. They glanced into our windshield, didn't recognize us. The breezy, first-day-of-summer scene made me cheerful, but I already felt like a tourist.

The road terminated at the park, with its glistening pool and new playground swirling with noise and activity.

As we unloaded our towels and swim vests, we could hear the shouts and laughter from the pool. I saw pink and white birthday party balloons and streamers in a stately granite pavilion. We walked around a new playground to the pool entrance and questioned why it was blocked with a temporary construction fence. Mom and I examined the blackened remains of plastic melted to a tall play structure. It looked like those vinyl shade sails had been set on fire.

"Maybe it was struck by lightning?" I offered, feeling uneasy. After the smashed signs, the torched playground was a startling first impression.

The attendants in the pool house window just waved us through, clicking a silver counter. The city pools were free for opening weekend.

Here were the neighborhood children missing from the MLK natatorium. This pool had more kids than water. Maybe twenty children splashing in the pool, twenty more running around, and twenty adults attempting to relax on the deck.

Guy and Bruno knew what to do. First one in the water wins.

The pool was shaped like a big, friendly squiggle that ranged from zero to four feet deep. In contrast to the MLK natatorium, you couldn't swim laps here if you tried. The pool was shallow, designed for kids and nonswimmers to play, not exercise. I wore a swimsuit, but I wouldn't need to get in the water with the boys.

In my photos of the scene, the sky is rippled with rainclouds. Out of a dozen people in the shot, half are looking at me, the other half are gazing toward the two white boys that resembled twins with their matching blue vests and dirty blond hair. It felt like we had invited ourselves to a backyard swimming pool in the middle of a family reunion. No one spoke to us, but I wouldn't say we were invisible.

Before I had a chance to even spread out a towel on a lawn chair, it started to thunder. The lifeguards blew their whistles. Raindrops vanished on the wet pavement.

It was kind of a relief. The lifeguards started packing up. Parents stuffed their beach bags and stood to stretch. Kids piled onto the playground equipment that was supposedly closed for repairs. I watched a boisterous cluster of children in bright swimsuits crowd onto a spinning merry-go-round. Two long-legged tweens spun them into a rainbow.

My sons joined a handful of younger kids at the splash pad, which for some reason, wasn't considered a risk for lightning strikes. Bruno scurried around karate chopping the streams of water with a pool noodle. Guy took turns straddling different fountains, pressure washing his crotch, a favorite activity of every kid at every splash pad I've ever seen.

Since Centennial Olympic Park's ring fountains opened in 1996, these water features have become a popular alternative to swimming pools in Atlanta. The Parks and Rec program lists four in the city as "a fun and popular way for kids to 'beat the heat' without swimming." Splash pads are cheaper than pools because they don't require paid attendants. The kids won't drown, but they also won't learn to swim.

In a nice part of town, a splash pad can rival an amusement park, attracting families from all over the city. We hosted Bruno's third birthday party at one in the Historic Old Fourth Ward Park. This new park was on the Eastside trail of the BeltLine, at the heart of an area exploding with new condos and cafés, walking distance to Sephora and Williams Sonoma. We didn't get a permit, just showed up early to claim a picnic table for the cupcakes. The park was packed with joyful children and their watchful parents that morning.

The closest splash pad to our house is at Perkerson Park. We visited one morning and interrupted a man bathing in the fountain. What makes a pool or a park or a splash pad into a welcoming, safe, thriving place?

Jane Jacobs said that a neighborhood park is a "creature of its surroundings." Around this time, I was reading her 1962 classic *The Death and Life of Great American Cities* and highlighting lines like this. I wanted Jacobs to tell me it was okay to explore all these public parks and pools, to tell me where to swim.

She included a whole chapter about what makes a neighborhood park a "vital and appreciated" asset or a "breeding grounds for delinquency." Swimming pools, Jacobs wrote, invite "a sufficient sequence of welcome users." She said a good pool, like an ice-skating rink or a golf course, will attract users from beyond the neighborhood.

Furthermore, unlike playgrounds and splash pads, swimming pools are staffed with lifeguards and attended by parents. The surveillance by responsible adults made the difference between a lively park and an open space for muggings.

While Gramma stood under an awning, watching the boys scuttle around the fountains, I visited the pool house. Two four-foot steel peace signs adorned the doorways near a photo montage of the life of Reverend James E. Orange. He was a civil rights activist, an aide to Dr. King, and longtime resident of Oakland City. In 1963, young James Orange joined with Dr. King and Reverend Ralph David Abernathy in Atlanta to plan the March on Washington. He spent his life leading unions, fighting for immigrant rights, and raising a family in Southwest Atlanta.

Black-and-white images of the tall, young James Orange, marching in Selma, then leading Dr. King's funeral procession. Color photos of the white-haired reverend speaking into a microphone, praying over King's tomb. There were no captions, but they would've been hard to read anyway. The memorial gallery was bolted near the ceiling, out of reach of vandals but too high to read.

The city renamed Oakland City Park the Rev. James Orange Park in 2011, and by 2012, the Friends of RJOP group was raising money to demolish the old pool and build a new playground. Mayor Kasim Reed, who had staked his campaign for mayor on reviving Atlanta's public parks and pools, said in 2010, "Creating places where young people enjoy safe and fun recreational activities in their communities is a top priority of my administration." He pledged resources to rebuild the pool and pool house and install a new splash pad.

At the park's rededication in July 2015, Mayor Reed said, "Rev. James Orange Park was abandoned, and an area known for criminal activity when I took office. It is now a place that the community can be proud of." While swimmers dashed into the water, Reed made a statement about the mission of the Parks and Recreation Department as providing more than exercise and leisure to Atlanta's youth but also "facilities just like this that nurture academic success and character development."

Jane Jacobs was critical of the ability of pools and parks to accomplish such goals. She called this "the doctrine of salvation by bricks." She wrote, "When we try to justify good shelter on the pretentious grounds that it will work social or family miracles, we fool ourselves."

We just came to swim. As I searched the internet to find information about this park, it was hard to look past the continued violent crime in the area. In 2016, a year after the grand opening festivities, the naked body of a nineteen-year-old woman was found in the park. She had been shot multiple times and dumped by the basketball courts. One day in June, gunfire near the

Orange Park pool prompted the early closure of several pools across the city. The top news stories about the park overshadowed the mayor's narrative of character development.

"Too much is expected of city parks," wrote Jacobs. "Far from transforming any essential quality in their surroundings, far from automatically uplifting their neighborhoods, neighborhood parks themselves are directly and drastically affected by the way the neighborhood acts upon them."

The park was full of people, laughter, and music, with the pool and the playground at the nexus of activity, but the whole project felt like the smashed signs for Colonial Hills—a surface attempt to add value to a neighborhood where the economic problems ran much deeper.

I looked over at the charred playground. Candy wrappers tangled in the fence. A stray flip-flop, a waterlogged teddy bear, face down on the concrete. Kids being kids, setting fires, but also powerless kids testing their power. Was this normal rebellion or a message of resentment toward changes coming to the neighborhood, changes that brought white people like me to the park?

I was comforted by how Jacobs focused on the economics of the city, not the habits or morality of park users. "Deterioration, crime, and other forms of blight are surface symptoms of prior and deeper economic and functional failure of the district."

In a more affluent community, broken signs and damaged playgrounds were easily removed and replaced. Litter and vandalism happened everywhere, but here they lingered, evidence of the tremendous resources required to maintain a well-used park.

May 28   WATER BALLET

The most interesting pools are the abandoned pools. You imagine all that missing water, the flirting and floating that happened there. An empty pool says summer's over; the empire has fallen. A kind of psychic energy remains.

Freestyle skateboarding was born out of the decaying swimming pools in the backyards and hotels of Southern California in the mid-1970s. Abandoned by foreclosure, drained during drought, these empty pools were the first half-pipes. Before pool skating, the sport resembled surfing without a wave, there was the downhill slalom and novelty ground tricks. In each new pool, skaters invented new tricks. And because you could only drop in one at a time, your turn was your chance to experiment, express your style. What these skaters created was more like a performance on a dance floor, less like a competitive sport with points and teams, and it quickly gained international popularity. Skaters occupied the rot of suburbia, made urban exploring into an art form.

Today, in many concrete skate parks, you'll find a bowl that resembles a smooth swimming pool with a deep end and shallow end, often including a strip of decorative tile around the coping as a nod to their aquatic inspiration. The bowl is often the steepest, most intimidating feature of the park, where only the most experienced skaters and riders can drop in, gracefully carve around the bowl, and fly out. I know from experience that climbing out is a tough, running-start scramble. I spent hours hanging around skate parks while Jason aired out the bowl on his BMX.

In the early 2000s, Jason and I lived in Greenpoint, Brooklyn, near McCarren Park, where a grand, football field–sized swimming pool had been drained, chained, and left to decay. Funded by the WPA, it opened in 1936 and lasted until the early 1980s. It was closed, along with many other WPA era pools, due to budgets cuts and rising crime. We lived two blocks from the pool but didn't know it was there until Jason's BMX buddies invited us to come help build some ramps inside.

From the outside, overgrown and barricaded, densely tagged with graffiti, it looked like many of the industrial ruins of North Brooklyn at the time. Eddie Rios, a humble but legendary former BMX pro, showed us a break in the fence where you could duck in. Skaters and riders trucked in wheelbarrows and lumber for their DIY skate park, but clearly the graf writers had found a way in first. They had been there for years; the pool was an immense, illicit museum of street art.

Jason brought a screw gun; I brought a camera. Inside was a vast open space that rivaled any park in the city. When I was roaming the floor of the pool amid the wildflowers and spray paint cans, taking photos of trees shooting up through the ancient tile, I had never heard the term *gentrifier*. I did not imagine that we had any power, that this was the tip of the invasion. There's a tendency for the artist to take the credit and the blame for way neighborhoods shift from working class to trendy and exclusive. But the wandering graf writers and skaters preceded the artists, then yuppies who would really settle down and remake neighborhoods as attractive and safe again. Eventually, people with money start to see the appeal.

In 2004, Noémie Lafrance, a Williamsburg choreographer, asked the NYC Parks Department if she could stage a dance performance in the McCarren Park Pool. She was surprised when they agreed. For years, the city had plans on the shelf to restore and reopen the pool for public use but no funding to make it happen. Lafrance's proposal came at the perfect time. She partnered with a big concert promoter to raise the $250,000 that NYC Parks required to clean up and stabilize the venue so that she could stage the performance.

Her production, *Agora,* premiered the next year, and introduced a new load of hipsters to the marvels of the McCarren Park Pool. It literally opened the floodgates of events and happenings in the empty pool. By then, Jason and I had moved back to Atlanta. I remember reading with envy the unbelievable lineup of summer shows in the pool—Feist, Sonic Youth, Blonde Redhead, Deerhunter, the Yeah Yeah Yeahs, TV on the Radio. Again, how did I always miss out on the party?

A few years later, I was amused as young concertgoers lamented that Williamsburg was "losing its soul" when NYC Parks retired the venue to resurrect McCarren Park Pool as a swimming pool again. The development and displacement cycle is so fast in New York City. Today families swim there again. Every generation thinks they knew and loved the real pool.

■ ■ ■

I was thinking about all this—urban pioneers, disaster porn, poverty tourism, skaters and dancers, and artists and gentrifiers—when I heard about a dance performance to be staged in an empty pool in Atlanta in September 2012. Choreographer Lauri Stallings created a piece for the Atlanta-based performance group glo in the dry bottom of Maddox Park Pool. I had no idea there was an abandoned pool in there. The idea of a white artist exploring Bankhead blight made me uneasy.

Maddox Park was right next door to Bankhead Manufacturing, the metal fabrication shop my father managed for the last decade. Dad's workplace was one of a string of heavy industrial sites connected to the railroad corridor, flanked by junkyards, boarded-up storefronts, and demolished housing projects.

At some point when I was worrying about Dad's blood pressure, I recommended that he walk over to Maddox Park on his lunch breaks to get some exercise. I changed my mind when I visited the park and saw its postapocalyptic edges—houses half-burned and collapsing, boarded-up apartment buildings reclaimed by squatters and kudzu, dumped tires and couches, stray dogs. I asked if he ever considered carrying a gun.

Bankhead Highway was notorious for the sprawling housing projects concentrated along its length, from Bankhead Courts, Bowen Homes, Hollywood Courts, and Perry Homes to the nation's earliest public housing project, Techwood Homes. Intensely poor, segregated, and isolated from the rest of the city, the projects were fertile ground for creative exchange and expression. Bankhead gave rise to influential rappers who name-dropped the neighborhood and developed their own subgenre of Dirty South hip-hop. Kids videotaping Westside block parties created dance moves copied around the world.

The street was renamed for Judge Donald Lee Hollowell in 1988, and the projects were all demolished by 2009, but a steady stream of visitors still stopped to pose and take photos in front of the giant letters of the BANKHEAD sign in front of Dad's metal shop.

And right in the middle of this scene was Maddox Park. Opened in the 1920s with a two-acre, bean-shaped swimming pond and granite pool house, it was one of Atlanta's oldest public parks. At some point in the 1970s, the pool was renovated, but it had been fenced off and abandoned for all of Dad's Bankhead years.

Alas, glo's dance performance was yet another thing I missed, one of a hundred cool shows and happenings around town that I slept through in 2012, my first year of motherhood. I found some YouTube footage of seven dancers in retro swim caps and bathing suits jittering in the empty, blue-lit pool. That show probably put Maddox Park on the mental map of an entirely new set of Atlantans who had never experienced Bankhead as a neighborhood, just as it elevated the pool in mine. I credit Stallings for having a creative vision for the place and for shining a light on our underfunded infrastructure. But suddenly, white people with money were looking at the Maddox Park Pool again.

■ ■ ■

Fast-forward to 2018, and that pool was newly renovated and full of water. On Memorial Day, we visited the Maddox Park Pool. Our third new pool in as many days.

Jason drove north on Lowery Boulevard, in and out of rain showers and puddles. I kept warning the boys that if it was raining, we wouldn't be able to swim. "We're just going to check it out," I promised, and they echoed me.

"We're just gonna check it out!"

We turned left on Bankhead, past Dad's old sheet metal shop, then turned into the historic entrance of Maddox Park. The driveway led alongside the railroad tracks but didn't connect to the pool. We had to circle the park, under the old railroad tracks, over Proctor Creek. The houses we passed looked vacant and half-collapsed.

"Whoa," said Jason, eyeing a muscular pit mix trotting down the street. "Are you sure about this park?"

I was sure. The properties were all investor owned, in limbo. Just waiting for the neighborhood to flip.

We found the pool entrance and spotted some lifeguards in their red shorts through the wrought iron fence. It was raining but just barely. The pool was open. We walked through the stone pool house, a dim narthex before the sparkling blue swimming pool. No admission fee, no questions asked.

It's hard to describe the unbridled glee of my children with each new pool discovery. "Don't run," I kept pleading. "No running by the pool." They ran anyway, crashed into the water.

The rainclouds scudded to the east. The sun-toasted pavement steamed brightly. Monumental steel sunflowers sprayed one "beach" of the L-shaped pool. The boys ran into the mushroom-shaped fountains and danced inside the curtain of water.

To be here for free, racking up some quality time with the boys and seeing a new corner of the city, it felt like I was getting away with something. Any minute, the thunder would break out.

Everything was new—the pool and the concrete around it. The blue lounge chairs and big canopies. It was hard to tell what part of the granite pool house was historic and what had been renovated. The pool was hugged by these glorious old oak trees and crape myrtles that could have been planted in the 1920s, when the park was built here. You couldn't see the crumbling neighborhood through the branches.

At first, it was just us and a young Black family. A little girl, maybe four years old, I think she said her name was Sara, was delighted to have some other kids to play with. Immediately, she was frolicking with Guy and Bruno in the fountains like they were old friends.

As the skies cleared, more families started to show up. White, then Black, alternating. I saw some folks that looked like grandparents, but mostly it was families like us, with young kids. I was honestly surprised and a little curious about the white people. Did they live in the neighborhood now? Were they buying up houses in Grove Park and English Avenue? Grad students at Georgia Tech? Or were they like me, venturing from other neighborhoods, just looking for a nice place to swim on the first sunny day of summer?

A few years ago, I worked on a master plan for the city of Atlanta focused on Westside neighborhoods like Maddox Park. It was my job to attend all the public meetings and interview residents about their neighborhood, to try to come up with a community-based history of the area.

These meetings happened in church fellowship halls and city recreation centers. In Grove Park, I interviewed a sixty-six-year-old retired navy vet, a Black man whose family had moved to Grove Park in 1964. His high school and the parks were just beginning to integrate. Even though Atlanta's public pools officially desegregated in June 1963—a fistfight at Maddox Pool was the sole incident reported on opening day—he told me that the pool was still segregated a year later.

"They didn't want us to get in the swimming pool," he said. "When we got in the pool, they got out of the pool."

I never forgot that. The swimmers at Maddox Pool never really integrated; they just switched from white to Black. Working on that plan, I saw maps of the racial makeup of Atlanta illustrated with census block data. A sea of green dots for Black residents filled the west and south of the city; the north and east were made up of blue dots for white. Based on the stark segregation in those maps, I would venture that there has never been much integrated swimming in Maddox Park Pool. Until now.

I played Ring around the Rosie with Guy and Bruno and Sara. Over and over. We all fell down and ducked underwater. Sara craved my attention; she wanted to show me her toenail polish and hold my hand. The novelty of a parent in the water, an adult with different-colored skin. Sara's mom seemed suspicious; she kept yelling at her daughter to get out of the water and stay in the fountains. Likewise, it made me nervous when Guy started trailing another dad, a tattooed Black man racing his daughters across the shallow end.

"Tell Guy to leave him alone," I said to Jason.

We talk a lot about how Guy has no social instincts, no sense of other people's patience, interests, or personal space. He'll throw his arms around a girl in his class, no clue that she's trying to shake him off. He'll get right in the face of any kid on the playground and ask a string of questions, or any dog for that matter. Behavior that's cute in a toddler but worrisome in a seven-year-old. On one hand, I love that he's sweet and guileless. But Guy had to learn some respect for the unknown before he got hurt. Not every stranger wanted a skinny kid climbing on his back in the pool. Or worse, maybe they did.

"Give him some space," I told Guy as I pulled him toward the shallow end. "That is not appropriate."

"But I like him," Guy whined.

Every pool is part of trying to teach him how to be around strangers.

I aimed him toward the pool's edge, where his brother was in a cannonball contest with two Black boys. Maybe he could join them. The pool strips away of lot of the stuff that children otherwise use to assess each other. He gets a few minutes before they notice that he's different.

■ ■ ■

Somehow it was rainy enough to cancel our camping trip but not too rainy to hit the pools. Without exactly planning it, we swam in Atlanta's three newest pools in the first three days of summer. I picked them because they were new, and in the news; all had been renovated and reopened with great fanfare by Mayor Kasim Reed's administration. I began to think of them as the Reed Pools.

MLK, Orange Park, Maddox Park—when Reed took office, all three were in bad shape or abandoned. The new pools were very different from the austere, 1970s pools they replaced, with sharp edges, deep ends, and diving boards. The Reed Pools, with the latest trends in pool design and water features, were meant to be welcoming to children and inexperienced swimmers.

In terms of political optics, these pool reopenings were huge wins. The ribbon cutting ceremonies put a spotlight on Reed and his lovely wife and daughter in a tiny pink swimsuit while Black grandmothers demonstrated a water aerobics class and Black children splashed into fountains. They were expensive projects presented as Reed's largesse, his personal gift to the Black families of Atlanta. But that's also how I learned about the pools and why I felt comfortable venturing into historically Black neighborhoods to swim. The sparkling new pools were attractive, safe, and designed for families with young children.

As I lounged on the deck of the beautiful new Maddox Park Pool, I couldn't just chill and enjoy it. Could the reopening be the first time the pool was racially integrated in any meaningful way? Were sunbathing white people on Bankhead a sign the slumlords were waiting for?

At the same time, Black families were being pushed out of the city.

The Atlanta BeltLine project was in the background, gaining steam. The BeltLine would convert the unused railroad on the edge of Maddox Park into a linear trail that looped the entire city. When the first sections of the BeltLine debuted on the north and east sides of the loop, the white parts of town, they touched off a tidal wave of new development, redevelopment, and skyrocketing rents. The conditions were already ripe for gentrification; everything from income levels and housing prices had been creeping up. The BeltLine gave it all an organizing framework, gave developers their marching orders.

Now everyone knew the BeltLine was coming to the historic Westside, to the Black side of town. Some people viewed it as an opportunity, others as a threat. The plans had been around since 2000—where would the money for implementation come from, and when? Planners had been talking about Maddox Park as one of the green jewels of the BeltLine's "emerald necklace" since 2004, but here on Bankhead, it all still felt unattainable, a mirage in the distance. Invisible investors bought old houses, then left them to rot.

In 2010, a master plan for Maddox Park and vicinity was produced as part of the Atlanta BeltLine planning process. It recommended reopening the pool and restoration of the pool house as a top priority for the park's rebirth. The new Maddox Park would be a "catalyst for new development" that would also "accelerate redevelopment in the area."

In the last years of Bankhead Manufacturing, Dad fielded countless phone calls and surprise visits from developers interested in the properties owned by the metal shop. The chief developer was a Mr. Totey, a name I heard as "Toady," because he seemed like a creekside lurker. He formed a nonprofit to promote the expansion of Maddox Park, construction of the Proctor Creek Greenway, and redevelopment of everything in between, at which point it became tough to distinguish developer-driven schemes from the community revitalization promised by an environmental nonprofit.

Just like in Greenpoint, the plans to restore the pool were already there on the shelf, amid a whole stack of plans, just waiting for a moment when public funding intersected with private demand. A dance performance demonstrated how exquisite and valuable the pool could be. It set everything, good and bad, in motion.

During my interviews for that Westside master plan, I met a white choreographer who lived and worked near Georgia Tech. She asked me if I knew of any cool, abandoned places to stage a performance. I took her card, said I would get in touch if I thought of any.

May 29 RAIN PARTY

School was out, summer camp hadn't started yet, and the boys were stuck at home with me. Of course, it rained all week.

Googling for indoor pools, I found Welcome All Park, only ten miles away. Same distance as Maddox Park but south, away from the city, into the suburbs. The owner of my local coffee shop had recommended it. "It's a really nice pool," he said. "In a really nice area." He told me he had learned to swim there.

We drove in the rain outside the perimeter, the interstate boundary that marked the city from the suburbs. Past our nearest Target-Lowe's-BJ's-Publix compound. Past the Barnes & Noble–turned–BeautyMaster, a rare Southside Starbucks, and the busiest LongHorn Steakhouse in the country, into a part of Fulton County that had just incorporated as a city. Through the windshield wipers, I noted one well-tended subdivision after another; most looked like they were built in the 1970s and '80s.

Following the lead of North Fulton cities like Crabapple and Sandy Springs, but without the distinctive name, the new city of South Fulton was formed to represent all the unincorporated areas left in the county. For years, there were rumors that Mayor Reed wanted to annex this area into Atlanta, to add middle-class, Black residents to the city voter rolls. Instead, South Fulton residents formed their own city. With a majority-Black population and leadership, the new city of South Fulton would look more like Stonecrest, another experiment in Black cityhood in the eastern suburbs of Atlanta.

Welcome All Park was busy for a Tuesday afternoon in the rain. Ballfields spread out beyond the recreation center; the parking lot was full.

An attendant in a blue polo, embroidered with the new CITY OF SOUTH FULTON seal, greeted us with a clipboard. "That's two dollars for him and him and three for you," he said. "Cash only."

I didn't bring cash.

He explained that today was South Fulton's first day operating the facility, and they hadn't set up credit card readers, yet. He started to give me directions to the nearest ATM.

What are the chances? A new day for an old pool.

The boys protested returning to the car. But we haven't even seen the pool yet, they whined. I found enough quarters in the car cupholders to cover admission.

Inside the huge cinder-block natatorium was an Olympic-sized pool, diving blocks at one end, lifeguards at the other, white pennants stretched across the pool where it dipped to six feet, then nine feet deep. Half the lanes were reserved for lap swimmers in bright latex caps. The other half was open to the moms and babies gathered in the shallow end, teenagers clowning in the deep end. I saw a man teaching a girl to swim, maybe a father and daughter.

All the patrons and staff were Black. Everyone was bopping along to the music, Hot 107.9 piped in from somewhere. I recognized Drake and Migos; the rest was new to my ears.

There were a few steamy windows over by the square kiddie pool and out-of-order waterslide, but most of the light poured in from above. The ceiling had these soaring skylights that cast a dramatic spotlight on one corner of the pool whenever the clouds parted. Those skylights are so clear, I thought. How did they clean them way up there? I watched airplanes cross the sky, one after another.

The boys wore their swim vests and bobbed around in the shallow end for a while, then moved over to the kiddie pool when three little girls about Guy's age showed up.

Guy was awkward. Floppy, unself-conscious. An imitator and provoker. He wanted to play with them so badly.

I watched the girls try to assess him. To figure out if he's joking. What is he doing? Why is he jumping around like a little kid? I see them scan the faces around them for clues and confirmation that this kid is weird but harmless. What is wrong with him? How old is he?

White kids found him unsettling; I saw them avoid him. At a recent birthday party, I overheard a little girl warning another kid about Guy. "He's seven years old, but he doesn't act like it." So far, the kids who gave him a chance were Black. I suspected they wrote off his quirkiness as general whiteness.

I chatted for a while with a shy, very pregnant young woman in a bikini as her daughter played Marco Polo with my sons. Her belly was taut and round as a basketball, her bulging belly button would never be the same again. She was soft-spoken and anxious as she talked about her impending due date. I tried to say something encouraging. Having two is a blessing. Look at them play together. Everything is much easier the second time.

But I recognized that fear and fatigue in her eyes. Labor is savage; babies are relentless—there is no way around it. And yet she could do it; she was already doing it, in part, by finding this pool. The water lifted the burden. Her daughter in a hot-pink life preserver, free to frolic. These afternoons floating in the water would seem like a dream if they remembered them at all.

Eventually, it started to rain again, and Guy pointed out that the roof was closing. With a mechanical whir, several translucent panels were sliding into place to cover the sky. I realized they weren't skylights but sky.

A few of the panels stayed open. A gentle shower fell into the pool.

"It's a rain party!" yelled Bruno. Raindrops. Drop tops. We were smitten.

"Half of them don't work anymore," said one lifeguard.

"When was this built?"

"Before I was born," she said. "At least twenty-five years ago."

This made me feel old, like everything lately. I swam under a fortieth anniversary banner for the recreation center, 1972–2012. South Fulton's old natatorium was a generous, well-built facility that had held up for decades. I liked the nostalgic elements—the huge, tile mosaic on the wall of Fulton County's oak tree logo. Even the dysfunctional roof panels were charming.

Unlike all the other inner-city pools that were closed and abandoned as neighborhoods declined, Welcome All Park's pool had benefited from the sustained, year-round investment of its middle-class, suburban community. This was an all-Black pool that had never been marginalized. I felt like a guest in a beloved place, not a threat.

May 31 POOL PLANS

The rain moved out. The temperature climbed. Friends saw my photos of pools and started asking for advice about where to swim. Kristy was bored with the Y. John asked about swim lessons for his toddler. Rebecca said she needed to get her eight-year-old in the water. Where should we go? They texted. How much does it cost? Is it safe?

I was becoming a scout, an ambassador for uncertain white people curious about public pools.

It was a lot to research. Local government websites were often unreliable, so I never knew exactly if and when the pools were open or if cash was required. If the weather shifted and it started to thunder, the pool could abruptly close, no refunds.

Try to be flexible, I advised them. Accept that you might get ten minutes in the water, or you might get three hours. The public pools would kill your plans, but they're cheap.

I recommended the Grant Park Pool for beginners. It was big and fun and unpretentious, with a kiddie pool and lots of lounge chairs. It was centrally located in a desirable historic neighborhood where they were unlikely to be the only white people in the pool.

I took the boys to Grant Park on a Thursday night because it was open until eight. I told Jason to meet us there after work and we would go out for pizza.

Another good thing about Grant Park was that you parked on a street that overlooked the pool. Through the oaks, you had a view of the pool and everyone in it. If the pool was closed for maintenance or crowded with teenagers or half-reserved for a swim team practice, you could see this before you even left your car.

The boys liked to squat in their little flip-flops and preview the action in the pool from this vantage point, like watching a football game from the bleachers.

I led them down the redbrick sidewalk, past dreamy Victorian palaces, to the very 1970s-looking bunker bathhouse. As I stood in line to pay admission, the boys clambered on two life-sized concrete dolphins that stood sentinel by the entrance.

In front of me, I overheard a terse interaction between a white Grant Park mom and the Black pool attendant behind the desk. Apparently, she didn't bring enough cash.

The City of Atlanta had changed its prices, explained the teenage attendant, and the credit card machine wasn't working.

Bummer. I knew the feeling very well. It was a long hike back to the cars.

"Don't you think you should honor the prices on the website?" argued the mom. There was some back-and-forth. And then she asked to speak to a supervisor.

At this point, I had never heard someone called a "Karen," but I recognized the script. I held my breath, wished she would reverse course. This didn't need to be a fight.

The supervisor wasn't answering the phone. The daughter started whimpering, either about missing precious pool time or in response to her mom's anger. I checked to see if Guy and Bruno were picking up on the tension. For me at least, it was instructive to have a front row seat for this exchange.

"Why would you turn them away?" said the mom, gesturing to her kids. Pinched wad of cash, pinched face. The attendant could do nothing but apologize.

I thought about offering the mom some cash or telling her the CVS across the street had an ATM. But she didn't need money. She needed to be right.

The woman stormed off, trailing her bawling children like ducklings. I stepped up to the desk with an apologetic grimace and exact change. Why was rule following so important to my people? Is it because we are stuck in mom mode, forever tasked with managing discipline, enforcing fairness for our children? Or was this whiteness bristling against Black authority? The boys and I zigzagged through the locker room and burst out onto the pool deck.

The broad, turquoise pool shimmered in the late-afternoon sunlight, hugged on all sides by Grant Park's beloved oaks.

A cluster of white parents, fully clothed, gathered in the shady northwest corner of the pool. Toddler swim school, I guessed. We headed the other direction. I did not make the same mistake as that summer when I brought the boys to this pool alone, without floaties. This time, they wore their little PFDs and leaped into the warm kiddie pool without me.

Right away, they joined forces with a boy named Houston or Austin, some western city, who was bare chested, blond, rambunctious, and five years old, he told us. Almost six! They took turns shouting something silly as they bounded into the pool.

"Bootie-Butt!" hollered Bruno. Splash.

"Donald Trump!" shouted Houston. Splash.

I sat on the edge of the pool scooping stray catkins from the water with my toes. At my elbow, a dark-skinned boy afflicted with hypertonia, struggled across the shallow end. I noticed his muscular little body, his mother's protective arms. For the second time in an hour, I tried to communicate telepathically with another mom. Guy had the opposite diagnosis, hypotonia, or low muscle tone. The mother watched her son only. Where else do you see disabled bodies, really see them? Or even such a range of bodies, half-naked and vulnerable, moving slowly in the sun and through the water.

Houston was swimming without floaties, which inspired Bruno to take off his vest. I climbed into the water and freed his buckles. Then Guy wanted to match his little brother.

Here's where they surprised me by doing something that resembled swimming. Jumping off the side of the pool into my arms, then paddling back to the wall. Climb out and repeat.

This is part of how kids learn to swim. Competition. Peer pressure. Watching other kids. I remember that feeling; it was what compelled me to finally let go of the edge of a pool.

Is this the greatest pool? I asked. Yes, they agreed. Every day's pool was the best pool, but the combination of abundant sunshine and friendly children bumped this one to the top of the list.

After an hour of this, Jason appeared on the pool deck in wilted office attire.

"Honey, I'm home."

"Finally," I said. "I need backup."

The boys showed him their new swim stunts while I gathered towels and water guns and swim vests. Found my grocery bag of dry clothes sitting in a puddle. Jason corralled the skipping boys into the men's locker room.

I met them back at the pool entrance, fully dressed with spiky wet hair. I asked them to climb on the concrete dolphins for a photo. My children each straddled one and grinned at my camera, exhausted and content from their accomplishments.

They were fountains once, these statues; their brass noses were nozzles. Later, when I started digging into the history of Grant Park, I spotted them in a photo from opening day in June 1974. That's when the pool finally opened after a decade of delayed promises and opposition from white neighbors who wanted "to preserve trees and prevent more noise in the park." Two skinny Black boys in cutoffs held their arms in the spray from what looked like a sea lion.

The original Grant Park Pool, established in 1902, was a spring-fed lake nearly seven acres long, divided for boating and swimming. They called it Lake Abana. Thousands of white swimmers enjoyed the lake for decades. In 1960, the city drained the lake and filled it with dirt. I found the details deep in the legal notices published in the back of the newspaper: a city advertisement for bids to haul thirty-eight thousand cubic yards of dirt from the Key Golf Course to the Grant Park Zoo Development while "filling the swimming pool with the hauled dirt." Zoo Atlanta's current petting zoo and Wild Planet Café sit in the shady lowland where swimmers used to splash.

The first animals to arrive in the new zoo? Six seals housed in the old pool.

Every time we go back to the Grant Park Pool, those statues look like seals to me, not dolphins. They remind me of the animals the city imported rather than allow Black children to share the lake.

June 2 POOL HOPPING

Emboldened by our pool discoveries so far, I made a list, a map, and a goal—visit every public pool in Atlanta before the end of the summer. We had already seen four of the city's nineteen public pools, and it was only June.

The next pool on my list was South Bend. It was only a few miles away, but it felt much farther because it was on the other side of I-75 and I-85. Sixteen lanes wide, the ironically nicknamed "connector," highway divided Atlanta like a river, but worse. People at least like to look across a river. This highway was a harsh, gray dead zone.

Aunt Myra and the cousins met us at the South Bend Pool, which we both found scruffy but appealing. Thankfully, she's a fan of midcentury design and could appreciate the modest upswept "Googie" style bathhouse architecture. None of it looked like it had been updated since the 1950s.

There was no furniture on the deck, so we spread our towels in a shady spot of concrete against a chain-link fence that ringed the pool. Two steel life-guard stands held red umbrellas.

There were no fountains or kiddie features, but the shallow end was crowded with children and teenagers, some hauling their toddler cousins and siblings. I saw very few adults anywhere. We were the only white people, which was no surprise at this point and didn't seem to register with the kids. If we were swimming, we didn't feel out of place. A middle-aged man in big shades hanging out solo by the pool stairs looked more suspicious than we did.

The boys shared their water cannons and goggles with the other kids, which made them momentarily very popular. I investigated the deep end, so deep it made my ears pop when I tried to touch the bottom. That diving depth—eleven feet—was another indicator of the pool's age. Myra stayed in the shade in her shorts and sunhat, posted photos online that we were "pool hopping."

The place was such a vivid time capsule, later that summer it would serve as a shooting location for the retro horror series *Stranger Things*. All they had to do was put up a sign that said Hawkins Community Pool, add some lounge chairs, and fill the pool with white extras, and it was 1985.

We swam for nearly an hour before the lifeguards whistled for safety break. The crowd grudgingly lifted themselves from the water onto their towels, opened bags of Takis, and checked cell phones. My sister produced Ring Pops for our crew. Wrapped in towels, they eyed the other children impatiently.

I paced barefoot, studying the pool.

There was a plaque in the breezeway of the brick pool house, dedicated by Mayor William B. Hartsfield in 1953. This pool was built for the white swimmers of Lakewood, a neighborhood near a distinct bend in the Southern Railway line. It had to be one of the oldest unrenovated pools in Atlanta. Forty names on the dedication plaque, all of them men with first names like Ogden, Earl, Dowse, Milton, and Raleigh, except one: Lillian Everett, Secretary. What would they think of this summer scene, still segregated but not officially and not for whites?

I asked one lifeguard how long the safety break lasted, and he couldn't say. "I don't even like to swim," he said. "I'm just here to meet females."

Judging by the aroma of the pool office, he was high. But I understood. The females that day were distracting.

The surface of the pool turned to glass; puffy clouds stalled overhead. I did some math. At sixty-five years old, this leftover pool had lasted longer than the grand Lake Abana.

Two teenage boys swam out to wrestle over a floating basketball, and no one stopped them. A kind of happy rulelessness prevailed. Typically, this would drive me crazy, but I was outnumbered by teenagers. And it was so hot. The warm concrete burned through our towels, made the kids drowsy.

Eventually, a lifeguard pulled a water sample and disappeared with the vial.

Safety break, which was supposed to give the lifeguards a quarter-hour for water testing and rest, was downtime for me. I had overscheduled our Saturday. That morning, I took the boys to a birthday party. I can't remember why, but the hostess loaned me a very old hardcover of Lillian Smith's *Killers of the Dream*. Maybe she heard me blabbering about our segregated swimming pools to one Black dad who was running for mayor of College Park. On the edges of birthday parties, this is the kind of exchange that happens, and you barely remember what was said because you were half-minding your children, trying to get them to use a tissue or finish a juice box.

Anyway, I had been chasing little boys all day, while Jason was working through his never-ending list of weekend yard and house chores. It was pleasant to just watch the shifting treetops over the placid clearing, sublime old oaks, poplars, sycamores. On one side of the parking lot, up a steep grassy hill, loomed a fenced dog park. There was a cluster of granite boulders where dogs perched regally, a fine view of the skyline. On the other side of the pool was a bushy cliff where a creek, some tributary of the South River, cascaded down a ravine. You could hear the crashing water but hardly see it through the dancing kudzu. I liked knowing it was there.

Music drifted over from an ice cream truck, which was just a tan Econoline with a magnet sign that said ICE CREAM TRUCK. Again, what year was it?

Safety break stretched on forever; groups of kids started to leave. We gave it another half-hour, then abandoned South Bend too.

June 20 SUMMER SOLSTICE

The temperature hit one hundred degrees on the solstice. It was the middle of the day in the middle of the week, and everyone huddled in this Southeast Atlanta coffee house was sheltering from the heat.

I was waiting to meet a grad student studying community resiliency and water security. That she thought I had some insight to offer on this topic was amusing to me, but I was always willing to meet residents, students, and potential allies for lattes and talk about urban creek projects. Sometimes I visited several coffee shops a week for these conversations, which seemed to balance out all the meetings with politicians, developers, planners, and economic development people that packed my days.

I preferred mismatched, gritty cafés like this one, with a wall covered in community flyers and local artists' work for sale, beat-up sofas, and folding chairs. They attracted fewer corporate types fielding sales calls loudly on their Bluetooth headsets, more students quietly studying and grooving under their headphones.

A young man and woman took a small table next to me.

I heard him ask about the day's plans, and she said, "Are there any places to swim that aren't gross pools?"

I looked up. The speaker had long, peroxide blonde hair. A baseball cap that said OBITUARY. I couldn't see the man's face, only his long dark hair. Both wore all black with lots of tattoos.

"Well, there's the Chattahoochee River," he said.

"That's like, nature. Snakes and shit. And don't they open up a thing at a certain time every day?"

"The dam?"

"Yeah."

"Hmm." They both flicked their devices, searching for water, I suppose. They looked like roadies or riggers on their off day from a concert tour.

"You can never find a damn swimming hole in the South," she said.

I stared intently at my laptop. She was voicing the problem of water access so perfectly—public pools were "gross"; nature was risky. I stopped typing whatever email I was writing so I could listen.

"I mean, I get it, it's a city," she went on. "But even in Florida, you can put your feet in the water. If there's a creek near here, you can't touch it."

Were they on a date? She was filling the silence with chatter. I couldn't help myself. I loved her broadcast.

"You could make a million dollars," she mused, "if you built, like, a lazy river–type thing. Like a glorified pond."

She was describing the "Little Hooch" at White Water, the water park of my youth. Or the lazy river at the South Cobb Aquatic Center. Both would be clogged with kids on rafts.

She followed her thought to the same mental image.

"Just spitballing here. . . . There would be, like, a limit to how many people were in it at a certain time, how many people a day. So, you're not abusing the facility. You'd be like, I own this beach."

"You only have to drive forty-five minutes to get to a place on the river," he offered. This guy knew Atlanta.

She stopped for a minute, looking at her phone.

"The hardest part would be someone has to pay for it."

He showed her something on his phone, and she said, "Ooh, an aquatic center!"

"Wait, never mind. It's a disgusting public pool."

She moved on. Started telling him about her latest thirty-day cleanse.

I felt indebted to the blonde and her castoff comments. She wasn't wrong. Any urban creek was too contaminated for swimming. Any public pool on a hot summer day would be swirling with strangers, like this coffee shop. To swim in the private lakes and private pools of Atlanta, you had to know someone with a membership, a dock, a condo, or a key. Someone who owned a beach.

If I could've volunteered any advice without seeming like a creepy, eavesdropping weirdo, I would've told them to visit a downtown hotel with a rooftop pool, several of which sold spa passes starting at fifty dollars an hour. Maybe I had called the Mandarin Oriental, the Four Seasons, and the W on a whim one afternoon and pretended to be a guest to find out how this worked. This option was too expensive for my unpicky little swimmers—it would be cheaper to take my kids to White Water—but maybe the roadies had money to burn.

They left before my date showed up, letting a blast of warm air into the room. I hope they found a pool, but I imagine they dropped the idea. Privacy is expensive.

June 21 SWIMMING IN EAST POINT

The morning was bright and muggy by six thirty. Excited about starting swimming lessons, the boys woke up early, slipped into their swimsuits, goggles, and flip-flops, and commenced arguing over the television remote control and the last two Pop-Tarts.

We were an hour early for our lesson with Miss Michelle, so I hustled the kids into the car and drove to the East Point Historical Society.

"Where are we going?" The constant backseat refrain.

I turned by a big grassy field a couple blocks from our house.

"I'm gonna show you where our swimming pool used to be."

The boys spilled out of the car, no water in sight. A lovely, hundred-year-old white Craftsman that housed the East Point Historical Society sat in the middle of the three-acre lot, flanked by crape myrtles and brick pathways.

Before I had children, I used to walk down here often with my border collie, unclasp her leash, and let her chase Frisbees in the field until the sun slipped behind the trees. The lawn was always mowed, but there was little activity besides me and my dog. The EPHS held open-house hours a couple Saturdays a month.

"This," I said, spreading my arms out across the field, "is where the pool used to be."

Somewhere between the parking lot and the magnolia, the old pool spanned the empty field. I did my best to show the boys the scale of it, where the diving board was and the kiddie pool. I estimated the pool's footprint from studying old maps and aerial photos.

The boys didn't believe me. Who would plant grass on a giant swimming pool? they asked. Why? When? I could show them where the pool used to be, but I couldn't explain what happened to it.

The first time I wandered into the EPHS house, some aimless Saturday morning, also pre-kids, I was greeted by a six-foot-wide photo of a swimming pool over the mantel in the living room–turned–gallery. The dim walls and shelves were cluttered with framed black-and-white photos of houses and factories and men in suits, rusty plaques and farm implements, architects' sketches and high school pennants, but the image of the wide blue pool was the centerpiece of the museum.

When a volunteer docent told me the pool was once located on this property, I was surprised and curious. I didn't know there used to be a pool in my neighborhood.

A professional photographer was hired to document the grand reopening of the swimming pool in 1954. The city's original pool had been closed for years due to cracks and failing filtration. Rather than attempt to bring it up to code, the city built a state-of-the art pool right next to the old one. It took a wide-format camera and a distant perch to capture the full width of the huge new facility.

The black-and-white photo had been hand-colorized—redbrick bathhouse, green grass, a yellow car on the street, pale blue water. There were a hundred happy people in the water, a hundred more along the edges enjoying the scene, all meticulously painted pink and tan. The pool was clearly segregated.

The more I thought about this, the more bitter I felt. On a hot summer day, a history museum was a poor substitute for water.

Of course, I suspected the pool was destroyed during the 1960s during integration, but for a long time, I had no proof. All I had was that giant photo and the oral histories scattered in comments on the EPHS Facebook group, a patchwork of memories from its mostly white membership. Their consensus was that this generous swimming pool was the most wonderful and memorable part of growing up in East Point in the fifties and sixties. It was peacefully integrated and lasted well into the seventies, they remembered. The pool was ultimately demolished when it became too expensive to maintain. Racism didn't figure into the pool's regrettable demise.

Most commenters were satisfied with this story, but like my kids, I was incredulous. If the pool was so beloved, how did it fall into disrepair? Who stopped maintaining it and why? And beyond that, why were there still no public pools in East Point decades later? The City of Atlanta sustained nineteen public pools—from basic concrete pools to fancy new aquatic centers—but East Point couldn't marshal the political support or resources to build a single pool. Why? Why was I driving my children to a private backyard pool in College Park for swimming lessons, instead of walking down the street?

Perhaps most telling was this grassy expanse, the pool's complete erasure. Why bury the place that delighted so many people for half a century? It felt like a cover-up.

It was hard to picture anything here but a boring grass lawn. The boys darted around in their swimsuits and goggles, pretending to swim in the air, little blotches of orange and blue on a green canvas.

■ ■ ■

Thanks to the EPHS, I could piece together the history of swimming in East Point from the city council minutes. Deep into these recordings of motions and recommendations and reports, I found the first surprise. There were two pools.

In 1953, the city solicited bids for two new pools—a 450,000-gallon capacity "white swimming pool" on Spring Avenue and a much smaller "colored pool" on Randall Street in the East Washington community. Those terms, *white pool* and *colored pool,* were in the minutes. The newspaper said, "Negro pool." I flinched each time I read them, as though they were slurs and not legal designations.

The Black pool would be one-third the size of the white pool. Why didn't they just build two equal pools? I mentioned the disparity to a white volunteer at the East Point Historical Society.

"Of course, they were different sizes," he said. "There were twice as many white residents as Black."

I was taken aback. Did he really believe it was about numbers? He was an amateur historian who dressed up for Civil War battle reenactments on the weekend. He told me that his family never swam in public pools "because that was mixed bathing."

By now, I was reading *Killers of the Dream,* in which Lillian Smith broke down exactly how segregated spaces project a clear racial hierarchy. Regardless of population numbers, the segregated Black schools, neighborhoods, churches, and even cemeteries were always inferior.

"Every little southern town is a fine stage-set for Southern Tradition to use as it teaches its children the twisting turning dance of segregation. Few words are needed for there are signs everywhere. White . . . Colored . . . There are signs without words: big white church on Main Street, little unpainted colored church on the rim of town; big white school, little ramshackly colored school; big white house, little unpainted cabin; white graveyard with marble shafts, colored graveyard with mounds of dirt."

I kept flipping back to the copyright page, where it said, "1949, First Edition." I couldn't believe a white woman in the 1940s was writing so vividly about "the authoritarian system of white supremacy twisted up with Christian fundamentalism," using terms that only came into my vocabulary after the most recent presidential election. As new segregated facilities were being funded and constructed, facilities like East Point's swimming pools, Smith was warning her readers that Jim Crow was injuring our neighbors and corrupting our own souls.

East Point's miniature "colored pool" was state-of-the-art, but it reminded me of those "mommy and me" sets, which include a woman's outfit and an identical child-sized version. As if white taxpayers had kindly provided this little pool as a favor for their dependent neighbors across the tracks. On the contrary, the Black taxpayers who lived in East Washington joined the East Point Community Civic Club to raise fifty thousand dollars toward a pool on Randall Street. According to the *Atlanta Daily World*, these citizens purchased the land and donated it to the city to create the park. At the time, most of the streets in the East Washington neighborhood were unpaved.

I stumbled over the capitalization. Why was *white* lowercased and *Negro* capitalized? They were describing two specific groups of people, not a color palette. In first grade, Guy learned to capitalize proper nouns, and even he would see that this didn't make sense.

That lowercase *w* had the sneaky effect of making whiteness generic and invisible, the default category. Not *White* like a proper noun, a distinct identity, but *white* like a color, the gesso of a canvas, devoid of meaning. What would happen if I started capitalizing *White*? I wanted to see the word anew. It ought to make me flinch.

By late 2020, after the police killing of George Floyd in Minneapolis and the uprisings that followed, most major American media outlets began capitalizing the *B* in *Black* when it referred to a racial or cultural identity. Capitalizing *White* was less widely accepted. The *Washington Post* and CNN switched to the big *W*, but the Associated Press and *New York Times* suggested that capitalizing *White* legitimized hate groups. A number of concerned friends and editors pointed this out to me while correcting my capital *W*. Most of them were White.

After a while, I found plenty of compelling arguments for capitalizing *White*. Historian Nell Irvin Painter confirmed my line of thinking that naming *White* as an identity "makes white people squirm." She wrote, "No longer should white people be allowed the comfort of this racial invisibility." The Center for the Study of Social Policy went even further, saying that exempting "White" as a race was "an anti-Black act which frames Whiteness as both neutral and the standard." Eve Ewing, sociologist and author, used an unforgettable metaphor when she likened Whiteness to an invisible force field that has to be tested and mapped. "Where there appears to be nothing at all, there is, in fact, danger."

I choked on the word at first. It felt like shouting after a lifetime of whispering about race and denying its function in my life.

■ ■ ■

Both pools opened in June 1954, a high-water mark for the City of East Point. There were speeches and beauty queens in swimsuits at the ribbon cutting for East Point's "new, modernistic" pool on Spring Avenue.

A few weeks later, the Randall Street Pool was formally dedicated with "a mammoth parade" led by the South Fulton High School band, a ribbon cutting, prayers by the Reverend R. B. Rowe, "trick swimming and a pool program." I found some great photos of the day in the *Atlanta Daily World,* featuring sweaty dignitaries in light suits and straw hats posing while, in the background, a crowd is enjoying the pool. Two swimmers hovered mid-dive over the water.

The pools were popular with families from day one and became the heart of summer activity in the Black and White community, respectively. In 1956, the Parks Department organized the first annual Water Show and Beauty Parade at the Randall Street Pool, featuring water safety demonstrations, "fancy diving," and a "fashion revue." At the Spring Avenue Pool, there were "Dive-In" movies every night of the week, from "dark till close," which would've been pretty late in the summer. "I've been concerned for a long time," said parks superintendent Roy Grayson, "over the fact so many people were missing the enjoyment of night swimming."

For this delightful concern, and for all his creative programming at both pools, Grayson was beloved as the city's parks director. There's still a baseball field by my house named after him. But in 1959, Grayson was involved in a scandal at the Randall Street Pool that cost him his job, and more. When two teenaged White girls, swim instructors with the American Red Cross, stepped into the water for a safety demonstration in front of a crowd of hundreds of Black residents, it caused an uproar.

East Point was not ready for accidental integration or the media attention that surrounded it. Grayson was suspended, then fired. The mayor demanded sworn affidavits from all the instructors that "whites and Negroes" were never in the pool at the same time. His son Jim Grayson told me that the KKK burned a cross in their front yard and called their home with death threats.

The family left East Point. Roy Grayson may have built the pools and overseen their maintenance and operation, often organizing volunteers and employing his own children in the effort, but his most important job was maintaining segregation. Hearing about the impact on Jim Grayson's life convinced me that parks and pools are ultimately social spaces, and in the 1950s, the job of parks director hinged on maintaining social order.

The Spring Avenue Pool admitted four Black swimmers on Sunday, July 5, 1964. A jeering crowd and fistfights were reported at the scene. One former lifeguard claimed that these integrationists were outside agitators, not Black swimmers from East Point. The next day, city council voted unanimously to shut down both public pools due to "the Breach of the Peace which occurred at our Spring Street Pool yesterday and the discharge of an explosive near our Randall Street Pool last night." This astonishing line in the city council minutes is the only reference I could find of a bombing at the Randall Street Pool. An article in the *Atlanta Constitution* the next day altered the story significantly by applying the word *explosive* to the crowd.

Council recommended that both swimming pools remain closed "for the present and the future," and the mayor appointed a committee to consider "the best method of disposing of the swimming pool properties." The city attorney advised the council to sell the pools. Swimmers received refunds for their season passes.

Cooler heads prevailed, and the following season, the council voted to reopen the pools with one creative new rule—swimmers had to register at the recreation center in their respective community to purchase swim tickets. In other words, you had to live in a White neighborhood to swim at Spring Avenue. By restricting swimmers to their segregated neighborhoods, the city could maintain segregation in the pools a little while longer.

But after these scandals and violent episodes, many White swimmers never returned and withdrew their support of the pools. Lester Maddox, segregationist firebrand who published editorial rants within ads for skillet fried chicken at his Pickrick Restaurant, put it this way: "Integrated pools? Yes. The federal judge says if they are operated by Atlanta, they cannot be operated segregated. GOOD. Fill them with soil and by spring they can be filled with beautiful plants, shrubbery. . . . If we must share the pools, will bathtubs be next?"

Charles Strickland, a former president of the EPHS, told me it was a case of "if we can't have it to ourselves, then we ain't gonna share it."

White swimmers found other places to swim. They built private swim clubs, backyard swimming pools, and exclusive community pools. Between 1950 and 1970, suburban development fueled many innovations in pool construction and financing, resulting in over 800,000 new private, backyard pools across America. Meanwhile, Black families were systematically denied access to suburban housing and home loans. Jeff Wiltse documents this nationwide trend in his book *Contested Waters: A Social History of Swimming Pools in America*. "This represented a mass abandonment of public space and was caused most directly by racial desegregation. . . . The primary appeal of club pools was that members could avoid interacting with people who were socially different from themselves."

In East Point, those who could afford the dues joined the Lakeside Country Club, established in 1959 on the rural western edge of the city. With a swimming pool, an eighteen-hole golf course, and Saturday night formal dances with a full orchestra, Lakeside membership was a mark of status. A newspaper covered the formal summer opening of Lakeside in 1960, a black-tie affair, noting that it was "one of the latest additions to Atlanta's growing list of social clubs." I found a photo online of the marbled cover of *By-Laws and House Rules* published by Lakeside Country Club, Inc., in November 1959. Did the pages inside mention racial restrictions? The membership at Lakeside was exclusively White.

If a country club was too pricey, for twenty-five dollars a month, White families could swim at East Point's Elks Club pool near Greenbriar Mall. There wasn't a WHITES ONLY sign hanging by the big outdoor pool, but it was completely segregated. My neighbor Martha Kimes told me that her family joined the Elks Club in the summer of 1974, and it took a month before she understood that it was segregated. Her son invited a Black boy to join them one Saturday for a swim.

"It didn't dawn on us that it was restricted," she said. By the mid-seventies, her East Point neighborhood and her sons' elementary school were racially integrated, but there were still unspoken rules about which facilities belonged to which groups. It's like the Civil Rights Act forced people to remove explicit racist language from their by-laws and membership rules, but the unspoken rules were just as effectively enforced.

"It came to my attention—some adult made some comment—and I had to backtrack. I didn't want to embarrass the boys," Kimes told me. "Once we figured out the policy, we didn't go back."

East Point fire chief Corey Thornton shared a similar story about persistent, de facto segregation in East Point, long after the pools were legally desegregated. Thornton's parents grew up in the all-Black East Washington community, and even in the 1980s, they forbid him to swim in the formerly White pool on Spring Avenue.

"It was a group of us would ride our bikes around. My mom always told me, 'Corey Deon Thornton, do not go to that pool.' You know, when they call your whole name back then, that means pay attention. So, when she emphasized that, I knew that was a place I couldn't go. But it wasn't until I got older that I really understood why I couldn't go."

Thornton was a strong swimmer. He worked as a lifeguard at the Boys Club pool and spent summer days swimming with friends. "My pool was at John Milner Park on Randall Street. All the Blacks swam at Milner Park. That was the only place that we were allowed to swim." He never took a dip in the Spring Avenue Pool.

He told me that when his parents moved to Carriage Colony, a subdivision in East Point with spacious ranch houses and a community pool, they were one of the first Black families to move to the neighborhood. As other Black families moved in, the community pool was sold and destroyed. I found the pool in a historic aerial image, hidden way back against the power line easement. It appears in 1968 along with the new houses and then disappears from the 1993 photo. Another pool filled in with dirt, erased and forgotten.

In 1982, both of East Point's public pools were closed for repairs. Voters defeated a referendum that would have raised $770,000 for renovations to the aging pools, plus built a third pool at Sykes Park. The newspaper reported,

"City officials can only speculate as to why the referendum failed, citing economic difficulties and unemployment as possible reasons why voters chose not to allow the expenditure."

That oversized print of the White pool hung in the office of Lowell Hollums, the director of parks and recreation, even after the referendum failed and the pools shut down. Explaining the high cost of pool maintenance, he said, "A pool is like an iceberg, with 10 percent above the surface and 90 percent below." White voters who were now paying to swim in private clubs or investing in their own backyard swimming pools were not interested in funding public pools. Black voters still remembered their parents' warnings never to go to Spring Avenue. Just like on Tybee Island, the public debate was focused on cost, but more complex motivations remained below the surface.

■ ■ ■

Once the city demolished the pools, it commissioned a new plan for the three-acre property on Spring Avenue in collaboration with the newly formed East Point Historical Society. According to Charles Strickland, locating the EPHS on the site was "a case of building a battle memorial on an old battlefield."

Their vision for a historical park included a horticultural conservatory, gardens, outdoor exhibits like a steam locomotive, and the EPHS house, relocated from downtown to make way for a strip mall.

The pool photo wasn't simply hanging on the wall of the museum, in a position of prominence. The EPHS curator told me she wanted to move the photo, that it gave the wrong first impression, but it was literally built into the wall. Its frame was made of molding.

After a few research trips to the EPHS, I spotted an eight-by-ten-inch black-and-white photo of the Randall Street Pool hanging below the big photo, obscured by a lectern. It would be hard to think of a better example of Lillian Smith's explanation of White supremacy: big color mural, little black-and-white photo.

The stately old house had settled into its new foundation, surrounded by shaggy rose bushes and mossy brick paths. Out back, an ornate little fountain incubated mosquitoes in rainwater. The whole site was slow to drain and somewhat marshy, maybe because there was still a ton of pool concrete under the grass and the old spring still bubbled underneath Spring Avenue.

The historical park vision was only half-implemented. Maybe it was the timing, the budget, the aging and fleeing EPHS membership, the heat of the summer, how it saps one of urgency, stamina. Maybe, as a city, our heart wasn't in it, because it only represented a dwindling segment of the population.

There are two histories of East Point. I mean this literally—there are two history books that sit side by side on my shelf, the Black history and the White history.

I got the first book at the EPHS, a coffee-table hardcover with the city seal and EAST POINT PICTORIAL HISTORY stamped in gold foil on the burgundy cover. It was compiled by the first officers of the EPHS and published in 1982, the same year the pool closed.

It covers nearly a century of locals and landmarks, back to the earliest days of photography. Flipping through page after page of formal portraits of the founding families, politicians, businessmen, camp meetings, and school classes, it appears there were no Black people in East Point, or that their lives were not significant enough to be included in the official record.

I get what they were doing, these early preservationists. They were scrambling to rescue the historic remains of a downtown that had been carved up by urban renewal highway projects; gutted by the construction of a station for MARTA, Atlanta's new rail transit system; threatened by airport expansion; rendered obsolete by shopping malls and suburban sprawl. America's historic preservation movement, galvanized by the demolition of New York City's Penn Station in 1963, was slow to come to the capital of the New South. The state passed the Georgia Historic Preservation Act in 1980, authorizing cities to create historic preservation commissions. East Point's new historical society put forth a heroic scavenger hunt to document and preserve a crumbling core that by its centennial was facing complete erasure.

But the commission was all White, and what it gathered centered White pioneers, their property, achievements, and memories. It assumed that anything outside of that experience, everything since the era of White majority was marginal and not worth documenting. The pictorial history was published in 1982, a paper memorial for the White community that had fled. As the book was heading off to the printers, the pools were sitting closed and neglected. No one took responsibility for this loss, but the newly formed EPHS contributed to both pools' unremembering.

When I described this injustice to a friend who works at the Georgia Trust for Historic Preservation, he pretty much laughed at me. "That's all of history, I'm afraid." White history, it turns out, was what most of us had been taught.

Mayor Patsy Jo Hilliard, East Point's first African American mayor, first woman mayor, and the city's longest-serving mayor, leading from 1993 to 2006, decided to do something about this one-sided storytelling about the city. "The one thing that really angered me is they had a book, they wrote a book about East Point, and the only Black person in there was a man standing there with a broom." Hilliard commissioned Herman "Skip" Mason, a scholar of African American history, to compile and publish another East Point history in 2001. "I said we need to tell our own story."

Mason's book is part of the Black America Series, one of those paperbacks you see perched by the cash register in quaint gift shops and visitor centers. Mason's book is replete with the faces of East Point's Black entrepreneurs, athletes and coaches, teachers and principals, funeral directors, domestic workers, mill workers, pastors, and Sunday school classes. Casual snapshots alongside formal portraits. Children and elders, unknown faces and celebrities. From the first freedmen and women and pioneers to the first Black elected officials and public servants. It's a record of a self-sufficient community forged by segregation.

It contains the stories and photos that are missing from the 1982 White history—not just a supplement but a rebuttal. I bought it because it had several photos of the Randall Street Pool. There's a photo of a dozen boys in swim trunks lined up with their swim instructor, chests puffed out, faces serious while a few girls in white swim caps smiled from the back row. On the adjacent page, the East Point chapter of the KKK is pictured parading down Main Street in satiny white robes.

Flipping between these two history books, the White pool and the Black pool, ours and theirs, I kept thinking about that third pool proposed in 1983 at Sykes Park. That was our chance, our one aborted attempt at building something new, something designed for everyone. Instead, in 1986, our city leaders turned the pool into a museum and memorial to a lost battle. They failed to imagine that newcomers would want to swim here together, that we would choose East Point precisely because we chose integrated public spaces over gated suburbia. They didn't have a mural-sized vision of what that could look like.

■ ■ ■

Which brings me to the summer of 2018. East Point was a pool desert.

Spring Avenue Pool was a lawn. The Carriage Colony Pool was covered with grass and junk vehicles. The Elks Club building was still standing, no pool in sight. The Boys and Girls Club no longer had a pool. Lakeside Country Club's golf course had been redeveloped into a master planned subdivision called Lakeside Preserve with a community pool at the center, but it was for homeowners' association members only. The homepage of the neighborhood website featured a little Black girl floating in an inner tube in a swimming pool.

After swim lessons with Miss Michelle, I dropped Guy and Bruno off in Hapeville for "summer camp," which was just day care with extra crafts and playground time. No swimming or archery or bonfires.

The morning was already spent, I was late for work and getting later, but I took my time driving back home along the railroad tracks. I drove through the East Washington community, the neighborhood designated in 1912 for East Point's "colored" residents and brought to life in Mason's Black history of East Point.

I found John Milner Park and the site of the Randall Street Pool, now a parking lot on the corner bordered by willow oaks. It was easy to match the location to the views in the photos in Mason's book. The old houses were gone, replaced by a public housing complex, but the railroad tracks and industrial factories hadn't moved. I tried to imagine the joyful noise of the pool over the thunder of the nearby recycling plant.

I could make out a grassy depression near where the pool used to be and, beneath that, a stream in a pipe. In 1953, construction crews were surprised to discover an unmapped sewer line and manhole during excavation at this site. The pool had to be moved slightly, away from the brick pipe that carried not sewage but a stream. The water flowed from some timeless spring near the railroad tracks, under the asphalt on its way to the sea. The pool came and went, but the water was still down there.

June 23 URBAN SPRINGS

No pool today. I woke up bright and early and donned my tour guide outfit—dark T-shirt, men's Walmart work pants, waterproof hiking boots, sunblock, coffee in a tumbler. I was meeting a group at the Outdoor Activity Center, a city-owned nature preserve in Southwest Atlanta. We were going on a bus tour of three challenged urban creeks—Proctor Creek, Intrenchment Creek, and the Flint headwaters. These three creeks represented the three river basins of Atlanta—the Chattahoochee River, the Ocmulgee River, and the Flint. I was the tour guide for the Flint.

A yellow school bus idled in the gravel parking lot of the wood-paneled nature center, its slanted roof nestled in the shady oaks. Piles of mulch and gardening equipment lay jumbled by the entrance. The mid-1970s design of the place reminded me that this was the product of Commissioner Ted Mastroianni's vision of nature preserves across the Southside. This one, the "OAC"—twenty-six lush, wooded acres surrounded by a working-class neighborhood—became a beloved part of the community as the idea for Lake Charlotte unraveled.

Aboard the school bus, a talkative group of thirty or so people slid into their seats—colleagues and students, neighborhood activists and scientists, water professionals and park designers, an almost entirely Black crowd. It didn't slip my notice that this was something unique. Across the country, environmental groups fretted about the Whiteness of the conservation movement and organized symposiums on how to engage people of color to save the great outdoors. They created "hoods to woods" and "streets to peaks" programs to recruit urban youth into hiking trails and kayaks. Here in Atlanta, the same concerns were passed between White staff and panelists, but the urban conservation scene was not completely Whitewashed.

I collaborated with a handful of Black-led environmental nonprofits focused on issues like green jobs, urban farming, and environmental justice. It was still rare for me to find myself in the minority as a White person during outings or meetings, so when it happened, as it did on that bus, I paid attention. I watched how Black leaders welcomed Black residents through their stories, their songs, their laughter and talkback, even their choice of clothes and the snacks on the refreshment table, all choices that were subtly but insistently different from what I would choose as a White organizer. They welcomed people into the room and the conversation through the common experience of being Black. And through the slow and deliberate act of listening, treating residents as valued consultants, not a resource to be mined.

Daryl Haddock, cofounder of West Atlanta Watershed Alliance and master of ceremonies for the morning, was one of those leaders. He brings a solid, middle-aged dad presence in his cargo pants and untucked polo and uncool glasses. But I have seen him steal the show as the only Black man on a panel of NASA scientists at a national conference. And then win further cred by posting his original comic series on Facebook featuring posed GI Joe figures in action scenes with plastic dinosaurs. Haddock spoke with a slight New Jersey accent, but he knew more about Black Atlanta than I did. It was Darryl Haddock who pointed out how the Atlanta Child Murders haunted the city's residents and wild spaces, teaching a generation of Black Atlantans to fear and avoid the woods and creeks. Through his stories, I learned how people of color can have a fundamentally different experience of wilderness than I do.

As much as I begrudged working on a beautiful Saturday morning, when Haddock started to talk, I felt a rush of gratitude and thought, I can't believe I'm getting paid to be here. Almost everyone on the bus was receiving a stipend to participate in the program. Along with half the tour group, I pulled out my phone and started recording Darryl's lecture. As the bus lurched along Northside Drive toward downtown, Haddock stood backward in the aisle and delivered the most elegant and logical explanation for Atlanta's urban form I've ever heard. Most Atlanta history starts with the intersection of railroads, a story that begins with White settlers, surveyors, and industrialists. Haddock took us back even further, to why Muscogee (Creek) people had settled here in the first place.

"Back then, this area would have been open, with deep streams that the Indigenous peoples could paddle through and get to the interior lands but also get back out to the North Georgia mountains."

We looked out at the passing skyline and tried to picture it.

"Europeans called them the Creeks because they settled on the creeks, but they didn't call themselves Creeks. All we know is that they spoke Muscogee. They could get from the Chattahoochee to the Gulf. They could cross over to the South River, eventually get to the Atlantic."

"Eventually, the Europeans, the colonists, started to think that this could be a transportation hub. Not for streets and highways, for boats. The realization that this must be a great place that could connect people was something settlers saw very early on because of the Indigenous people."

Underneath Atlanta's intersecting interstate highways and railroads, the creeks and waterways that defined an Indigenous network of roads are still flowing. From Five Points, in the heart of downtown Atlanta, you can walk in three different directions and find the location of three different springs leading to three different major watersheds. It is unusual for a major city to be situated at the headwaters of two rivers and a half-dozen creeks instead of on the banks of a major river. But Georgia is unusual in its wealth of rivers. If you saw a map of major river basins, color coded, most states would have two or three colors. Georgia has twelve or fourteen, depending on how you count, with exquisite tongue twister Muscogee and Cherokee names like Ohoopee, Ogeechee, Ochlockonee, Withlacoochee, Tallapoosa. The state is furry with rivers and their tributaries. Atlanta is a little bald spot in the northwestern corner of the Georgia map, high ground on the subcontinental divide where one could move freely across the region.

"Originally, the Chattahoochee River was authorized to move steamships, just like the Mississippi River, with ships moving up and down the river corridor from the Gulf of Mexico. But the grade was too steep; they couldn't get big boats up here, and you can't move commerce in canoes. They needed a different kind of technology to move lots and lots of commodities up here. Does anyone know what that is?"

Railroads. The railroads followed the ridgelines, marking the watersheds and sketching out the pattern of development for the next two centuries.

We stopped at the Vine City MARTA station, along one of those ridgelines, and walked to a windy high point in front of Mercedes-Benz Stadium, Atlanta's futuristic football–soccer–monster truck arena. The view from here—no water, few trees, the downtown skyline, the rooftops of westside neighborhoods. The stadium gleamed with steel triangles like a spaceship dropped on the edge of the city.

Haddock explained impervious surfaces, how stormwater floods a landscape like this. We stood on a thin strip of littered grass. "If you were a raindrop, where would you go?"

When juicy summer thunderstorms rolled through, the water rushed downhill into homes on English Avenue. Meanwhile, the football stadium and the massive Georgia World Congress Center sat along the historic rail corridor, high and dry, surrounded by parking lots, while the Black neighborhood downstream turned, temporarily but violently, into a detention pond. This was a pattern that continued through the tour—all three urban creeks had the massive weight of public infrastructure and parking lots sitting on their headwaters. The springs of Proctor Creek were buried under the Georgia World Congress Center, Intrenchment Creek was piped under Atlanta–Fulton County Stadium, the Flint headwaters were trapped under the Atlanta Airport. Downstream, Black neighborhoods absorbed the floodwaters.

Next stop, Peoplestown, a historic downtown neighborhood in the shadow of Turner Field, the stadium that hosted the 1996 Olympics and later the Atlanta Braves. We climbed off the bus to visit a renovated city park built on a former landfill that used to flood. D. H. Stanton Park, one of a string of new and revitalized greenspaces along the BeltLine, was engineered and LEED certified to manage large volumes of stormwater through its fields and playgrounds.

The bang and buzz of construction echoed from up the hills where new three-story houses were being erected. The dominant look was modern farmhouse squeezed next to shabby bungalow. It was hard to say what unleashed gentrification on the neighborhood, the BeltLine or the baseball team that, by relocating to the suburbs, set off a massive redevelopment of the Turner Field area. But our eyes landed on the park. The city's investment in the park was a signal to affluent buyers that this attractive but rough-around-the-edges Black neighborhood had potential. Peoplestown was overwhelmed by new construction, new residents, and investors.

A guest speaker joined us to give a brief history of Peoplestown and the new park. He spoke with pride about how he and other neighborhood leaders championed the park's development.

I noticed that one member of our tour, an older Black woman in a peach windbreaker, had drifted back over to the bus. As I went to speak to the bus driver about lunch plans, I stopped to check on her.

"Not interested in the guest speaker?"

She said she already knew the story.

"I was raised up right here on the corner," she said. "We lived in this park. Didn't no one come back over here. And now look at it."

I was confused by her anger. I saw families carrying bright gift bags to a birthday party. Colorful playground equipment. Toddlers on a splash pad.

Moms and dads—White, Asian, and Black—pushing strollers through the candy-colored shadows cast by the translucent panels of the pavilion. This playground here used to be unsafe and overgrown. In 1999, a girl was injured by an explosion when the static created on a playground slide ignited methane seeping up from the landfill. The transformation of the forgotten playground into an attractive park seemed like a success story. But this woman saw a place she didn't recognize.

"I wouldn't come here. I don't feel welcome."

Before I could formulate a question about why, about what park amenities might make her feel more welcome, she read my mind.

"When we show up, the police show up too."

Indeed, an officer was there on patrol.

"They profile you," I said.

She nodded.

"If my mama was alive to see this." She threw up her hands in disgust. "They down here playing *soccer.*"

I almost laughed, but she was not joking. I pondered the threat of soccer and the invasion of affluent, White newcomers, as I rejoined the group.

The talk had veered into the subject of gentrification, rising property values and taxes. Our speaker received constant calls, letters, and texts from investors offering to buy his house. He said he wasn't going to sell for less than top dollar, at least three hundred thousand. He was trying to talk tough, but that number sounded low to me. Didn't he realize the new McMansions sprouting up around the park would be listed at half a million? The prices were like a runaway train barreling through the neighborhood.

Our group marched back to the bus for boxed lunches. A few minutes later, I asked a legacy Westside resident if she sees this at her park by her house on Lindsey Street.

"See what?"

"White kids' birthday parties." She knew I was asking about gentrification.

"No. The only time I see White people is when they're from a church. Volunteers. Handing out sack lunches."

I was speechless.

"I tell my kids to go on and get a free lunch," she told me. "I'm not proud."

We ate our sandwiches and chips on the bus as we headed south to East Point. The bus was lively with chatter, but I felt somber.

What if we did everything right, restored the creeks and built the right kind of natural infrastructure in the right places. Cleared out the dumped tires and built rain gardens full of native grasses and floodplain parks full of butterflies and birthday parties. What if we succeeded at converting the worthless floodplain into the jewel of the neighborhood and, after all that, discovered that we harmed the people who lived there for years through the floods and sewer spills and dumping and drug trafficking. Harmed them because as their neighborhood shifted around them, they were marginalized in their own backyards, profiled by police, or could no longer afford property taxes. We would've saved the creeks from city poison and underground obscurity. We all benefit from clean water. Would the benefits eventually trickle downstream, to the suburban neighborhoods where the displaced people settled?

■ ■ ■

Cutting through Southwest Atlanta on my way home, I passed over Utoy Creek.

Hey, that's my creek! I thought. I taught my boys their watershed address—South Utoy Creek, Chattahoochee River, the Gulf of Mexico, but I hardly ever saw the Utoy Creek. I made a U-turn and pulled over on the low concrete bridge, aged and aristocratic with its lichen-spattered stone and veil of English ivy.

I took a few photos, which immediately felt pointless. Utoy looked like any other urban creek in Atlanta—a clear, shallow stream winding through brown silty beaches, steep banks bound together by kudzu and dumped tires, a rusty sewer pipe marking the eroded floor of the creek. It could be the Flint River, the South River, Proctor Creek, or Intrenchment Creek. The two-lane road curved out of sight into a bushy forest dripping with wisteria, cicadas pulsing to the sound of rushing water. You could squint and forget that you were in the city at all.

A low black car pulled up next to me, all windows down, two guys smoking in the front seat and someone in the back.

"Ma'am?" the driver shouted. I couldn't see his face in the dark car.

"This is private property. Why you out here taking pictures of my family's private property?"

I looked around. Looked down to make sure my boots were, technically, in the public right of way, on the shoulder of a public street in the middle of a bridge over a creek that certainly no family owned, but I decided not to argue with him. He sounded mad.

"I'm looking at the creek." Lamely, I gestured to the water.

"You can't be out here taking pictures of my family property."

Hard to explain why I wanted to see Utoy Creek. Sir, I'm a professional creek finder.

"Okay, thank you," I said, not thankful at all. I started back to my car.

They drove away slowly, weed smoke trailing out of the windows.

Driving home, it sank in that the aggressor was me. Me with my sweaty T-shirt and muddy boots and iPhone photos and unfathomable motives. One White-skinned prospector, and there goes the neighborhood.

I underestimated how my presence was freighted with menace. In these parts, the people who study creeks are getting paid.

July 6 NATURAL BODIES

We interrupted our tour of Atlanta pools and creeks to visit my mother in the mountains of East Tennessee. We did this every year for the Fourth of July—traded Atlanta, broiling hot and rife with backyard gunfire, for Gramma's rural village with its adorable Main Street parade and fireworks by a lake.

I watched the dashboard thermostat drop fifteen degrees as we gained altitude driving up the mountain. The cooler temperatures of the Cumberland Plateau, and the complete lack of mosquitoes, made it an ideal place to spend July. Before the Civil War, the town's founders chose this location for its abundant natural springs and elevation above "the Malaria line." For centuries, the area was a summer getaway for wealthy southern White families from Nashville, Atlanta, and Birmingham. And now it was a getaway for us.

We celebrated our nation's independence with popsicles and explosives and, the next day, took the boys for a swim at Lake Cheston, a small, murky pond not far from Mom's house. The boys dragged their cheap rafts across the pebbled and grassy beach, littered with a few cardboard discs from spent fireworks.

As Jason stood belly deep in the lake, tossing the boys into the water, I took photos of them midair. Arms outstretched, Bruno's tiny ribcage, Guy's awkwardly bent knees. God, he was throwing them high. They weighed no more than forty pounds; they froze above Jason's head. They screamed with delight and clamored for another turn.

This was the first time they'd been swimming with their father that summer, and it was a notable change from my cautious supervision. It was the only time they dipped into a natural body of water all year.

Or was it natural? The water looked and felt like sweet tea, layers of warm over pockets of ice water. There were fish and turtles, lily pads and cattails. Did a majestic tulip poplar belong on the edge of a lake? Some trees flourish in wetlands—sycamores, willows. This one looked happy lakeside. The legend of the southern swimming hole was that it was someplace wild and pristine, just a rope swing and fishing pole, like nature intended. But swimming holes are almost always man-made. Someone dammed a creek and made a private oasis.

Up here in the mountains, all the lakes were reservoirs. Some were enormous TVA projects like Lake Nickajack. Whole valleys flooded; villages sacrificed to deliver electric power deep into Appalachia. I had to take deep breaths each time we drove the long span of Highway 24 over that lake, try not to think about flipping the car off the bridge. The local reservoirs for drinking water or recreation were not as visible or accessible. You had to know the footpath to Saint Andrew's Lake, or "The Rez." I swam in the lily pad–capped Lake Dimmick a few times before I learned I was floating in the municipal water supply. There were dozens of small reservoirs on the mountaintop, all of them built after the 1950s with dam technologies that were refined during World War II.

Mom insisted that Lake Cheston was a natural lake, and we had a whole debate about what makes a lake natural. It reminded me of a similar debate we had over a book she was reading about the sinking of the *Lusitania*. She was sure it was "historical fiction." I argued it was a true story, so the book had to be some kind of narrative nonfiction. Didn't matter. It felt like a novel to her. And this felt like a "real" lake.

I pointed out the long earthen dam where a man was walking his Labrador retriever.

"Look for the flat edge of the lake, and that's usually a dam."

"But what creek did they dam?" she asked, disbelieving.

I couldn't find it on a map. The creek or spring was nearly invisible, some ephemeral tributary of Wiggins Creek. It only made itself known as Lake Cheston, which was named after the dam builder. I liked thinking about water like that, defined by its container. The container was almost always temporary.

■ ■ ■

The next day, we made a two-hour road trip to north Alabama to visit my friend Natalie Chanin near Muscle Shoals. It could've been a day trip, but Natalie, having heard plenty about my keen interest in swimming pools, suggested we stay the night at this palatial Marriott on the riverfront. She described its over-the-top hotel pool with waterslides and rock waterfalls. She and her daughter lived nearby and had recently booked a room there just for the pool and spa.

But if it's on the waterfront, I said, why not just swim in the river?

"Oh, I won't let my kids swim in there," she replied, kind of sadly. "There's a nuclear power plant upstream, chemical plants. It's a very industrial river."

As we drove west along the Tennessee River, I could see what she meant.

We passed locks and dams, smokestacks, and nuclear reactors. I forgot how big rivers looked like industrial superhighways, so different in character from the tumbling whitewater rivers of North Georgia or the swampy blackwater rivers near the coast. This river was a mile wide, a gleaming muscle flanked by sharp-edged cities, gaining strength as it rushed toward the Mississippi. In Florence, I spotted a narrow public beach, but what were those silos holding upstream?

Meanwhile, our hotel pool was dazzling. While Mom was checking us in, I led the boys into the dim hotel bar for a view of the courtyard swimming pool below.

The two wings of the hotel, six or seven stories tall, embraced a small-scale water park. From above, we could see a series of large pools joined by a faux rock waterslide and tunnel structure in the middle. The decks were crawling with pink bodies; dark wet heads bobbed in the water. All the resort features were tastefully designed into the mix—a tiki bar and hot tub for the grown-ups, zero-entry beach with fountains for the smaller kids. Beyond the pool were three rows of lounge chairs, a hill of begonias, an emerald golf course, and beyond that, the Tennessee River. The boys were practically vibrating with anticipation.

We spent all afternoon at the pool among the tourist families and bachelorette parties and conference attendees. I sipped a virgin piña colada while Jason caught the boys at the bottom of the waterslide. There were kids of all ages, in floats and goggles, ruffles and flippers. One girl was flopping around in a full mermaid tail. We dragged the boys out the next day to explore Muscle Shoals's famous recording studios and downtown Florence, but there was nothing they wanted to do more than swim.

We met Natalie for lunch, and she recommended that I read *A Pattern Language*, the influential 1977 book that breaks down the elements of good architecture and city building. Each short section of *A Pattern Language* referenced other numbered sections, and the reader was supposed to leap around within the network of concepts, like surfing a hypertext. The book has become a kind of source code for both urban designers and software designers.

Eventually, when my used copy arrived in my East Point mailbox, I flipped to section 71, "Still Water." I thought of that decadent Marriott swimming pool in North Alabama in July and its relationship to the Tennessee River.

Children can play in the water safely when the edge is gradual. A baby crawling into a lake comes to no abrupt surprises; he stops when the water gets too deep, and goes back out again. . . .

But a swimming pool, and any kind of water with a hard and artificial edge, has none of this gradualness. A child may be running along at top speed, when splash, suddenly he finds himself in six feet of water.

The abrupt edge, most serious for children, has its effects in psychological terms for adults too. . . . The presence of an ecologically wrong kind of abruptness is disconcerting—and destroys the peace and calm which water often has.

The hard edge of an earthen dam, over time, softens and vanishes under reeds and moss. Is it a natural body of water? Here, as the Tennessee River was engineered for greater navigation, industry, and power generation, it took on some of that "ecologically wrong kind of abruptness."

Meanwhile, the swimming pool was designed to mimic nature—plastic ferns, concrete beach, fiberglass rock outcroppings, thatched roof bar. It's like designers switched the fundamental ideas of *A Pattern Language* to redefine pools and rivers. The result was a radical new kind of pool, more private and exclusive than ever, and a highly engineered river, visible to all but forbidden to touch.

■ ■ ■

On our last morning, the pool opened at 8:00 a.m., checkout was at eleven. We had a couple hours of pool time left and woke up early to take advantage. We were the first ones wading into the placid, turquoise water. Patio music leaked from some tucked-away sound system, a morning playlist featuring Aretha and Otis, Muscle Shoals gospel.

I carried my coffee to the little kiosk where two young pool attendants were stationed, a Black man and White woman with a high brunette ponytail. They smiled and prepared themselves for good customer service.

"I have a question," I said, politely. "What's the wildest thing you've ever seen happen here?"

They glanced at each other. She stifled a laugh.

"You mean in the water or just out here?" She gestured around at the golf course, the bar.

I shrugged. "Both."

They shifted, relaxed a bit. He was quiet.

"I saw a grown man jump off that thing," said the woman, pointing to the faux rock waterslide, "Then he swam over to his children."

"Was he injured?"

"No. He was intoxicated."

I chuckled, I wanted more. This was why public pools never allowed alcohol.

"Lot of vomiting," said the guy. "I once saw a lady change her baby's diaper in the shallow end."

I nodded. "That's a code brown."

"I can't even tell you."

"Have you ever had to rescue anyone?"

They looked serious. "We're not lifeguards. It's posted: no lifeguard on duty," he said. "I mean, if someone is in trouble and no one else is helping, we would jump in."

"Of course."

"But we're not lifeguards. It's on the rules: no children unattended at any time."

I glanced at the rules, all caps on a nearby poster. "So, people leave their kids for you to watch?"

"All day long!" she burst out. "Or I'll see the parents sitting up on their balcony, drinking beers, just waving at the kids. They're like, 'I'm here, I'm watching.'"

"Are you a good swimmer?"

"I was on the swim team," she said proudly. "At the pool on Royal Avenue. That's our public pool."

Then she remembered her job and pulled out a clipboard. "Actually, we're checking wristbands this morning. Can I get your name and room number?"

With this information, she handed me three blue rubber bracelets. More early swimmers were starting to show up with their rolled white towels and sippy cups. Our interview was finished.

"Is this a souvenir? Can I keep it?"

"No. It's so we know you're a guest."

I chased down the boys and slipped the wristbands on them. They paddled away, happy as tagged otters. This was the system to mark who belonged and who didn't.

■ ■ ■

During our last day in Tennessee, Gramma and I took the boys to a public beach at Tims Ford Lake. At ten thousand acres, Tims Ford Lake looked limitless, the kind of inland sea that generates electrical power, real estate value, and generally sweetens life in landlocked Tennessee.

We found the dump truck–made yellow sand beach, and the boys galloped into the swirl of moms and kids and cartoonish inflatables. The water was still and shallow, and they were wearing their little blue PFDs, so I spread my towel on the grass and closed my eyes.

Someone was blasting 1990s country music from an amp wheeled out onto the sand on a hand truck. Was that the scent of cat shit, toasting in the sun? I peered under my straw hat. Goose poop. It was everywhere. *Way down yonder on the Chattahoochee, it gets hotter than a hoochie coochie.*

The young women by the water were tattooed and labor scarred, pink skinned and brown. I listened to them supply commentary for each other's children in pure East Tennessee accents passed down from their grannies. It sounded like a loud, joyful style of collaborative mothering. They called each other Sherrie and Shae and T. One woman wading knee deep used a Walmart bag to patiently skein small fish. My boys joined the clutch of saggy-diapered toddlers reaching in to pet their slippery fins.

Speedboats buzzed by in the distance. Heat shimmered over the bridge. My mom waved from her inner tube in the lake.

Once sweaty enough, I joined Gramma and the boys in the water. The shallows felt surprisingly warm, as hot as tap water. Thinking about flesh-eating amoebas, I urged the kids to wade a bit deeper, swim out where it's cooler. Over here, I called, by this young couple, entwined in the water up to their shoulders and holding suspiciously still for a very long time. Pretty sure they were having sex.

The amp rumbled. *And you'll be sorry that you messed with the U.S. of A. / 'cause we'll put a boot in your ass. It's the American way.*

Into the second hour of our visit, a busload of disabled adults in swimsuits arrived. A couple caregivers in scrubs hung back under the shade of the picnic pavilion. What was it about the swimmers' jerky limbs and unrepressed yelps that announced their developmental differences? It's not like everyone else on this beach was a model of social grace and inhibition.

As two large men frolicked violently into the water, roaring with plea-sure, some parents called their children up onto their beach towels. One man splashed repetitively, moaning, arms like windmills. The effect was as if a shark had been spotted in the lake. We too ceded the waters to these men. Produced some Doritos and distracted the boys from the unpredictable newcomers.

The dystopian future where access to water is a luxury—it was already here in the South. Natural bodies anyway. Maybe up north it's different. Somewhere like Vermont or Michigan or Minnesota, where there are count-less glacial lakes with clean water and public beaches. Here in this corner of the South, beaches and pools were either privatized and sterile, available for a price, or free and public like this beach at Tims Ford Lake, the Coney Island of Winchester. Murky hot and overtaxed with humanity. Too many people with no other place to swim.

July 8 PAY SWIM

Pittman Park Pool had an impressive sound system. Or maybe it was that the pool itself was built like a concrete box; it felt like we were inside a booming auditorium. The pool was an Olympic-sized rectangle surrounded by sizzling pavement and eight-foot concrete walls. The acoustics were such that as we marched down the long ramp from the rec center to the pool, I distinctly overheard a boy yell, "Ooh, White people!"

What could I do but shoot my hand up and shout, "Hi!"

They laughed and ducked underwater, thrilled that I heard them.

The music was not loud exactly but expansive. It reverberated off the surface of the water and made it feel like a massive club. It was some heavy trap music that I was not young or cool enough to identify. There were no commercials, and these were definitely the uncensored versions, so I imagined one of the lifeguards had an iPhone plugged in somewhere, a playlist of summer hits. If I spent eight hours here, I would make a playlist too.

Where was everyone? We got there around four; the pool closed at seven.

In this whole giant pool, there were about six young teenage boys in a roiling huddle along the far swim lane, not exactly swimming but tumbling along together in the water, wrestling and splashing. The entire time roasting each other, cursing nonstop, a relentless trash-talking battle that echoed into a jumble that to my ears sounded like its own distinct language.

I considered the risk of my sons overhearing profanity and deemed it not only impossible to mitigate but harmless. They go to school; they live in a city. Didn't the boys hear worse language coming from Dad's studio on the weekend? Jason and I have tried to discipline ourselves since becoming parents, to clean up our dirty language in front of them, but neither one of us has deleted the "explicit" versions of songs from our playlists. Music is art, lyrics are poetry, and shouldn't they hear the artist's full expression? Some days the plastic Kidz Bop versions of pop songs seemed more obscene than the original.

This was my thought process as I dozed with my head under a towel, blocking out the blazing sun and turquoise sky. Every fifteen minutes or so, I felt the rumble of a freight train passing by.

We had the entire shallow end to ourselves. No one had to studiously ignore anyone—we were that far away. Guy and Bruno started out with their vests on but quickly realized they could touch the bottom and tossed their PFDs on the deck. Good, I thought. Real practice.

I thought they would be bummed that there were no other kids to play with, but they didn't mention it. Just the rollicking preteens on one side and a small child by the lifeguard stand, fully dressed and tempting fate by toddling along the edge of the pool.

A mother shouted to her son to get out of the pool before she "beat his ass" and then switched to "butt," probably for our benefit. She covered her mouth and giggled.

After a while, our invisible DJ switched up to "grown folks" music. Chaka Khan, Isley Brothers. Whoever sings, *Oh, Casanova* and *Steady rocking all night long.* I suspected this was also for our sake—less cussing.

When the teenagers filed out, flip-flops smacking, towels popping, we were virtually alone in this massive pool. Just a lifeguard under the distant umbrella and his partner dangling her feet in the water, a baby girl sleeping in a stroller in the shade. Between songs, a surge of cicadas.

I imagined everyone left because of us, the White people who invaded and ruined everything. Party's over.

I lay on my crispy towel on the unforgiving deck and smelled the sunblock baking off my skin. I watched the boys play in the shallow water. They tested how long they could hold their breath, slipping under the floating lane markers. They invented a game where they ducked underwater, counted 1-2-3, and now let's double fist-bump, now a high-five, now let's bump butts. No one taught them this. It loosened a little memory I had of making up similar games with my cousin in the shallow end of Meema and Papa's swimming pool. Now let's have a tea party, 1-2-3, now let's do a flip, now let's do handstands. I lay there and watched them sideways, the jagged light in the water, weeds sprouting up through the cracks in the pavement, puffy clouds scooting lazily along the treetops.

It felt kind of postapocalyptic to be lonely in this enormous open space in the middle of the city. The sun stood still overhead.

After an hour or so of this, the heat started to feel worrisome. Our skin was roasting. It took a long time and many bribes to convince the boys to get out of the water and dry off. We wandered around the huge pool yard. Tall weeds and abandoned lawn chairs. The old diving pool, thirteen feet deep, was fenced off and growing reeds. Deep inside, a volleyball and a tennis shoe bleached white by the sun.

We made our way into the blinding dark of the damp pool house. Three Black lifeguards had big smiles for us. They looked like high school girls to me.

"Where is everyone?" I asked.

One young woman shook her head, "Nobody comes to this pool." Emphasis on the *No.*

"Really?"

"Not on the weekend when you have to pay. During Free Swim it's busy."

"When is Free Swim?" I asked.

"Weekday afternoons. There's usually fifty people, but"—she paused, thought about how to warn me—"there's a lot going on."

"This is an incredible pool. It's weird to see it empty."

She chose her words carefully.

"It's this neighborhood. A lot of these kids are impoverished, and they aren't going to pay to swim. On the weekend, there's nobody here."

How did I not realize this sooner? That the pools in Atlanta's poorest neighborhoods sat fully staffed but deserted during "Pay Swim" hours. It cost ten dollars for a family like ours to swim. Ten bucks, plus my whole afternoon. The more serious investment was all my hours of pool research and swimming lessons.

I thanked the girls and helped the boys change clothes in the damp locker room.

That this enormous public facility would be fully staffed but virtually deserted on a glorious day in July seemed like a scandal, or at least a waste. I could start a campaign—free pools for the summer. Reach out to the parks commissioner, talk to the manager. Could they create a program of swim vouchers for qualifying families? Why have these empty, sparkling pools just out of reach?

As we pulled out of the parking lot, I realized that the music wasn't coming from the pool's speakers but from a truck parked around the corner at a barbecue. The barrel of a barbecue smoker hitched to the truck puffed like a locomotive. A few men dozed in lawn chairs in the shade, stilled by the heat and the meat. Will the boys remember any of this? This big empty pool that seemed to go on forever? Could they hear the trains or the bass underwater?

It was only on leaving that I looked at the neighborhood. Pittsburgh, one of Atlanta's worst for violent crime, was like any old, hilly Atlanta neighborhood dense with trees and cars. You can only see as far as the block in front of you. We rolled through a tight grid of streets stacked with old houses, gingerbread cute next to burned-out ruins. On one corner where only a rough foundation remained, I saw a shrine of colorful paper tubes—the remains of a homemade fireworks show.

Cars parked on both sides of the street, so narrow that they became effectively one-way. Up ahead, a Lincoln was stopped and a brown elbow propped out the driver's side window; someone on a porch leaned out to chat. I reversed and tried the next block, where an evening church service was starting. A white-haired woman climbed slowly out of a sedan, while a man in a three-piece burgundy suit took her arm, dabbed his neck with a handkerchief. He forgot it was over ninety degrees. I forgot it was Sunday.

July 17 NEXT-DOOR NEIGHBORS

This afternoon at the gym, Nicole invited us to be her guest for "Family Night" at the Conley Rec Center pool. At this point, everyone who knew me was offering to help me find a pool.

This outdoor pool in College Park was very close to our house, but I hadn't yet figured out how to swim there. It wasn't like Atlanta's pools, where we just showed up on the weekend with a few dollars and our towels. I took the boys to Conley pool one sunny Sunday and was disappointed to find the gate was locked.

You had to be a College Park resident or have a pool pass to swim there, so when Nicole mentioned the opportunity, even though our Tuesday night was overbooked as usual, I said yes. Let's squeeze the juice out of these long summer evenings, I thought. Let's add another pool to our list.

My acquaintance with Nicole consisted of friendly patter in the gym parking lot before and after workouts. She was a Black woman about my age, a teacher who lived in College Park with her husband and a daughter close in age to my sons. For a couple years, we showed up at the gym at the same time. We had roughly the same goals—to wrestle back some of the energy we took for granted and the jeans we wore before having kids.

Sweating together was a form of intimacy, so swimming together was no big deal.

■ ■ ■

The pool manager was a muscular, dark-skinned city employee who knew everyone by name. He wouldn't let us in until Nicole climbed out of the pool and introduced us as her guests.

College Park's pool was an unlikely oasis set between City Hall and the football stadium. The depth of the deep end suggested this was an older pool, where the diving board had been removed at some point. A shallow kiddie pool with mushroom-shaped fountains had been added. A handful of families spread out around the picnic tables and lounge chairs, a cluster of teenagers around the shallow end.

Streaks of laughter cut through the sound of fountains as the MARTA train hummed by in the distance.

The manager strode briskly around the perimeter of the pool, joking and chatting with each swimmer. Unlike the silent, probably stoned teenage lifeguards in Atlanta, this guy was a gregarious grown-up, a bit intense about the job. He nearly tackled a kid for running from the bathroom.

I forgot the boys' vests, and the shallow end wasn't shallow enough, so I had to stay in the pool with them the whole time. The water was startlingly cold. Was it one of those spring-fed pools? I encouraged them to run around on the splash pad, where two boys wielded Supersoakers. Floating, Nicole smiled and waved, her copper skin and amethyst one-piece glowed against the turquoise water.

I don't live in College Park, but this block felt familiar and welcoming. I had been to College Park Library to vote, to the Historical Society for a lecture, and to City Hall for meetings about the Flint River project. We attended a couple of kiddie birthday parties in the city's dignified old gymnasium, with a soaring wood beam ceiling that seemed to inspire flight.

The pool was at the heart of a complex of municipal buildings on Main Street, on the site where Cox College, a fancy women's conservatory and the city's namesake, stood at the turn of the twentieth century. The college closed its doors during the Great Depression, but the name remained. The thought of demolishing that Victorian wedding cake of a building seemed tragic, until you calculated how the buildings that replaced it have served more people, more democratically and joyfully, for twice as long as the college.

Like East Point, College Park received WPA funds to construct a swimming pool in the 1930s. Like Hapeville, the pool finally opened in the late forties, after years of delays. Unlike both of those neighboring cities, College Park's pool is still there. Of the three "Tri-Cities," which share similar geography, history, and demographics, College Park managed to maintain its original swimming pool and add a new outdoor swimming pool on Godby Road in the 2000s. I envied College Park's pools, but more than that, I envied the community that valued and funded them, the functional government that built and managed them.

Any time the lack of swimming pools in East Point surfaced on neighborhood Facebook or NextDoor pages, a naysayer would suggest that building a pool was a waste of taxpayer dollars, that money should be spent fixing potholes in the streets and cracks in the sidewalks, hiring police officers or giving teachers raises. Pools were an extravagance—too expensive to maintain and staff and insure. And even if the city found funding, pools would be a nuisance; they would attract delinquency and traffic.

I rolled my eyes. You only had to look next door to College Park to see that it was possible for a small town to manage a couple swimming pools for its residents. It was generous, but it was worth it.

In the background of my sunset pool photos were a series of tiny airplanes. The constant jet noise never becomes romantic like the sound of trains passing in the night. However, at a certain distance, planes gaining altitude make elegant shapes against the clouds. Sitting on the warm concrete with our feet in the cold water, Guy and I guessed their destinations—Honolulu, Cairo, Seoul, New Orleans. Living next to the world's busiest airport isn't too bad when you can share a nice swim with friends.

July 19 BACK TO FOREST VALE

Every time I saw Allison that summer, in the school parking lot or at the gym, she invited us to go swimming. One afternoon, almost a year after our first visit, we made it back to Forest Vale Club.

The afternoon was the muggy prelude to a rush hour thunderstorm. Like last time, when we arrived, she refused to let us pay and brushed off our thank-yous, all southern hospitality with a very Yankee shrug.

At this point, swimming lessons were paying off. Both boys could manage their own tentative swimming style, achieving enough buoyancy and coordination to move through the water.

Bruno demanded that Jason give him "the bootie throw," repeatedly launching him into the air. Guy wore a mask and let his arms trail behind him as he gazed around underwater, his mind full of underwater sounds, little snorkeler without a snorkel. I took up my position poolside near a couple moms I barely knew. Today the pool was hot and boring. The trees were very still, wilting in the humid air. At the bottom of this freeway valley, the icy pool sparkled with its inner light.

One woman was a special-ed teacher.

"It's an inclusion class so I have another teacher with me," she said. "Twenty-three students; six to eight have an IEP. We start inclusion classes at third grade."

I asked her a string of questions about special ed at her school, rekindling the unending conversation about schools that every parent seems to share on the edges of soccer fields, swimming pools, and birthday parties. I had a feeling public school special-ed services were not enough for Guy. He was happy but clueless about what was going on in kindergarten and first grade.

If I could add up all the valuable intel I have gathered during these conversations, I could publish a report and market myself as an educational consultant. At times, I whine that we moms can't, or won't, talk about anything else. Then I remember politics is poison, the weather is worse, and I can't follow any exchange about television or sports. I wasn't going to pass up the chance to grill a couple special-ed experts.

The fun of this summer, I realized, has been in the chase, in discovering new pools in neighborhoods I might never otherwise visit. My kids have been learning to swim, but I've enjoyed the unpredictability, the anonymity, of each public pool. Did I want to join a private pool and go to the same place every summer? Talk to the same moms about the same stuff every week?

Allison asked me to watch her daughter while she swam to the deep end with the boys. They took turns on the old-school springboard. Bruno shouted out "Cannonball!" every time, whether his form resembled artillery or not. I laughed at Jason's silliest jump. He dove headfirst and grabbed his ankles, sending an enormous wave into the shallow end where I dangled my feet.

Meanwhile, the girl bobbed furiously along the invisible line where the shallow end began to drop off.

"Gracie, come back this way," I suggested.

She didn't seem to hear me, but Allison did. She recognized Gracie's hop-hop-hop as a technique she'd been taught to keep her head above water. Before I was in the water, Allison and Jason were swimming over to the girl, hoisting her up on the deck.

"God, I'm sorry," I said. "I didn't realize she was struggling."

She shrugged it off. She saw her children testing their pool skills daily. But I was shaken. I had read too many articles about drowning, how it happens and who is vulnerable. Drowning is often quiet, one said. People silently slip under the water. I forgot that swimmers don't thrash and shout for help when they're trying to breathe. It was happening right in front of me.

Pool play resumed. Cannonballs moved to the shallow end. Mixed in with my blooming alarm and guilt was a trace of anger. All these kids in the water, and where was the lifeguard? There were no lifeguards here, I figured, because this was a private pool.

Eventually, Bruno complained that his chlorine-singed eyes were "soggy." Blue-gray clouds rolled in, darkening the pool deck. Dinnertime loomed.

As we packed up our towels and goggles, a big family arrived, a couple adult women with children and teenagers. Or maybe I assumed they were family because they all had the same brown skin and black hair. There was no interaction between this group and ours as we hauled towels and beach bags back up the hill to our car.

By the time we left, every head in the pool had black hair, and I could hear shouts in Spanish over the white noise of the freeway. That's promising, I thought. The membership is not all White. But it a was neat exchange of space, not exactly the picture of racial integration.

■ ■ ■

Allison told me to talk to Tania, who had been a member of Forest Vale "for-ever." She could answer my questions about its history and membership rules.

The tables were packed with Hapeville's multicultural daytime crowd. A dozen meetings in progress, trendy professionals who could be real estate agents or airport contractors, mixed in with casually dressed students and locals between errands. Tania was one of the second group. Curly blonde hair pulled back in a ponytail. She wore a sleeveless shirt that showed off her strong, tan shoulders and faded tattoo. She met me on her way to a doctor's appointment and ordered a big iced coffee with whipped cream on top. I had no idea we shared, as she put it, "contempt for the covert and overt racism and socioeconomic systems that are the realities of why these pools exist."

As we loaded up on caffeine and sugar, the southern accents came out. Tania was a teacher who spent summers at the pool. I noticed the instant familiarity of speaking to another White woman who grew up in the same Southside Atlanta milieu at the same time, but because she was a couple years older and inches taller than me, she also reminded me of those pretty, athletic, older girls who had intimidated nerds like me back in middle school.

Tania had joined the Forest Vale Club when she moved to Hapeville fifteen years ago.

I started asking the same questions that any potential member might ask because I was, in fact, a mom looking for a swimming pool. She explained the pool season, the fees, the process for joining, and the expectations for members. I asked the basic questions first, before I steered toward the issue that had sparked my curiosity—why the pool resembled a relic of the Jim Crow era.

"Allison offered to nominate me, but I kind of wanted to know if the pool was still segregated."

She reassured me that the pool was open to all nominees. "I've never seen anyone not voted in."

"I mean, I'm not trying to call out Hapeville," I explained. In the years after desegregation, White people built backyard pools and private clubs like crazy, and not just in the South. If this pool was built in the late sixties, it fit into that national trend. "This happened all over the country."

"Okay, I'm sure it used to be all-White. But it's not anymore."

She said there had been a conscious effort to make the pool more inclusive.

"I've seen the change since I joined. We have same-sex couples now, more biracial couples, more diversity in terms of race. I remember the first gay couple who joined. I remember the first Black person to join. His wife volunteered to be on the board just to make sure the pool was inclusive."

"All this has happened in the last fifteen years?"

"The younger people are changing it. I make a point to nominate people like Melanie and Shawn from the yoga studio. I get a kick out of pissing off the founders. We have completely turned their purpose on its head."

There it was—their purpose.

"I have a theory," she went on. "It used to be, the person who was nominated had to be there when we voted. The founders wanted to see the nominees before they voted."

"Now they don't have to be present. The old folks from the original families still show up when we're voting on new members. You don't see them any other time. I don't know why they come."

Tania went on. "I love living here. We have such a good mix of blue collar, white collar, racial diversity. It's a vibe. Like at the pool, we've got a neurologist, lawyers, next to teachers, artists. You don't see that at other private clubs."

I agreed. I knew that vibe and appreciated it too. That hard-to-balance blend of longtime residents and newcomers. Not just Black and White but Korean, Mexican, Cambodian, neighbors all with a common southern accent. Bonded by our interminable green and humid landscape.

Tania brightened as she told me about her love for the pool.

"When I first started going, there were no kids. My friend would go with me, and we would drink and lay out. Now it's free babysitting. My daughters learned to swim there; they had no formal lessons. I can read a book while my kids play all day long. We keep shower stuff at the pool; we take their pajamas."

Tania continued. "I'm a teacher. I've never worked in the summer. The pool is our summer. It's my happy place."

I was nearly sold, ready to join, but the air of secrecy still bothered me. I knew, without anyone telling me, not to identify the location of the pool on social media. Allison waited until the last possible moment to give me driving directions.

"So why does the pool have this reputation of being 'the secret pool'?"

She sighed.

"It depends on who you talk to. There's a contingent that wants to keep it exclusive, and that is tinged with racism. The old folks."

"Is there a waiting list?"

"There's never been a waiting list since I've been there. They like us to stay under eighty families, and we're at around seventy-two. It's a lot of wear and tear on the pool."

"So, it's not too crowded . . ."

Tania shrugged.

"I think some people are afraid of lawsuits. I mean, if someone drowns, we own the pool—we are all liable."

She sipped her iced coffee and shrugged. "Maybe it's about taxes or something. You'd have to ask a board member."

Changing the subject, Tania told me about another pool on the Southside. "It was in Fairburn. Looked exactly like Forest Vale. Same style pool, clubhouse, everything. What was it called. . . . It's closed now."

I swiveled my laptop around and pulled up Google Maps on the slow café Wi-Fi. Scrolled southwest where she told me to go, from Hapeville into the suburbs of Fairburn to the intersection of East Campbellton and Spence Road.

"It was on the right. You drove up a steep hill."

I switched to satellite view and watched the image of a forested plot load. A white trapezoid was carved into a red dirt clearing.

"That's it!"

We zoomed in. The base of a diving board looked like a stray tooth. It pointed to a deep end dark with leaves and shadow. It was the film negative of Forest Vale, its evil twin. Not sure if Tania felt the same little burst of excitement peeking at the image of the abandoned pool. It must feel different when you swam there.

"We spent all summer there," she said. "Everyone from my church were members."

I looked up the property tax records and found that Wildwood Recreation Club, Inc., had bought the property in 1967 and sold it in 2003 to a nearby Christian school. We discovered all this in ten minutes from our little table in Hapeville.

"Wildwood!" Tania clapped her hands. "That was the name. I bet it was built by the same people who built Forest Vale."

Wildwood and Forest Vale certainly looked alike and were built around the same time. Tania and her White, South Fulton neighbors were the connection. Like Forest Vale, it was a working-class club that operated quietly for decades on nothing more than word-of-mouth and church networking. I swept this story into a corner of my brain that was increasingly convinced that the segregated doings of White southern churches were actively eroding American democracy.

Tania followed the trail of her memories backward.

"And there was Duncan Park Pool in Fairburn. I learned to swim there." She sighed, "It sat for years in disrepair."

I had a flash of déjà vu, or was I just starting to hear a common refrain? Pool in disrepair, the good old days lost, like Jack Greene crooning, *There goes my everything.* Where had I heard about Duncan Park?

It was here, in this same coffee shop, hollering over the espresso machine, that Wesley Bolden told me about it. Wesley, who was Black and a native of College Park, and Jamie, who was White, were co-pastors planting a church in East Point. I saw them often at the café, and we joked that it was our office.

Wesley must have asked about my summer, and I told him about visiting lots of swimming pools.

"Do you know about the pool here in Hapeville?" asked Jamie. "The 'secret pool'?" He made the air quotes with his eyebrows.

"It's finally getting to be a little more diverse. But when I was a member, it was all White. I joined when I moved here, about 2006. I went there for a couple years, but with what we were trying to start with the church, it didn't make sense."

What they were trying to start was a racially integrated church.

Wesley hadn't heard of the secret pool, but that didn't surprise him. He grew up with the impression that Hapeville was an all-White town.

Wesley asked if I had been to Duncan Park Pool in Fairburn. "I swam there as a kid because I liked to swim laps and the College Park pool was too small. It's like a play pool. I needed a real pool. I've always been a swimmer."

He said Duncan Park pool had been renovated with a couple big waterslides. I added it to my growing list of pools to visit.

"Duncan Park reopened," I told Tania, happily. "It's supposed to be really nice now."

■ ■ ■

I had the information I wanted and more. Forest Vale Pool was integrated. The club's mystique was the result of its hidden location and some obscure legal issue that even the members didn't fully comprehend. So why was I still hesitant to commit myself to this group?

The first thing I did after our conversation was look up the legal definition of public and private pools in Georgia. I had no idea how they were regulated, taxed, and who is liable for accidents. I might have even Googled this on my phone, in the car, in the parking lot.

I found the answer in the Fulton County Board of Health's two hundred–page document, "Rules and Regulations for Public Swimming Pools, Spas, and Recreational Water Parks."

"Assurance of clean and safe public pools," it begins, "is partially due to the permitting requirements and routine inspections performed by Environmental Health Services. All public swimming pools are permitted annually, and inspections are performed routinely."

The first dozen pages were a glossary of terms from *A* to *Z*, or *Abandoned Pool* to *Water Quality Monitoring Device.*

Public Swimming Pool was defined as any "artificial body of water shared and used by the public for swimming, diving, wading, recreation or therapy." It included municipal, school, hotel, or motel pools; apartment complex pools; pools and spas operated by camps, country clubs, and all kinds of organizations. Forest Vale met the criteria.

I always thought *public pool* meant owned by a city or county, funded by taxes to serve everyone in the community. But here the term was much broader than that, and it included just about any place where groups congregate in a man-made swimming hole.

Older pools designed and constructed prior to this big book of rules could get grandfathered into a permit, but by law, they still needed a permit and an annual inspection. Furthermore, "the operating permit shall be framed and displayed in a conspicuous place as close to the pool entrance as possible such that it is easily readable by the public at all times."

I would later look for an operating permit posted at the pool but couldn't find one. Instead, on the bulletin board, there was a one-page history of the pool and a framed photo of its founder, Earl D. Knight.

Earl D. Knight, "Hapeville real estate man," was appointed to the Hapeville Housing Authority in 1953, served as Chamber director in 1957, and rose to be chairman of the Hapeville Planning Commission. At the same time, Knight was one of nineteen Hapeville residents who put in $250 to purchase the land for a private park in the late 1950s. He led the fundraising drive to build the pool and "establish a private Country Club that almost any Hapeville family could afford."

Hapeville's public pool, another WPA-funded facility, was required to desegregate in 1963, the same year that Forest Vale opened. While Hapeville's public pool closed in the late nineties, Forest Vale, the exclusive club Knight had helped establish, was still in operation.

The more I thought about it, operating without a permit—and the assurance of safety it represented—was a dealbreaker for me. How could I let my kids swim in a pool that didn't meet the "minimum design, construction, and operation requirements for the protection of public health and safety"? Everyone seemed okay with this situation, I suppose, because no one had been injured by it.

Exempting the pool from government oversight struck me as an evolution of the same protest that led segregationists to withdraw from public spaces during the civil rights era. I couldn't fight my first impression that even though the club had amended its bylaws and was now welcoming non-White members, it was still secretly, stubbornly, operating by its own set of rules.

July 22 DISADVANTAGED YOUTH

Breezy, hot July Sunday. We parked by a playground at the Thomasville Heights Community Center. It looked like there had been a party the night before. The ground was littered with candy wrappers, cigars, and watermelon rinds. A styrene clamshell with crinkle fries floating in it. Fries never die.

I waved to a couple men leaning back in folding chairs under a tree. Acted casual, like I dropped by the neighborhood often. Perched on the hilltop, they had the kind of panoramic view that's hard to find in Atlanta. To the east, a deep green valley scarred by remains of the old housing projects; to the west, the towers of downtown.

Thomasville Heights was built in the 1950s with urban renewal funds, a complete, master planned village with much needed housing for "Negro expansion." It had apartments, a library, community center, elementary school, churches, parks, and a pool. It remained a self-contained, mostly Black neighborhood today.

This is the pool that made me uneasy, made me question the wisdom of my swim-in-all-the-pools project. Not because we were the only White swimmers but because we were the only swimmers at all.

As we flip-flopped down the littered sidewalk to the pool, two tiny kids, one on a bike, one on a scooter, swooped over to examine us.

I said hello and asked them if the pool was open.

"Naw, it's closed," they yelled as they wheeled away. But there was a white Ford Focus pulled up on the sidewalk by the pool house. I saw the door open and close, discharging a cloud of smoke.

"It's Pay Swim," said the pool attendant, as if that would deter me.

I dug for my wallet in the towel-stuffed tote bag.

"Which ones you paying for?" she asked. The scooter rider was back, along with two more small children now gathered at my elbow.

"These two," I pointed at my sons. "You know. The White boys."

She jumped, yelled to the other lifeguards. "She said the White boys!"

They laughed and coughed.

Might as well say it. We were conspicuously, blindingly White. And we didn't belong here.

She opened the iron gate to the pool deck, shut it behind us, alone. There were no fountains, no lawn chairs. The water rippled in the breeze, two bright-blue rectangles that merged in a Tetris shape. It wouldn't feel crowded with fifty swimmers.

Another lifeguard, a shirtless young Black man with thick dreads and Adidas slides, sauntered out of the pool house to protect us.

Guy and Bruno were all business. They hopped into the shallow end and dunked underwater. I spread a towel on the scorching concrete not far from a stray sandal. I thought about those hipsters at the coffee shop, right up the street from here. They were desperate for a place to swim but wouldn't consider "a gross public pool." Meanwhile, we had this enormous pool all to ourselves for ten dollars. It felt like we had temporarily made a private pool out of a public one.

One little boy in jeans and a wife-beater stayed by the gate watching us through the black bars like we were an exhibit at the zoo. I considered passing him five dollars for admission. It was hot; I had cash. But I didn't want to get stuck babysitting, not with water involved.

I saw two boys sail by on a bike, one standing on the back pegs, on their way to the basketball court, where some other children were waiting. One little girl had a baby on her hip. The neighborhood houses encircled the community center, the pool, a tiny library, the basketball courts, and the playground, so it's possible that the parents could supervise their kids from their front doors and kitchen windows.

I paddled around with the boys for a while. Floated on my back while solitary, upswept clouds moved overhead. Let my ears fill with water.

The lifeguard edged around the pool with a long-handled skimmer net.

"It's so quiet," I said to him. "This is like the most peaceful place in Atlanta right now."

"Be glad you not here during Free Swim," he replied in a deep drawl. "There's a lot of cussing."

I learned this a couple weeks ago at Pittman Park.

"During Pay Swim, there's nobody here?" I offered.

"Oh, they jump the walls."

The walls looked ten feet tall. Vertical concrete and steel bars.

"Do you kick them out? Or, uh, make them leave?"

He replied thoughtfully.

"I ain't about to put my hands on nobody's child," he said. "There's a kid that's seven years old over there shooting dice."

"Doing what?"

"Shooting dice."

"Huh. My oldest is seven," I said, waving at Guy. Guy in his snorkel mask and Speedo vest. How could these kids be living such different versions of a childhood in Atlanta?

A young blonde woman wearing an American Pools T-shirt walked out on the deck. She squinted in the sun and waved to me, like I might be lost.

"I never see anyone here on a Sunday, during Pay Swim."

I told her we were visiting all the city pools. I clung to my project like it was a permission slip.

Her name was Hannah, same as me. She was a supervisor for the contractor that operated Atlanta's pools during the summer. They staffed the lifeguards, serviced the pool equipment. I had so many questions for her. First, how she ended up with this job.

"I grew up near Baltimore, and I was on the swim team when I was this tall," she said, holding her palm low. "But a lot of kids around here don't know how to swim."

They didn't know how to swim, but they could ride a bike, play independently, tend a baby. Guy and Bruno couldn't yet do any of those things.

Her wife arrived. I noticed their matching tattoos. Before they left, Hannah recommended some other pools, the ones that we already knew and loved—Grant Park, Candler Park, Maddox Park. They had good attendance during Pay Swim. They were the same recommendations I would make. Some pools were designed to attract visitors, and some were not.

The Thomasville Heights Pool looked exactly like Pittman Park and Anderson Park, where we swam last weekend. Same stainless-steel pool coping, fluted concrete fences and blocky blue concrete, windowless pool houses. Wide, bare concrete decks with no shade, furniture, or umbrellas, about as welcoming as a prison yard. I dubbed it "quarantine chic," before I knew anything about the pools' history.

Like so many pool-related trends I noticed in Atlanta, Jeff Wiltse's book *Contested Waters* explained that what I was seeing was part of a trend happening across the nation. Lots of stark urban pools of the 1970s were funded and built in reaction to the "race riots" that flamed up in the late 1960s. Cities that saw violence in poor, Black parts of town, from Chicago to Detroit, including Atlanta, later received federal anti-poverty grants to build swimming pools. In fact, in 1966, Martin Luther King Jr. advised Chicago mayor Richard Daley that swimming pools would help alleviate some of the tensions that had caused a riot over a fire hydrant.

"Many municipal pools constructed during the late 1960s were small, austere facilities, located in out-of-the-way places that essentially quarantined minority youths," wrote Wiltse. These pools "were intended to cool down angry Black Americans and stop them from rioting." They were not designed to be welcoming or open to families like me, who lived outside of the neighborhood.

This explained everything about the way I felt visiting Anderson Park. Atlanta's so-called race riot broke out during the heat of June 1967 in Dixie Hills. Afterward the city dedicated resources to build a park to serve the area, opening the Anderson Park Pool in 1970. On opening day, the *Atlanta Voice* quoted a twelve-year-old swimmer: "I'm glad it's open. I think it'll keep me out of trouble." Vice Mayor Maynard Jackson was on hand for the occasion.

Wiltse said this pool building spree in poor neighborhoods had forever shifted the perception of public pools. From then on, "swimming at a municipal pool marked you as socially marginal."

No wonder these pools felt forbidding and stark. They were designed to be holding tanks for Atlanta's "disadvantaged youth." At Anderson Park Pool, like Pittman and Thomasville Heights, we were the only swimmers who showed up during Pay Swim. It was just us and the lifeguard and his tinny trap music on a Bluetooth speaker. Technically the public pools were for everyone, and we had every right to swim in them. But it felt wrong to have the lifeguards sitting there, waiting on us.

It's that the local kids couldn't join us. To them, the pool was closed.

July 28 DEMAND GOODS

Piedmont Park is Atlanta's Central Park, a 185-acre Frederick Law Olmsted–designed oasis in the heart of Midtown and the central meeting grounds for every big Atlanta event from the Pride parade to the Peachtree Road Race. Tourists and locals flock to the park for festivals and concerts, first dates and kickball leagues and family reunions. I figured Atlanta's signature public park should have the greatest public pool in Atlanta.

I made the mistake of taking my family to the Piedmont Park Aquatic Center on a Saturday morning when it was ninety degrees outside. Hundreds of families woke up with the same idea.

The parking deck was packed, cars crawling through the levels because kids were everywhere. I watched moms and dads loading toddlers into strollers, stuffing tote bags with floaties and sippy cups and diapers. I was starting to streamline this process, bringing less gear with every pool expedition, but it was still a hassle.

As we followed the path down, always down, to the pool, we heard the shouts of children playing in the water. Before we even saw the pool, we saw the line. It stretched from the pool house along Lake Clara Meer, where ducks huddled in the shade. *Trust me,* I told Jason. *It'll be worth it.* This pool was designed to handle crowds.

We joined the line, and the couple in front of us said it was "members only" until noon. People were lined up an hour early. What's a member? I thought this was a public pool.

Bruno took my phone and sat down with Guy on a swing by the lake, watching *Teen Titans Go!* Jason stayed in line while I strolled over to the farmers' market to procure popsicles.

A jazz trio played on the porch of the 1920s stone bathhouse, now the park's Visitors Center. I found some shade in the Piedmont Park Conservancy tent and started paging through a coffee table book about the park's history.

White people have been swimming here since the park was created in 1887, when exposition planners dammed Clear Creek to create a pond. By 1911, the pond had been expanded and named Lake Clara Mere. It took me a while to figure out this name was a creative translation of "clear sea," not a reference to a woman. The four-acre lake was designed to be a resort for the masses, equipped with a wooden bath house, slides, and platforms for diving and sunning. Hundreds of swimmers could splash in the pond, while a hundred more spectators looked on from shaded benches and grassy banks.

The "pool" saw many upgrades for safety and permanence over the decades, but this was the same grand facility that was forced, by federal court order, to admit Black swimmers by June 1963.

In black-and-white photos of the carefully orchestrated, heavily guarded integration of Piedmont Park Pool, I saw the same stone pool house and gazebo sentinel by the lake where my kids now stood in line. A crowd of horn-rimmed journalists and officials in suits—all White—gathered lakeside to watch history in the making as three young Black men approached the bathhouse. In their pressed slacks and tucked-in button-up shirts, the swimmers looked so slim and vulnerable, clutching only a rolled-up towel for protection.

They were photographed wading into the huge pool alone while the crowd supervised. A wider shot showed three White children knee deep in the shallow end, a couple more White swimmers farther out by the slide, all turned toward the Black swimmers as they dove in, braced as if there might be an explosion.

Nothing happened that day, but the pool, predictably, fell into disrepair. Attendance plummeted; budgets were slashed. In 1973, the city overhauled the facility, which was one of the last "bathtub pools," with no filtration system. The pool was one of those grim seventies concrete-and-steel designs, smaller and safer, and relocated to a less prominent setting. When I was growing up, visiting the park for the Atlanta Arts Festival in the eighties and the Pot Festival in the nineties, I had no idea there was a place to swim in Piedmont Park. Later a Black friend told me that the Piedmont Park Pool was a very special scene for Atlanta's young Black swimmers.

The current iteration of the Piedmont Park Pool is a state-of-the-art aquatic center that opened in 2008, after "a group of concerned citizens unwilling to accept the decline of their beloved park" took over. A private nonprofit, the Piedmont Park Conservancy raised the funds for the renovation. For their efforts, members got exclusive prime time for their paying members from eight to noon on Saturdays.

I wandered over to the restrooms of the Visitors Center above the scene of splashing, squawking swimmers. It was a splendid oasis—zero-entry beach, splash pad, lazy river, four lap lanes. From my perch, it was hard to see any detail, but the only brown skin I saw was a lifeguard. The public-private partnership saved the pool but inevitably created this awkward condition of seg-regated swimming in a public pool.

■ ■ ■

By the time they gobbled their gourmet popsicles and we sponged the choco-late from Guy's chin, it was our turn to enter the "aquatic center." We put on our Tyvek wristbands, color coded with our allotted swim time. Inside, the pool area was crowded and wild with children. Fifty lounge chairs lined the fence overlooking Lake Clara Meer, all of them occupied.

Jane Jacobs wrote that pools are supposed to operate as "demand goods," in neighborhood parks. They should not only serve the local neighbors but also attract visitors who bring the park to life with additional activities and spend-ing. The good news was Piedmont Park Pool was delivering on that concept. It was by far the most crowded and lively public pool we'd seen all summer. Even during Pay Swim, it was packed with a crowd that looked and sounded like a truly integrated public place.

The bad news was I had a hard time keeping my eyes on Guy and Bruno. They kept getting swept into the jam-packed lazy river. But they had their vests on, and they loved the chaos. And there must have been six lifeguards on their feet, pacing, watching, and intervening to keep heads above water.

I nabbed a chair by the lake, the original Piedmont Park swimming hole, jade green and untouchable. Here was a pool design trend popular from Mus-cle Shoals to Malibu to the Mediterranean—gazing at a natural body of wa-ter while you float in a chlorinated box. It seemed to me part nostalgic, part unfaithful. Like fantasizing about an old flame while you make out with your husband.

Jason watched the kids for a while; I watched the moms. I saw two very pregnant women waddling in tiny bikinis. I saw another mom distracted while her pale, synthetic boob sprung out of her bikini top and stayed there for a while. It seemed okay, like there was a different set of rules for modesty in-side these gates. I saw a woman cradling a teenager with severe cerebral palsy. She held him in the shallow end and spoke to him in Spanish. We all tried not to stare at the different bodies on display.

It was overwhelming to be there together, all of us roasting in the sun, ba-sically in our underwear. The suits were skimpier now, but it has always been like this. Public pools were erotic spaces just by allowing men and women to "bathe" together. All those grainy opening day photos from the 1930s showed girls lined up by the pools in their skimpiest suits, beauty pageants, fashion shows, posing on the park director's lap. Gawking at bodies has always been part of the experience of public swimming. What makes pools exciting also makes them dangerous: they are primarily social spaces. It's why they were the last battleground of segregation.

It was part of the scene in 1963 as three Black men, not women, stripped down before the watching eyes of a crowd of media and entered the water. Their bodies were perfectly fit and respectable. They had to be.

There was a quote in the Piedmont Park Conservancy's book from Martha Porter Hall, a neighbor who was there that summer. She remembered it the same way I measure time—by pregnancies.

"I was pregnant with my first child, had just had an appendectomy, and couldn't get in the water. But I had a maternity bathing suit, so I would go in my bathing suit and sit on the edge of the pool to make sure it was not abandoned. I think there were only two white people there. I would go there and make a statement."

It took me a while to unpack her statement, who it was for and what it meant. Whenever I heard *show up* as a term for anti-racist action, I wanted a better verb, something more specific, more active. But Hall literally just had to show up at the pool, which was something other White swimmers refused to do. She put her White, pregnant body on display to show her support for integrated public spaces.

What did she know about the force field of White motherhood? Maybe she understood that no one would mess with her. While minding my little ones, I felt both invisible and protected.

But another mom was watching me. A White woman, about my age, freckled and ponytailed, asked me where I had bought my swimsuit. It was a basic black one-piece with boy shorts.

"It's the shorts, isn't it?" She laughed and agreed. It made no sense that we had to wear panties in public. It wasn't practical.

The boys swam for forty-five minutes before it started to thunder, and everyone had to get out of the water.

August 4 THE SWIMMER

The rain went on, day after day, morning, noon, and night. Today was the last day of summer vacation. Next week it would be kindergarten for Bruno, second grade for Guy.

Today's gray light made me appreciate how summer storms typically blew over in an hour, scrubbing the sky brilliant blue and knocking back the heat. This ever-present warm drizzle made my hair frizz and the house smell like wet dog and funky socks.

I was running out of days to hit all the city's "seasonal pools," when this sprawling storm system parked over Georgia the last week of July, swelling the creeks and streets with steady rain. By the time it stopped raining and we made it to Rosa L. Burney Pool in Mechanicsville, the gates were locked, and a taut vinyl cover was bolted down over the pool. We had missed it.

It looked like a fun one too. Dedicated in 2010, it was one of Mayor Reed's pools. Curving forms, kid-friendly features, playful tile murals. My kids gazed longingly at the lazy river, then ran off to the playground next door.

Why was this fantastic, $2.3 million, LEED-certified pool closed already? Was summer over? Most of Atlanta's outdoor pools were open from Memorial Day to Labor Day, but half of them followed Atlanta Public Schools' schedule and only stayed open for the eight weeks of summer vacation. This pool, in one of Atlanta's poorest neighborhoods, was here to entertain kids while school was out. It was only open for forty days a year and only if it stopped raining.

We visited every public pool in Atlanta, but we didn't get to swim in all of them.

On top of the rain, the defeat of the locked pool, the end of summer malaise, I decided to revisit "The Swimmer." Was I like Ned, the foolish pilgrim of John Cheever's 1964 short story who tries to swim across the county, pool by pool? Was my quest to swim across Atlanta bound to become an existential nightmare?

Instead of rereading the story, I looked for a copy of the 1968 film version.

"Oh yeah, that's a great movie," said the concierge at Videodrome, the only surviving video rental shop in Atlanta. He led me to a shelf of 1960s classics like *Easy Rider* and *Cool Hand Luke*. "Very antisocial."

Jason was accustomed to my assignments—I finished a book, urgently needed to discuss it, and made him watch the film version so we could talk about it.

Driving home in the rain, I told him the story was about a man who swims from one backyard pool to another, crashing pool parties, all the way across the Connecticut countryside, and slowly realizes that the seasons are changing and his life has passed him by. He thinks he's an explorer, but he loses everything—his job, his family, his home. I remembered "The Swimmer" as a funny but haunting meditation on middle age. It's not clear how years seem to pass as Ned swims home in one midsummer afternoon, but I recognized the sense of disorientation, how time flies as we perfect our powers of self-delusion.

"You'll like it," I assured him. "It's one of those edgy sixties films. Depressing but somehow popular."

There were so many pieces of the film I loved—the snazzy fashions, the interiors, the dialogue. Ned invites Joan Rivers to join him "along a river of sapphire pools" and calls himself "a very special human being, noble and splendid."

The DVD "extras" started playing automatically. I listened as I stood in the kitchen, loading the dishwasher. Burt Lancaster wasn't a good swimmer. In fact, he barely knew how to swim at all. He trained for months with a UCLA coach so he would look like he knew what he was doing. For me, that bit of trivia added something to Ned's nakedness and vulnerability. By the end, everything was stripped away, his status, his strength. No watch or wedding ring. He's left with this quest he created for himself, a project that was supposed to mean something.

August 5   CARTOOGECHAYE

Today we had a small family reunion up the creek in Franklin, North Carolina.

Up the creek is one of those modest family terms that belies the value of a vacation property. To be more specific, my grandparents own a lush mountain valley just outside the Nantahala National Forest. The property includes two steep hillsides covered with mountain laurel and hardwoods and the valley in between, a meadow bisected by the Cartoogechaye Creek. No one ever mentioned it's about forty acres, but I learned how to look it up in the county tax records. I've seen their names on the deeds.

In my lifetime, the property has been a cow pasture and a cornfield and a campground. The creek flooded the valley once every few years, carried lawn chairs into the tree limbs and tumbled the fire ring stones into the field, so the only permanent structure on the land was a simple cinder-block pavilion, my cousin's Eagle Scout project, constructed in the 1990s for family picnics. We have hosted camping trips, picnics, and reunions on this land, festive gatherings that populated the valley briefly with trailers, tents, and campfires. As a child and later a teenager, I strolled through these happy scenes like I owned the joint, and we did.

Because our Memorial Day camping trip was canceled, summer was nearly over before I finally had a chance to visit my old friend, the Cartoogechaye.

After our potluck lunch under the pavilion, spiral-sliced ham, broccoli salad, red Jell-O, a bucket of KFC, and a watermelon, my cousins and our kids changed into swimsuits and clambered down to the rocky shoals of the creek. The water was high and cold, hiding boulders below. Guy commented that it must be high tide.

This is the creek where I grew up, wading, tubing, splashing and shivering, and digging for garnets. My kids were the fourth generation here today, running barefoot through the meadow where I learned to drive a stick shift, where my father planted rows of pines on the hillside, where my grandfather baled hay, all in the shadow of Podgy's mountain, officially named after his father, in honor of his years with the Forest Service.

What did it mean to watch my little boy in his blue life preserver, knee deep in the clear and icy creek, scooping and tossing stones at the rapids? What did it mean that my family owned a valley? That we owned a place that seemed timeless, changeless, cut off from the world? Even as a little kid, I knew it was special, a form of wealth. But I had no idea what it meant, how it bolstered my identity, my stability, my sense of ownership in the world.

I always felt like we owned this creek. At least this half-mile stretch, where I could take a bath if I wanted to. This stretch of stream looks like it must have looked to the Cherokee people two hundred years ago. Gold and black river stones, mountain laurel dropping pale cup-shaped blossoms in the swift water, shady banks held together by sycamores and black walnut trees.

In Cherokee, supposedly, *Nantahala* meant "land of the noonday sun." These valleys were so deep, they only get full daylight at noon before the sun slips behind the mountains and the temperature falls.

Occasionally, kayakers steered their bright boats down the Cartoogechaye on their way to the Little Tennessee River and sailed right through our campsite. We balanced paper plates on our laps and waved. They disappeared as quickly as they appeared. We owned the land but not the water.

■ ■ ■

Once, on a cool camping weekend with friends, sitting around the campfire, my friend asked, "What's the story with this property? Where did it come from?"

I told her it's been in the family forever. "Since we stole it from the Cherokee," I joked.

"I mean, was it a plantation or something? Did your family, like, own slaves?"

I don't think anyone had ever asked me that. I scanned the meadow for an answer.

"I've never heard about any slaves in my family," I answered slowly. "I don't think there were plantations in the mountains that were big enough to own slaves."

Even as I said this, it felt like a convenient story, a way to minimize my family's wealth. Where did I get that impression? My grandparents survived the Great Depression on the small family farms that their pioneer parents scratched out of the hillside. They were missionary, midwife, farmer, forester. No one ever used the term *land rich, cash poor;* it was impolite to talk about money or acres. Even if they had hard lives, they had a home, a sorghum mill, a springhouse, and a farm big enough to feed a big family. If they owned whole mountains, some unspoken number of acres, they weren't poor.

Didn't North Carolina "hillbillies" have to be drafted and forced into Confederate ranks? They had no investment in the system of slavery. Did I absorb that from the movie *Cold Mountain?* Where the Confederate hero deserts an army hospital because he didn't believe in the cause? Or from stories about my great-great-grandfather, a Confederate deserter who walked home to Macon County from a battlefield in Pennsylvania?

I learned that my ancestors were Confederates but not slaveholders. But they weren't abolitionists either.

Unsettled by all I didn't know, on our next porch visit, I asked Granddaddy how he came to inherit that beautiful slice of Nantahala floodplain from his father.

"I remember when Podgy was working on the trout hatchery up in South Carolina," he said, like I should know what that meant. My granddad peppered his stories with mentions of the Civilian Conservation Corps, the WPA, the Job Corps, the Forest Service. All the New Deal era government programs that put people to work and transformed this corner of Appalachia. In the South, these programs were all subject to Jim Crow laws, and they had the effect of lifting White folks like Podgy, my great-grandfather, into the middle class. I had to ask my dad in order to figure out that my ancestor's handiwork was still standing at the Walhalla State Trout Hatchery, still breeding trout.

"That was 1937, so I was eleven years old," he continued. "Podgy told me I was in charge. I milked the cows, hoed the corn, looked after the house. One evening, I had to go round up the cows that went up the creek to pasture. I rode my horse back there so many times, I didn't need a bridle. Old Maude knew the way. I looked around and thought, 'If this could be mine one day . . .'"

The dramatic afternoon light that rippled across the valley. The shuffle and plop of the creek, a breeze flipping the pale skirts of the sycamore leaves. There was no place I loved more.

"Many years later, Podgy asked me would I rather have the old homeplace or the land up the creek," Granddaddy said. "No question about it, I wanted the pasture."

"But how did Podgy end up owning that piece of land?" I asked, risking being rude.

"There was plenty of it," Granddaddy said matter-of-factly. The family's property extended across mountains and valleys, miles of land; they handed it out to sons like slices of pie. He described the property that went to his Uncle

Dick, Uncle Rufe, Uncle Hal, between this creek and that road, this neighbor's barn and that peak. Grandma gave one slice to a fair-haired cousin, always her favorite. Podgy had five siblings scattered all over the United States, but he was the only son who stayed in Macon County. We speculated that's why he inherited the prettiest valley on the Cartoogechaye.

As we talked, I knew I was going to research this more.

Podgy's father had inherited land through his maternal grandfather, Jacob Siler, who had the dubious distinction of being "the first permanent white settler in Macon County." Siler, a German immigrant, was part of a crew surveying lands "acquired by treaty" from the Cherokee around 1818. I found an artfully hand-drawn map of Cartoogechaye Township from 1958 commemorating 140 years since the land was settled, 1818 to 1958. Was there no celebration this year, the 200th anniversary?

I read that Siler bought land for twenty-five cents an acre from a Cherokee chief named Balltown George. The Cherokee people were forcibly deported from this area by the Indian Removal Act of 1830.

The result was that two hundred years later, my sons splashed in the Cartoogechaye Creek, learning to love the water. They were already reaping the benefits of this tremendous inheritance. From Jacob Siler, the European settler who was able to buy half the county, to the government programs that buoyed my great-grandparents during the Great Depression to my boys, wading in their own private, pristine mountain stream, a glowing and direct line of privilege and wealth. And me, too, with the freedom and gall to write a book about all this. Me, trying to divine the duties of that wealth, besides simply preserving it for my kids.

The more I read about these treaties as coercion, legal theft, Indian removal as deportation, and the Trail of Tears as genocide, the less I wanted to boast about hanging onto this property. The thought of our debt frightened me.

When we built the picnic pavilion by a shady bend in the creek, there was room around the structure for benches and picnic tables. Over decades of streamflow smashing into that bend, the rushing creek had clawed away at the bank. It stripped off the chicken wire fence so that the benches now dangled over the water. One day, the pavilion will slump into the floodwaters of the Cartoogechaye, taking my childhood memories with it. The creek was reshaping the land.

August 11 RESCUES

We hosted Bruno's fifth birthday party at the John A. White pool on Cascade Road in Southwest Atlanta.

We arrived at noon, just as a thunderstorm cleared and the pool reopened. I gave the attendants cash to cover admission for our guests and balanced Bruno's cookie cake on a lounge chair under a large umbrella. Jason carried in oversized floats shaped like a giant popsicle and a sprinkled donut. I set up a dozen little goodie bags that contained cheap goggles and Pop Rocks. As the clouds burned off, you could hear the sizzle of rain evaporating from the warming concrete.

I got the idea to have a party here last month when we visited this pool for the first time. This is a newer pool, renovated in 2014, and only a ten-minute drive from our house.

It looked like there was a family reunion happening that day. No matching T-shirts or anything too formal; they just set up their coolers and speakers and gathered forty people around this very umbrella, kids and grandkids in swimsuits and floaties. Teenagers performed a dance routine in the fountains as one aunt broadcast it from her phone. Adults posed for photos knee deep in the shallow end, kids ran to the two stubby waterslides at the other end of the pool. I avoided staring at this knockout woman in a lime-green thong, watched the dads sneaking looks instead. It was all laughter and beats and happy shouts over the running shush of the fountains.

At John A. White, people of all ages were having a blast. Maybe it was the neighborhood—Cascade Heights is an affluent enclave of stately old homes on generous wooded lots, home to a who's who of Atlanta's Black politicians, celebrities, artists, and civic leaders. And John A. White is the kind of park where you might spot a group of Black folks practicing tai chi in a meadow or the famous author Pearl Cleage walking her dog or a former mayor playing golf.

Maybe it was the splendid summer weather, a bright break in the rain, or that the joy of this family spread to the rest of us at the pool. Maybe it was that this new facility was designed for such a scene, to accommodate large groups of families and youngsters at play.

We were in the water for less than ten minutes when I saw my first save. A toddler in khaki shorts broke into the waterslide line and zipped down into the deep end. Before I could even consider if such a small child knew how to swim, a teenaged lifeguard hopped in and scooped the kid off the pool's bottom.

The lifeguard delivered the toddler to a woman who was in the shallow end holding another baby. She thanked him and fussed at the toddler in one breath. The party never stopped.

Some grandmas offered to catch my sons at the bottom of the waterslide. "We got a lot of babies out here," a woman with silver dreadlocks reassured me. "We're not going to let anything happen to them."

Suddenly, this was my favorite pool.

Through the crowd, I spotted a stylish young couple dangling their feet in the pool. She, thin, dark-skinned, him, pale and tattooed, taking turns inflating a raft with their mouths. Maybe it was this sprinkling of quiet hipsters on top of the already mixed and boisterous crowd. In a flash, I felt transported to Brooklyn or LA. Like I was in a real city, anonymous but welcome.

∎ ∎ ∎

Originally, this pool was built for White Atlantans. The Parks Department proposed the John A. White Golf Course as a potential pool site shortly after Cascade Heights was annexed into the city limits and specifically, to serve the White population moving here from the Mozley Park area. The new pool was dedicated in 1955, a big, basic rectangle with a diving board and a midcentury modern pool house with a barrel-vaulted roof.

By the late 1960s, Cascade Heights was a predominately Black neighborhood. In 1979, the pool was repaired at great expense by the city. Mayor Maynard Jackson lived in the neighborhood.

What's different about John A. White Pool is what happened next. By the 1990s, decades of deferred repairs to sewer infrastructure—combined with rapid pre-Olympics growth—meant that Atlanta's old pipes, which were supposed to contain both stormwater runoff and sewage, were failing in spectacular, disgusting ways. During storms, rainwater pushed raw sewage into parks, streets, backyards, and basements. It discharged human waste directly into Utoy Creek, along with all the urban creeks that flowed to the Chattahoochee River. The state EPD fined the city for violations of the federal Clean Water Act.

The problem was a reeking nuisance and health threat all over the city, but one particularly egregious example was the John A. White Golf Course, where a branch of Utoy Creek routinely flowed with sewage. In 1991, the city proposed a plan to build a "strain and spray" sewage treatment facility in the park. This solution was not only expensive and questionable, but it was also prescribed without community input. It would virtually ruin the park. Neighbors were outraged.

Southwest Atlanta residents—Black scientists, politicians, veteran civil rights organizers—mobilized to fight this plan. They formed the Environmental Trust in 1993 and developed their own solution—a system that separated Utoy Creek from sanitary sewer lines forever. The trust spent years refining this alternative plan and convincing politicians the investment would save money, spare the city further fines, and improve quality of life for residents. Its victory became a model for the costly but critical sewer repairs that followed. In fact, the work of the Environmental Trust actually predated the formation of the Chattahoochee Riverkeeper, a White-led environmental organization that was also born out of Atlanta's sewer crisis. Cascade residents led the way.

In 2001, Shirley Franklin, another Cascade Heights resident and veteran of the Jackson administration, successfully campaigned for mayor promising to fix the sewer system. Once elected, the first African American woman mayor of a major southern city, Franklin made this a major priority of her administration, declaring, "I am the sewer mayor."

The John A. White Pool was renovated and rededicated in 2014 by Mayor Kasim Reed. "This is the park where I grew up as a kid," he said, "So when we didn't have a pool that was appropriate for this community and this neighborhood, I decided I was going to do something about it."

At the ribbon cutting, he wielded a pair of giant scissors while the Black-Eyed Peas boomed from a sound system.

By "appropriate for this community," did he mean small children and non-swimmers? It cost $1.6 million to rebuild the pool as "more of a recreational experience," with a large, zero-entry kiddie pool and fountains; the deep end was only four feet deep. It was a place to play and cool off in the water, not for competitive swimming.

Mayor Franklin had done the dirty and unpopular work of rebuilding the underground infrastructure that made swimming pools possible.

When you say "Cascade" in Atlanta, people think of a residential area bisected by Cascade Road, from West End to the legendary Cascade skating rink. The word is synonymous with Atlanta's Black political establishment and the Black middle class that has shaped the city for the last sixty years. The name comes from the waterfalls of Utoy Creek.

Without the separated sewer system, the tedious, technical, nearly invisible work of the Environmental Trust and Mayor Franklin, the tenacious Black advocates of Cascade Heights, it wouldn't be possible to host a birthday party at John A. White Park. Twenty years ago, the thunderstorm that just rolled through would have flooded the sewers, contaminating Utoy Creek just beyond those trees. And these juicy thunderheads roll in from the west each afternoon like clockwork.

■ ■ ■

The birthday party was sunny, steamy. Our guests trickled through the gates and soaked in the scene. For most of them, it was their first visit to a public pool in Atlanta. Soon the pool swirled with children.

Out of nowhere, a little girl swam over to me, held her tan arm up to my tan arm, and asked if I was half-Mexican. No hello or anything.

I floundered. What am I? Scotch-Irish, German? Whenever I saw the term *Caucasian*, on a speeding ticket, for example, it struck me as comically outdated.

"Well, I'm half-Mexican," she said. "Look, we're almost the same color. I have to wear sunblock too."

While she was fascinated with my skin color, I was struck by the fact that she was eight years old. So tall and talkative, her social and verbal skills far beyond those of my seven-year-old, who had just struggled to tell me that a big storm cloud was under us. Over us, I corrected. He paddled away.

"He knows how to swim?" the girl shrieked, "How old is he?"

Guy was underwater, slipping between kids on the way back to his father. I cheered for him; the girl looked shocked.

I looked around at the pool full of children. Out of all the bobbing, hopping, splashing, playing, chicken-fighting kids, only a couple children were truly swimming. My kids showed up, ran straight into the water, and started swimming, no floats or vests this time. It appeared to be a kind of magic. No one saw the poolside barfing and tears at swim lessons. No one saw the work the boys and I had done to make swimming look effortless.

It made me sad to think that having access to water wasn't enough to learn how to swim. Kids needed instruction and challenge. Someone to show them how to do the difficult, scary work of learning to float.

Bruno's cousins and classmates and their moms gathered 'round—Anisa with Noah, Evy and Lalu from the gym, Danielle with Ike and his adorable little sister, Myra with Cecil and Geneva, Allison with her kids, Eve with Tripp and Jacque. After we sang Happy Birthday, I took the lifeguards fat squares of cookie cake, a little bribe to say, thank you, I hope it's okay that we had a party here.

August 12 DAD SWIM

School started. Bruno in kindergarten, Guy in second grade. They looked like little managers-in-training in their tucked-in school polos and tidy haircuts. I would've felt wistful about it—the end of summer, those first-day-of-school photos in the front yard—but the weather was so hot and summery. We could still go swimming.

Soccer practice started. Homework started. I still took the boys for after-school swims. Despite his disabilities, Guy was swimming independently. Bruno was less fearful but still getting the hang of it. During the last days of summer, we checked so many pools off our list—Candler Park, Adams Park, Mozley Park, Garden Hills, Chastain Park.

Candler Park was a 1950s pool that looked identical to South Bend, only the swimmers were White. We caught two frogs in the pool and released them through the fence. The pool rules said do not swim if you have an "open womb."

We went to Free Swim at Adams Park (renovated 1991, Maynard Jackson, Mayor), and it was just us and a family from Brooklyn. My dad told me he had welded repairs on an Atlanta pool made of aluminum. I finally found it when I elbowed the side of this pool, and it chimed like a bell. I spotted a pair of false eyelashes on the ledge of the pool, slightly more exotic trash than the ubiquitous waterlogged Band-Aid. The boys stood under an enormous red bucket that tipped water down on their heads.

At Mozley Park (renovated 1987, Andrew Young, Mayor), we saw sisters splashing in swim hijabs alongside teenagers in string bikinis. Boys were flipping over backward to impress them. During safety break, the lifeguards engaged in a brief diving contest. An ice cream truck parked by the pool house provided a music box soundtrack.

As one of Atlanta's "partner pools," Garden Hills was operated in partnership with a private, clearly well-funded nonprofit. Like Piedmont Park, that meant this was a grander facility catering to a much wealthier and Whiter neighborhood. I saw Speedos here for the first time, fit grandpas and grandmas, a giant inflatable unicorn raft. There was a tall, springy diving board where divers of all ages took turns showing off their moves. This was the first and only time I noticed what was likely a gay couple, two men sunning and reading magazines, at a public pool. I tried to make eye contact with a seventy-something grandma rocking the same polka-dot Target one-piece as me. Garden Hills was a lively social scene.

I nagged Jason to come to Chastain Park Pool with us, another partner pool. There were a lot of White dads there, which I associated with the posh neighborhood, and the classic rock station piped through the speakers. We swam to The Who, U2, Bruce Springsteen, all pleasant summer swimming jams. Again, the diving board signaled some alternate universe where legal liability wasn't a concern. The pale moms were skinny and fit, wearing stylish plum and sage bathing suits, all geometric and strappy. Never sitting, always lunging between their kids, handing out orange slices or a napkin, squirting out more sunblock.

We went to enough pools in a short enough time that I started seeing patterns. I saw the same American Pools lifeguards at different pools. I mused about their lives outside of this summer gig. Maybe they recognized me too.

I noticed the topography. Almost every pool had a creek running beside it; almost every park had a creek running through it. It became clear that urban parks followed the contours of the watersheds, always located in the soggy bottomland that couldn't be used for houses, strip malls, or cemeteries.

The pools always lay downhill, like a shining blue gem nestled at the heart of the forest. I felt the pull of the water, of gravity really, and the magic of knowing these pools were built on top of our original swimming holes and diverted creeks. The oldest pools were spring fed—Washington Park, Lake Abana, Piedmont Park, East Point. There was some memory of water that we kept renovating and rebuilding there.

August 24 SURF SAN FRANCISCO

Outside the low cinder-block wall surrounding our hotel, somebody lay face down on the sidewalk.

Should I tell the concierge to call 911? She could see the fallen from her desk behind the glass door. She buzzed us into the lobby, which we didn't realize was locked. This was normal in the Tenderloin.

It was Jason's idea to come to San Francisco for our annual honeymoon. We tried to plan a short getaway for our anniversaries. Every year, we came up with a road trip packed with our favorite pre-kid activities—art galleries, nature hikes, historical sites, record shops, fussy restaurants, bike rides, quirky lodging, and some form of water. Jason wanted to see the Magritte exhibition at the San Francisco MoMA, so that was the seed for this, our sixteenth anniversary. Because my birthday was the day after, I got to pick the next adventure—surfing lessons on Stinson Beach.

I didn't understand how much San Francisco had changed in the decade since we last visited, and I wasn't prepared for street scenes of open needle use and grown-ups passed out in the gutter.

Our motel, a midcentury motor court, had been renovated for traveling hipsters. Two stories of minimal guest rooms wrapped around a central courtyard. Every cherry-red door opened up to the main attraction, the small oval pool. It had black 69s tiled across the bottom, flanked by canvas sling chairs and banana trees and aloe plants in fat terra-cotta pots.

The concierge saw us gawking at the pool and told us it was heated. We giggled and hustled to our room on the second level. We skipped the anniversary champagne waiting on a table in our room, the anniversary sex this was all in service of. We changed into our swimsuits and, minutes later, recruited a stranger to take a photo of us cannonballing into the pool. He captured us midair, me plugging my nose and eyes closed, hair flying. Jason, grinning and executing a perfect tuck. I decided I did not look fat and gave Jason permission to post it on Instagram.

For the last couple of years, my social media feeds have been marked by the scenic fortieth birthday celebrations of my peers, trips to Iceland to see the Northern Lights, dancing on a backyard trampoline, 1970s-themed costumes, Caribbean cruises. My generation practices assertive memory making, not only advertising life's wins and milestones on social media but planning life around potential posts. I could blame Facebook for this affectation, but it was merely a more intentional version of our parents' Christmas cards and family newsletters, a way to broadcast how rich and fit and successful we were while also being a genuine time capsule of life's highlights.

The hotel pool was one of only two swimming pools in the country on the historic registry. The bottom of the pool was a tile mosaic titled *My Fifteen Minutes—Tumbling Waves*, by New York pop artist Francis Forlenza. When the hotelier commissioned the work in 1989, he didn't know that it was against code for a pool bottom to be anything but white. For years, there was no swimming allowed (officially) in the pool, and a sign nearby said, "This Is Not a Swimming Pool. This Is Art," which sounds exactly like the title of a Magritte painting. Eventually, he won an exemption to the rule. We had no idea we were immersed in a work of art.

It was not by chance that we ended up in this stylish hotel, leaping into the pool for the cameras. I think Jason art directed that cannonball shot months earlier, when we booked the room. Outside the frame was everything that came before and after that shot.

■ ■ ■

An email from the surf outfitters was waiting in my inbox, reminding me of our scheduled lesson including wet suit rental. It'll be fine, I told myself, compared to the Polar Bear Plunge. San Francisco was cold in August, according to Mark Twain, and everyone warned me about it. I heard war stories from the few friends who had tried surfing lessons. They were bruised, beaten, lacerated by coral, and stung by jellyfish.

I tested out this theory on a friend at dinner. We met Adia at a Jamaican place near her studio in Oakland.

"Perhaps," I ventured, over jerk salmon, "the cold water will keep sharks away."

Adia cackled. "Sharks love cold water!"

I got carsick winding up the coast from San Francisco to our destination. We made lots of stops at record shops and bookstores, found the Trader Joe's in Sausalito. When we arrived at the beach, I read signs warning about sharks and riptides. I couldn't back out of my own photo op. The lessons were nonrefundable.

Bright and early on my birthday, we met our instructor, Simon or Nigel. With his South African accent and sun-bleached curls, he looked like a surf instructor out of central casting. He told us we weren't going to see any sharks today, and I decided to believe him.

The other students were on their second and third lessons, and this made me feel better too. No one masters surfing in one lesson. We all looked funny lying on our boards on the beach. We practiced jumping up from our bellies to a squat, over and over. Nigel said we were ready for the waves.

It was surprisingly warm in my wetsuit. I could feel the sun forming freckles on my nose.

Thanks to Nigel and his young assistants, both Jason and I managed to catch, tentatively, many waves. We learned to push onto our boards at the right moment and balance for three or four seconds before the friendly waves delivered us to the shore. Dolphins swam with us. We spotted seals bobbing the waves. Afterward we ate victory tacos on the beach. The Pacific was golden.

That night, my shoulder ached so badly I couldn't sleep. I took some Advil, a toast to being forty years old. I missed the boys but didn't miss being a parent. Is it possible, I thought as I dozed off, that every vacation is an elaborate new attempt to get into water?

■ ■ ■

We were a couple days away from Jason's heart attack.

When I scroll through the photos from that weekend, it's obvious why we take these anniversary trips every year and document them—to remember why we like each other. The two of us jumping into the arty hotel pool, our silly superhero poses in wetsuits, Jason examining a redwood, running across Stinson Beach in the morning haze just to scatter a flock of resting gulls, I see us laughing, spontaneous, delighting in our still-young-enough bodies.

It took a couple days to be friends again. Random date nights were not enough. They turned into business meetings or an opportunity to fight about money, work drama, politics, our family, or whatever we couldn't talk about in front of the children. More than once this year, I ended a date early because I was crying or tired. I dozed off in the cushy chairs of more than one dark movie theater.

The photos show none of that. These missives to the public are curated to project a certain joie de vivre, proving to ourselves and others that after sixteen years, marriage could still be happy. But there was so much more we didn't document, most of it too precious and intimate—the road trip soundtrack winding through Muir Woods, the incessant gossip and debates. We met a couple on the beach and discovered it was his fiftieth birthday and my fortieth, so they invited us back to their rented mansion for cocktails, and it turns out he was a professional harpsichordist, and his lovely daughter named Hannah wanted to be a writer. Jason and I collapsed every night slightly drunk and goofy. Was it all a dream?

I look at our anniversary photos and think about what would've happened if Jason had felt chest pains in a gallery of the San Francisco MoMA and keeled over while studying a Magritte. I would've thought it was an elaborate prank. What if it happened while we were stuck in traffic on a bridge over the Bay? Or way out on Stinson Beach, a long and nauseating ambulance ride from any hospital?

Thankfully, it didn't happen in California. The weekend was dreamy and light, before the trapdoor opened.

PART 3

THE OFFSEASON

September 3 LABOR DAY

We went to Grant Park Pool on Labor Day at 5:00 p.m. It was the last day of swimming, the final hours before the city's outdoor pools closed for the season.

Through the fence, we could see that the kiddie pool was deserted, its placid surface a perfect mirror of the treetops. The big pool was full of swimmers and sunshine. Around forty people splashed and lounged and dangled their feet in the water, soaking up this poignant summertime scene one last time. A handful of latex-capped athletes moved purposefully north and south between the floating lane dividers.

"The kiddie pool is broken?" Guy asked. Not broken, just closed, I told him. For a long time, Guy asked questions by inflection instead of inverting the verb, as in, "Is the kiddie pool broken?" His inability to conjugate verbs made him sound like someone learning English as a second language or like a child much younger than he was. Around his neck, he draped a blue-and-white striped towel we bought on Stinson Beach.

As we approached the entrance, the bored pool attendants chanted, "It's free," in unison. We grinned and filed past the front desk. Jason and boys to the left through the men's locker room, ladies to the right.

I was relieved. We almost missed the last day of the season. I needed the diversion. What else are you supposed to do after someone in your family nearly dies?

Last Friday, Jason knew he wasn't having a panic attack as he biked to work, but he didn't tell me exactly what was going on. He texted me at 8:24 a.m., "Having chest pains. Called 911. At the corner of Sylvan and Murphy."

I missed this message, and the most frightening moments of this story, mercifully, because I was in the shower, probably shaving my legs and contemplating a packing list for our Labor Day weekend camping trip.

When I returned Jason's call, fumbling fingers, nightmare style, he answered. He was in the back of an ambulance headed to the ER, and his voice sounded normal. Maybe, I suggested hopefully, it was just anxiety?

Jason has had panic attacks since he was a teenager, triggered by stimuli like the swirling carpet patterns in hotels or the flickering fluorescents at the A&P. He told me about strangers' faces turning into plastic or, worse, family members turning into wax.

But this feeling he had while pedaling up the hill on Murphy Avenue wasn't a panic attack. He later described clear physical symptoms—shortness of breath, even after he dismounted and walked his bike, followed by chest pain, then a growing, crushing pressure, like a load of bricks on his chest. He lay down by his bike, dialed 911, and shouted his location to the dispatcher over the blasting horn of a passing freight train.

Oakland City Fire Station was across the railroad tracks, so help arrived quickly. The firefighters saw a middle-aged man having chest pains during physical exertion and assessed the situation instantly. They gave him nitro-glycerine, and Jason felt relief.

Maybe that's how I managed to race to the hospital, calling Jason's father and my father, then his sister and my sister, canceling plans and arranging new plans as I wove through rush hour traffic, how I could keep from scream-ing as I spiraled up the interminable parking deck in search of an open parking spot. Jason sounded fine; he was conscious; they were just going to check him out. But the medics had run an EKG during the ambulance ride to Grady. They told him the results looked "gnarly."

I navigated Grady, Atlanta's massive, utterly Gotham downtown hospital, and somehow located my husband sitting up on a gurney in a messy triage area, shirtless and sexy, looking mildly annoyed as a swarm of doctors and nurses danced around him. I counted twelve. His family history, combined with the EKG, had them scrambling.

Years later, during a dreamless predawn worry session, I would remem-ber that Aretha Franklin's funeral was playing on a large flat-screen television in the ER waiting area. Louis Farrakhan and Bill Clinton seated on the same stage were among the bizarre details from that day tucked away in my brain.

Once the crowd of nurses dispersed, we took a dazed selfie in the ER be-cause what else do you do with all the time waiting? I was wearing a blouse I bought at a boutique in San Francisco. We were still debating whether to can-cel our camping trip.

No one uttered the words *heart attack* until after the heart catheterization procedure later that afternoon. Cardiologists would run a tube from a vein in Jason's arm into his beating heart and then shoot it full of dye and study an X-ray in real time to look for blockages. I had to sign one of those forms on a clipboard acknowledging the risk of death. This was supposed to take twenty minutes, just to be safe, but I suffered at least an hour of *The Graham Norton*

Show blasting from a corner television. Only soothing beach scenes should be broadcast in the cardiac cath lab waiting room.

When the cardiologist came to speak to me, he used the terms *98 percent blockage, the widowmaker,* and *cardiac arrest.* He had just placed a stent in Jason's artery.

It took me all day to understand that my husband had had a heart attack, that it had nearly killed him. It was hard to believe. Jason was thinner, fitter, and healthier than he had been in a decade. He was biking to work every day, twenty miles round trip. He was forty-four years old. I thanked the doctor, found a bathroom down the hall, went into a stall, and cried.

■ ■ ■

We pulled three empty lounge chairs together into a patch of shade by the pool. Jason's arms were still bandaged from IVs and the heart catheter. He couldn't immerse himself in the water, only watch from the deck where he was supposed to be taking it easy. He frowned at his phone.

I didn't even think, why are we here? Why go swimming? Did we do this for the kids, or was it for me? I was too drained to care. It was hot and sunny. It was the last day, it was free, and it felt radically normal to be by a pool.

As usual, there were rowdy teenagers, lounging twenty-somethings, and busy moms, White and Black, all together but not interacting.

The children found each other. Bruno befriended a little Black girl in a pink swim vest. Or it was she who befriended him, with her My Little Ponies and red popsicles? They seemed to be about the same age, same skill level in the pool. Her name was Dior, like the French designer but with an emphasis on the *Dee.*

I was aware of how much I needed these boys to know how to keep moving day to day, how to make friends in public places. I was also aware that they wouldn't do this forever. They would grow ever more self-conscious, race-conscious, girl-conscious.

By six thirty, late-afternoon shadows were swallowing the pool, and the remaining swimmers thoughtlessly drifted to the patches of sunlight that lay across the water. We waved goodbye to Dior and to the lifeguards, goodbye to the pools for the year.

■ ■ ■

I couldn't understand if this medical event was a big deal or not. A near miss. Some of our family members went to pieces; some sent their love and carried on with their plans. After all, Jason was okay. People have heart attacks all the time; they get stents in their hearts. It was as common as a car wreck. People take cholesterol medication, carry around tiny glass vials of nitroglycerine pills. But for every person I knew who had survived a heart attack or heart surgery, I could think of one who didn't. Jason's father did; his mother didn't.

"You got a second birthday, dude," said one of Jason's visitors at Grady. "This is the first day of the rest of your life," said another.

I brought him a box of his favorite donuts, even though donuts are at the top of the list of foods one shouldn't eat after having a heart attack.

It's not clear what you're supposed to do in the hours and days after a near death experience. Especially when the kids still need to play and eat and hear stories before bed.

We carried on with our routine. Took the kids to school, to soccer practice. People from church brought us dinners and told us about their cardiac troubles. Jason started rehab, started filling one of those pillboxes with compartments for every day of the week. He wanted to go back to work, but it alarmed his coworkers, so he stayed home and folded laundry. The volume doubled with little red school polos, navy shorts, soccer socks, gym shorts, plus swimsuits and towels.

I felt like I was part of this club, the heart attack wives, and I wasn't ready. Last week, I was in my thirties. How were we supposed to change our lives? If our story were a movie, the heart attack be would a turning point. We would quit our soul-killing jobs and sail around the world, maybe move to the country and become vegans.

Mom suggested that our wild little dog come live with her, where she could run freely in a big yard with Mom's other rescue dogs. The puppy was almost a year old and had grown into a coyote-sized mutt with short, Oreo-speckled fur and striking blue eyes. She was undisciplined and aggressive, still chewing up rugs and shoes, stealing socks and snarling at the kids. Jason and I had opposing approaches for correcting bad doggy behavior, which, unsurprisingly, was closely aligned with how we dealt with bad kid behavior, but we were overwhelmed. After the heart attack, our thin patience for the dog was causing fights and stress we couldn't afford. She had bitten all of us at least once.

"She's not a bad dog," Mom said. "But she's not helping Jason."

Feeling defeated, I drove the pup halfway to Tennessee to meet Mom in a windswept Costco parking lot. I told the boys that we would visit the dog at Gramma's house. That was the only thing we changed at first, and it was not a sacrifice but a relief. It's like the animal absorbed our bickering and anxiety, and it made her mean. She brought out the worst in us, and we were glad to see her go.

September 16 DENVER ENVY

It wasn't even fall, but the boys' school was closed for "fall break." Despite Jason's health crisis, or because of it, we kept our plan to spend the week with our friends near Denver, Colorado. Karyn and Keith had two little boys and a guest bedroom waiting for us. Karyn picked us up at the airport in their red minivan, the car they would loan us for the week. She brought snacks and Colorado T-shirts for the boys.

In September in the Rockies, the aspens turned yellow, and the weather was ideal for exploring Denver's abundant parks and trails and cute neighborhoods. Driving into the suburbs, we could see snow on the distant Flatirons, but it was still warm enough to swim.

The first time we spent a week in Colorado with Karyn and Keith, they lived in a giant apartment complex in suburban Superior with a resort style pool. The swimming pool resembled a blue donut with a bite taken out of it. The donut hole was an elevated hot tub where you could gaze upon the reservoir to the east or the vast expanse of Rocky Flats Wildlife Refuge to the west. We ended many of our days in that hot tub, all eight of us, taking in a spectacular sunset over the mountains. The show was different every night.

During that first trip, we saw majestic elk bugling in Rocky Mountain National Park, touched dinosaur fossils at Dinosaur Ridge, cheered for the motocross in Morrison, and waded in the South Platte River in downtown Denver, but it was that apartment complex pool that the kids remembered and asked about. "When are we going back to Colorado?" they begged. "I really miss that swimming pool."

Karyn and Keith made it easy and affordable to take a family vacation to one of the most beautiful places in the country. But the boys themselves were getting easier. After that first trip, without diapers or nap schedules, I realized that traveling with the boys was no longer a chore but truly fun. They were always up for an adventure.

Our friends moved from one apartment to a house seven miles east, in Broomfield. They commuted seamlessly between a half-dozen cities daily, offices in Denver and Boulder, picking up the toddler from preschool in Westminster, running to Louisville for takeout, home to Broomfield. This mobility between city limits was not unusual for any large, metropolitan area, but it looked confusing to me. The landscape was so flat, and all the planned developments looked uniformly new and tidy. Trees planted in the 1970s shaded the clean sidewalks that ran continuously across the plains. I had a hard time keeping track of what city we were in.

I envied my friends' ability to move their family and adapt to new places as I became ever more steeped in my corner of Atlanta. Karyn, whose parents were born in Shanghai, grew up in China, moved to the United States at age ten, and lived in three different states before settling in Atlanta. Keith was from coastal Virginia. They met in Atlanta, where they played in a band together and worked for the same media company. Karyn wore red when they got married next to an iceberg in Alaska. I lived vicariously through their moves as I updated their address on our Christmas party invitations every year.

On the drive to Broomfield, Karyn told Guy and Bruno that they no longer had an apartment complex pool, but we would go somewhere even better—the Paul Derda Recreation Center. Only in Colorado would you trade a fabulous private pool for a city rec center.

Every year, I was culture-shocked by the parks and trails of Metro Denver. Cyclists pedaled along protected trails that followed the highways, connecting everything. You could wade in the creeks in downtown Denver or Boulder. There was a manicured, active public park or greenspace within a ten-minute walk of every home, and if you were willing to drive half an hour, you could hike or bike or ski in the mountains. The quality of the public realm compared to nothing I had ever seen in the South, including the most affluent suburbs of Atlanta, which tended to restrict amenities behind the gates of a private club. Here public space was the priority.

For example, outside the kitchen window of Karyn and Keith's house, instead of a fenced backyard, there was a small deck that led to Brandywine Park. A fluffy green lawn surrounded a playground and tennis courts and a walking trail that led to the public elementary school her son rode his bike to every morning. Keith joked about never needing to mow the grass. I laughed that we flew a thousand miles to visit their recreation center.

Built in 2003 for eighteen million dollars, the Paul Derda Recreation Center was an eighty-five thousand–square–foot family playground with award-winning architecture and dramatic views of the Front Range. We entered by the clocktower and passed, agape, through the soaring timber-framed lobby. Beyond the central two-story rock wall was a wall of glass with a view of the pool, which was more like a Rocky Mountain–themed indoor water park. We saw a tall tube slide through faux rock formations, a lazy river, a lap pool, a couple spas. The boys ran to the window to point and squeal about which feature to conquer first. In all our pool hopping in the South, we had seen nothing like this.

And it wasn't just a pool. The rec center had basketball courts, weight rooms, a gymnastics training facility, fitness studios, an indoor playground, a preschool, and a second-story indoor track that overlooked it all.

"The winters are so long here. We don't ski, so we come here all the time."

In minutes, we were all scampering into the warm and crowded flow of the lazy river.

If suburban Broomfield were a salad, White people would be the iceberg lettuce and everyone else—Latino, Asian, Black, and Indian families—the skimpy toppings. My blond-haired little tourists fit right in, while Karyn, with her black hair pulled up in a ponytail and her red polka-dot swimsuit, was one of very few Asian people at the pool that day.

We trailed the boys through the fountains and slides, under the waterfalls and rock tunnels, around the lazy river again and again. I spun down the waterslide with Bruno and felt choked with claustrophobia. They could navigate the pool without floats and without me, but I stayed close by, just in case.

Jason rested on a lounge chair on the outdoor patio under the scorched blue sky, watching prairie dogs through the fence.

■ ■ ■

One evening, we took Karyn's sweet old dog Sputnik for a walk around the eighty-six-acre open space, the Broomfield Commons, yet another marvel in her neighborhood. Why was Denver so different from Atlanta? I blathered. How were they funding all this?

She told me what she'd learned in the first months of living in the state— that the profits from Colorado's lottery were dedicated to public parks, trails, recreation, and conservation. "I would have loved the free pre-K in Georgia, but the parks here are pretty great."

In Georgia, lottery money paid for public preschool programs and college scholarships for high achievers at public colleges and universities. Which was great, in a way, but many people never saw a dime from the Georgia Lottery. If you or your children didn't attend preschool or college or opted for a private institution or didn't maintain the grade point average to receive a HOPE scholarship, you would miss out on the benefits of the Georgia Lottery.

By contrast, it's hard to imagine a single Coloradan who doesn't directly benefit from these lottery-funded public amenities, either by improved health and quality of life or property values. According to their website, since 1985, the Colorado Lottery has funded $3.4 billion in parks, trails, and greenspace projects across the state.

I looked at the lists of projects funded by Colorado's lottery programs and saw so many of the destinations from our weeklong visits, from city parks and playgrounds to creekside trails and state parks. Hundreds of millions of dollars granted, thousands of acres of land acquired.

Obviously, a steady flow of funding made this lifestyle possible, but property taxes played a role too. Karyn's modest three-bedroom house was worth triple the cost of my house in East Point. Real estate was expensive, and the cutthroat market meant not everyone could afford to stay and enjoy the civic flourishing of the region. I saw a T-shirt for sale at a record shop that looked like "Straight Outta Compton" but said "Priced Outta Denver," instead.

They were so lucky here, I mused. City planners had a blank slate on which to draw street grids and master plan a utopia. They inherited none of the segregated geography that haunted the urban form of the South. It's like they had no history, no memory of public parks and pools as declining, marginalized spaces.

At the same time, Karyn found it challenging to find and form community like she had in Atlanta. "Everyone leaves the office at four thirty on the dot so they can go mountain biking or kayaking," she laughed. "But I don't blame them. That's why we all love living here."

■ ■ ■

Each morning, I checked to make sure Jason had the tiny glass vial of nitro-glycerine in his pocket. The vial was so small, you could swallow it like a pill. In Karyn's guest bathroom, he lined up his pills with terrible-sounding names: clopidogrel, atorvastatin, metoprolol, pills he must swallow every day, the nurses warned us both, or he will die.

We returned to Rocky Mountain National Park. At an elevation of eleven thousand feet, I was pausing to catch my breath on every trail. I worried about the boys scampering along the edge of a waterfall. The aspens were all yellow and fluttery and unhelpful.

"You feel okay?" I kept asking Jason.

We shouldn't be here. Two weeks ago, we were at Grady, in a room overlooking the city, listening to Richard Pryor's set about his heart attack. I watched skateboarders on a rooftop, the Grady chopper descending, the distant tango of homeless Atlantans and DragonCon attendees on the streets below.

On the trail to Bear Lake, I said out loud what I was thinking.

"If your heart stops out here, I'm not going to be able to haul you out."

Jason didn't miss a beat. He said, "I'll die happy."

■ ■ ■

One evening, we stopped for artisanal ice cream in charming downtown Louisville. Karyn and I pulled on a layer of fleece as the sun dipped behind the mountains. The boys refused to wear jackets.

"When we first moved to Colorado, I so wanted to buy a house here," said Karyn, "But every home out here is worth like a million dollars."

Merry bungalows faced the tree-lined street. Blue, white, gray. From the outside, they looked a lot like my little house in East Point. But the cars were Range Rovers and Audi sport wagons. Zillow told us the average home price in Louisville was $826,415.

"How do these people have so much money?" I asked.

"I have no idea. I have no clue who these people are," she said, delightfully blunt, as usual.

I slurped organic mocha ice cream from my spoon. Guy dipped his whole face in a cup of chocolate. Ah, Louisville, Colorado. Nice to visit, couldn't live there if you wanted to.

Million-dollar houses meant a healthy tax base on top of the billions from lottery funds. Was the wealthy population bankrolling these tremendous public amenities? Or did good public policy generate wealth for all? Or was it the usual boon of stolen land, war profits, and tech money?

■ ■ ■

On subsequent visits, I learned that the grass wasn't always greener in Colorado.

During a safety break at the Derda Recreation Center pool, Jason checked his phone.

"Did you spend four hundred bucks at . . . King Soopers?" he asked.

"What's King Soopers?" I pictured a fancy soup café. This was before a mass shooting at a Boulder King Soopers added another tragic location to our national list that already included Columbine and Aurora.

It was a fraud alert. I bolted for the locker room, realizing that my purse had been stolen. Someone had used our debit card to buy sixteen hundred dollars in Visa gift cards at Colorado's most oddly named grocery store. The Broomfield police made a report, but the thief was never caught. At least the culprit was kind enough to leave my clothes in the locker. Not everyone in suburban Colorado was rich enough for artisanal ice cream and ski vacations.

Later I read about the Rocky Flats Nuclear Weapons facility, a Cold War era bomb factory that overshadowed Arvada, Broomfield, Louisville, and Golden, all the picturesque boomtowns we envied as we cruised around in Karyn's minivan on the way to our next adventure. Rocky Flats left plutonium in the soil, tritium in the drinking water, and radioactive waste gone missing.

Once the plant shut down, in the 1990s, the Department of Energy turned the factory's security buffer zone into a fifty-two hundred–acre wildlife refuge. The week we visited in 2018, the U.S. Fish and Wildlife Service made the controversial decision to finally open the refuge's trails to the public for biking, hiking, horseback riding, and cross-country skiing. At the time, we didn't know any of that history of contamination and cancer or the long history of collective protest for nuclear disarmament in the 1980s. We just saw a wild and vast nature preserve next door.

Suburban Denver looked pristine and ahistorical, but it had poison coursing through its groundwater too. The decision to make the Colorado Lottery function as a conservation tool was a policy response to the statewide environmental wake-up call of Rocky Flats.

After a few years, Karyn and Keith would eventually leave Colorado and come back "home," to Atlanta. The isolation of the pandemic and the way it exposed anti-Asian racism pushed them to reconsider raising their Chinese American kids among the overwhelming blondness of Colorado. Despite the great pools and schools and trails and snowboarding slopes, they came back to the imperfect place where they fell in love, where their boys were born.

In the fall of 2018, Georgia voters decisively approved the Georgia Outdoor Stewardship Act, which created the state's first dedicated funding source for protection of land for parks and greenspace through a tax on outdoor recreation equipment. The tax on a fly-fishing rod purchased in Atlanta, for example, could ultimately fund the preservation of trout fishing streams in North Georgia. It was a limited and somewhat convoluted mechanism but a start toward creating a culture of conservation and shared public resources.

October 11   THE OPPOSITION

Myra forwarded an email announcement from the city, subject line: "Proposed New Recreation and Aquatic Center Community Meetings."

The body of her message: "WHAAAAT?"

The flyer featured renderings of a bland-looking two-story building and floor plans, along with date and location for the upcoming hearings.

"Woo boo finally!!" I shot back. My sister deciphered my frantic typing. Finally, the golden age of pool rebuilding was coming to East Point.

All year long, I had imagined that I would contact the city council or the mayor or the Parks and Recreation Department with some conclusions from our year of swimming pool visits and would somehow make a compelling case for ending our long swimming pool drought. Judging from the renderings, no such plea was needed. If they already had a location, architectural plans, and were asking for public input, that meant the idea for a pool has been swirling for years and the funding is finally falling into place.

The invitation sparked preliminary cheers, questions, and predictably, complaints on the community boards on Facebook.

"Spend, spend, another reason to add an additional fee to the utilities bill."

"Interesting that the description says FOR Ward D rather than IN Ward D."

"That's great, but why not Ward B?"

"I volunteer to teach water ballet!"

Didn't they see this was historic? There had been no pool in East Point in forty years. I made plans to attend the meeting and express my support.

Asa G. Hilliard Elementary School looked elegant in the cloudless violet twilight. Sharp edges of the brushed aluminum and stacked stone columns. I followed the low-lit breezeway into a lobby with colorful seating and linoleum.

I crept into the meeting a few minutes late because I was cooking chicken noodle soup and helping the boys pull their soccer socks over their shin guards at the same time so Jason could take them to soccer practice as soon as he got home from work. We barely said hello to each other as I passed him at the door, dialing up directions to the meeting, night falling fast, by six thirty.

This is why people skip public meetings on weeknights. You must be significantly invested or impacted by the proposed development to hustle like this.

We met in the "cafetorium," a combination lunchroom with a stage, where I found a red circle stool fixed at one of those long folding tables that trigger lunchroom memories. Up front, the rows of chairs were already occupied with forty or so neighbors. The city manager was talking in front of the stage, the red velour curtains pulled back, six presentation boards set up on easels.

Perhaps anticipating the gripes I had read on Facebook, he was explaining how East Point's 8 percent hotel/motel tax would fund the construction, operations, and maintenance for this new forty thousand–square–foot facility. This money generated by hotel visitors was restricted to fund "destinations and tourist attractions" and could not be spent, for example, on hiring police officers or filling potholes. I felt buoyed. It's hard to prioritize fun in the city budget, but they had found a way to do it.

I tried to discern the city manager's accent as he spoke, some twinge of the islands, and I wondered if that accent costs him any credibility with this crowd of longtime residents, both Black and White, born in the South. A big, dark-skinned man with a commanding presence, he had no trouble slipping in some humor and slang to get a few chuckles from the attentive audience. Nearly everyone in the room was African American—the mayor, council, the director of parks and recreation, and the residents—but there was still tremendous racial, social, and class diversity. Divisions are harder to detect, and alliances aren't always obvious.

Next, he delivered a quick overview of the site evaluation process, explaining that the search area was focused to Ward D, as it was the only ward in East Point without a park. He brought up and quickly knocked down several potential sites already owned by the city or the county—a defunct middle school (too residential), three acres on South Commerce Drive (too small), another site on the western limits of the city (too far away from most residents).

I spotted a few kids and their parents in the room, but it was mostly gray-haired people in those chairs, longtime homeowners. Later they would announce their address and tenure in the neighborhood as they stood up one at a time to oppose the proposal. I was one of maybe a dozen White people in the room, and I soon learned that the oldest, Whitest man seated up front was the owner of the property in discussion.

While he was talking, I completed a survey about the East Point New Multi-Use Facility. It was a single page, printed on both sides, with a dozen multiple choice questions about what features we would like to see in our future recreation center. I checked swimming pool, community room, kitchen, meeting rooms, art room, gymnasium, all of the above.

I started to get confused when a young woman passed me a packet of stapled pages filled with photos of strip malls, a "Visual Preference Survey." We were supposed to circle *Like, Neutral,* or *Dislike* under each photo. A boxy, modern Panda Express, a dingy barn-shaped bar and grill. Many of the photos looked like they had been shot through the windshield of a moving car.

Who made this, and what were they hoping to learn with this survey? The local sentiments about vinyl siding, backlit plastic signs, flat or gabled roofs? It struck me as the kind of worksheet you give to children during church or at restaurants. A way to keep us busy. The answers wouldn't be worth the cost of those color prints. What did this have to do with a swimming pool?

I slowly gathered what I likely had missed during the first ten minutes of the meeting and many conversations that had led up to this one. The proposed recreation and aquatic center was part of a mixed-use development. The landowner was willing to sell a chunk of currently forested, undeveloped land to the city as some kind of trade-off for rezoning the entire parcel from residential to commercial. Rezoning would require a vote. The rec center parcel was his bargain with the community.

At this point in the meeting, I realized it was not going well. I had shown up so optimistic, just bursting with civic pride and swimming pool trivia, I didn't notice that no one else was smiling or nodding. In fact, the residents were muttering to each other, clutching their notes, waiting for their opportunity to speak. What is the use of history, of all that I had learned?

They were motivated, and they were organized. The intersection of Washington Road and Camp Creek Parkway was already a traffic headache. Backups at the traffic signal snaked a mile up Washington Road. These neighborhoods were squeezed between the airport on the east and the sprawling warehouses and big-box stores feeding off I-285 on the west. This patch of forest served as both a visual barrier for their backyards and a sound buffer between the flight path and truck traffic. Now the city wanted to rezone it, cut down the trees, and turn it into a Frankenstein multiuse facility and strip mall that no one was asking for. They saw the pool as a ploy to win their approval.

A middle-aged Black man stood up and issued a warning about needing to lock up your wives when these basketball-playing youths started hanging out in their neighborhood, a statement so not-in-my-backyard alarmist, I almost laughed.

Straight-faced, the mayor took the mic. "We can ask the chief of police to pull crime statistics at comparable recreation centers and see about that."

But we don't have any comparable rec centers in East Point, I thought. We have one small 1950s era gymnasium in the heart of a historic neighborhood. What they were proposing was a big facility with a huge parking lot and a strip mall attached. A rec center built on the big-box model at the intersection of a major highway and interstate would look and feel nothing like the model for neighborhood-scale facilities of the last century. It would be more comparable to the LA Fitness on Camp Creek, which was notorious for car break-ins.

The mayor and the city manager took turns repeating that the land was zoned for residential use but would never be developed into houses. No one would buy a house on that corner, they said, not with the airplane noise and the traffic. This struck me as a tone-deaf argument for a roomful of residents who lived there already and saw the value in preserving residential use. They said all the properties on Camp Creek Parkway had been rezoned as commercial, that eventually this piece would be too, even if the developer had to sue the city to do it. At least, they suggested, this way we could get a public amenity at the same time and some influence over the style of the commercial development.

Maybe some attorney had advised the city to accept these foregone conclusions, but I saw how they made the residents powerless to stop an undesirable development, a frustrating pattern they knew too well. They undermined the community's only lever of power—zoning.

A lot was happening in the Q&A that I could barely follow. Grievances about the clear-cutting and development of a big warehouse district north of their neighborhood, despite resident opposition. Who had been notified about meetings, who had skipped meetings. Someone accused the city manager of being "in bed" with the developer. There was a lot of history here, and it had nothing to do with the trivia I had collected about the Spring Avenue and Randall Street Pools.

The only indication that the mayor was a little rattled is that she grew long-winded in her answers, going off topic, steering into the speech that got her elected about a vision of growth without gentrification but not really connecting that back to the corner of Washington and Camp Creek. She kept saying, "That's why we're here, we want you to feel heard," which was nice but a bit like "I'm sorry you feel that way." Not at all the same thing as actually listening to constituents' concerns and changing course.

The pool I had already fallen in love with was starting to feel like bait in a much more complicated deal. The email invitation, with its blue-sky renderings of the aquatic center, certainly didn't mention a rezoning battle.

Why couldn't we build a few small, neighborhood-scale swimming pools? Why this mixed-use project, with a commercial strip baked into the deal? Should we go back to a different funding source to pay for our residents' actual needs, instead of contorting ourselves to accommodate a tourist-funded, developer-led, multiuse mega-facility?

I could see how this was going to be an uphill battle.

I left early, feeling like if East Point ever built a pool, it wouldn't be this pool, on this site. It had been forty years since East Point residents saw the joys of a municipal swimming pool, and all we could imagine was an LA Fitness.

October 14 CHURCH POOL PARTY

I joined the party late because Bruno fell asleep in the back seat of the car, and I didn't want to disturb him. After half an hour, I carried him, still drowsy, up the steps and passed him to Jason. Come on buddy, I murmured, you don't want to miss the pool party, do you?

Guests were gathered on the front porch chatting about the new Sunday school classes that just started. Most of us were new to the church. I sat down next to a slim Black woman about my age on the porch swing. She introduced herself as Shawn Green.

"Your son is in the back," she warned me. "There's a pool, and it's not covered. You or your husband might want to go back there."

I pondered this for a minute. Told her Guy probably wouldn't jump in.

"I'm just a lifeguard, and I worry," she replied.

I brightened. I didn't expect to find a lifeguard at a church shindig. I told her the boys had been learning how to swim, that we had spent the summer visiting all the public pools in Atlanta.

Shawn grinned. "Did you go to Grant Park and Candler Park? My boss was named Hannah."

"I think I met her."

Jason brought me a plate of barbecue. Shawn was a teacher and an avid swimmer. During the summers, she worked as a lifeguard and manager at the pools, first in the city of Atlanta and later in the suburbs.

I asked which pools she had worked at in Atlanta.

"John A. White, but there were some bad experiences there." She pursed her lips.

"Really? We loved that one. We had Bruno's fifth birthday party there."

"What time did you go?"

"As soon as they opened."

"When was his birthday?"

"August. We celebrated on a Saturday."

"I was long gone by then."

Trying to be helpful, I just said it. "I got the distinct impression that the lifeguards were high."

She burst out laughing. "Absolutely!"

"It's like a whole culture," she said. "Somebody should make a reality show about the pools."

I told her I was writing about our summer.

"You really went to all the pools? Some of them are just . . . concrete."

I admitted that we missed the one in Mechanicsville. We tried the Adamsville Recreation Center a couple times, but it wasn't open for Free Swim. Plus, the Washington Park natatorium was closed for repairs. But yes, we went to the concrete pools—Anderson Park and Thomasville Heights and Pittman Park.

She shook her head. "You are like the bravest person I've ever met."

Or stubborn. "Er, not really. They were empty during Pay Swim."

Shawn knew exactly what that meant. It felt amazing not to have to explain the difference between Pay Swim and Free Swim.

Someone called me to the backyard, where children were starting to swim. I left Shawn on the porch and helped the boys find their swimsuits.

A skinny blonde girl dove into the pool and swam out to a foam raft. One of those thick, squishy rafts that lasts forever—I haven't seen one in years. With a jolt, I remembered the helpless feeling of getting trapped under a heavy raft like that one in a backyard pool, during a similar church-related pool party. As if on cue, I saw this happen to Guy, saw him bumping under the foam roof and then sputter his way to the surface. I was proud to see that he figured it out, didn't panic, and kept on swimming.

The girl was only a year older than Guy, but she slipped through the water with this elegant dive and her freestyle stroke that was even and confident, side-breathing that made her look like a professional. She clambered onto the raft and shrieked with laughter, dog-paddling over to a floating water gun, suddenly a kid again.

That girl is on a swim team, I thought. That is what lessons look like, what pool membership looks like. This was privilege, thin elbows slicing through the water, swimming in a backyard pool in October, after all the pools have closed.

■ ■ ■

By fall, I felt like it was time to join the church. It started last summer with me dropping by on Sundays for worship. It was a rich and ornate historic church downtown. I decided to visit because it was close to our house, supported an overnight shelter for men, flew a rainbow Pride flag over its front door. I liked that the congregation was not all White, all straight, all young, or all old. That it was right in the middle of the mess of downtown, across the street from the state capitol's gold dome.

The church satisfied aesthetic cravings I didn't know I had—for stained glass and dark wood pews, for fresh baked bread and a massive pipe organ. I enjoyed the wavery voices singing old hymns, the sour blare of the organ, a reader leading us through the poetic scriptures, all the creaky imperfections of a church that was older and wiser than me. I wanted eloquent, biting sermons followed by soothing prayers. And here was a church that was outspoken about racism, immigration, citizenship, poverty, environmental justice. On my first visit, the Korean American woman pastor preached on the church's role in dismantling White supremacy.

A year after my first scouting visit, I was taking the boys to choir practice and Sunday school every week. Jason joined us for the worship service at eleven o'clock, and we usually stayed afterward for the bland cafeteria lunch buffet. I got to know other members, mostly through their children. Kids made it easy to get drawn into the routine of church, then the committees and classes and retreats. Guy loved the stories about God and death and heaven; Bruno stuck around for the Goldfish and juice boxes in Sunday school. The Presbyterian church seemed like a slightly more democratic and liberal version of the Methodist church where I was raised, and Central seemed like as good of a home base as we would ever find in this church-filled city.

Meeting someone like Shawn at a new-member gathering, a Black mom, seeking a church home just as I was and who, of all things, shared my fascination with swimming pools, gave me that rare but solid sense of being led.

■ ■ ■

I saw Shawn a few weeks later in the fellowship hall after Sunday school, before worship. She called out my name and reintroduced herself.

"It's me," she said. "My hair is straight today."

Of course, I remembered her. She called it straight, but her hair was neatly curled into a bob. Almost every time I saw Shawn, her hair was completely different and coordinated with her stylish Sunday ensemble.

"You must think I'm crazy, but I was so happy to talk about swimming," she said. "It's such an important part of my spiritual practice. And I feel like someone just needs to make a movie about the pool culture in Atlanta."

Could we skip church, I joked, and just sit here eating banana bread and talking about the pools? There was so much I wanted to know about her experience as a lifeguard, about the pools and how kids learn to swim, and in general, about swimming while Black in Atlanta.

I never would've thought to ask about hair, but it's the first thing she brought up. Shawn told me her teenaged son was an avid swimmer, but her daughter gave it up because of her hair.

"Does a swimming cap help?" I asked.

"Not really."

She told me that chlorine dries out Black hair.

"What if you had a natural hair style?"

"But that's not 'beautiful,'" she said, with air quotes.

How many Black women avoided the water because it damaged their hair? Were there statistics about this? Shawn maintained an immaculate coiffure and a devotion to swimming, but it sounded like a hassle.

The only way I could relate was my contact lenses. I might take the kids swimming, but I hardly ever went underwater for fear of losing a contact. At times, I even knocked them out of my eyes washing my face in the shower. Losing a contact was not only money down the drain, but it also made me temporarily blind. I wouldn't be able to drive home from the pool.

Shawn explained why she had left the city pools and took a job in suburban Tucker. She grew tired of the constant friction with the teenage lifeguards.

"At John A. White, I was the manager, but they acted like I was an outsider. But I lived up the street, right on Cascade Road."

I asked why, and she rattled off a list.

"Because I'm too 'bougie.' Because I'm older, I'm educated, I'm from Kansas. I moved here to go to Spelman."

"And the litter would drive me nuts. I'd say, *This is our pool, let's keep it clean. Enjoy your chips, but let's use the trash receptacles.* I would be out there in the morning before opening, picking up diapers in the parking lot. Every day. The kids would just look at me like I'm insane."

I remembered a big plastic trash can at John A. White, spilling over with trash, where I had jammed our box from the Great American Cookie Company.

"I warned them, they're coming. The White people are coming. They aren't doing the drive anymore, y'all. They don't want to drive from the suburbs. And these big, beautiful, houses are so affordable. They see the neighborhood looking trashy; they see an investment opportunity."

"Whoa, did they understand that?" Did I understand that?

I had to strain to connect cause and effect from litter to gentrification, but it was a story I had heard from community organizers before. In East Point, Ms. Lyles organized trash cleanups and cleared storm drains in the East Washington community. She tried to warn the young people who littered that they were going to get priced out of the neighborhood soon. This was a revelation to me. The only thing I understood even less than littering was real estate.

"After a while, I didn't want to fight with them anymore," she sighed. "I thought, this is their summer job, they want to have a nice summer. I'm not fighting with them. I'll just go someplace else."

The fellowship hall filled with people heading to the sanctuary. We stood to depart. Upstairs, the kids were waiting in their Sunday school classrooms.

As Shawn gathered her coffee and her purse, I stopped her. "What did you mean by swimming is a spiritual practice?"

"It's when I pray," she said. "I get as much out of swimming as worship. It's when I think."

She invited me to meet Coach Illonga at the Y in Southwest Atlanta. He coached the Masters swim team there, she told me. He organized open water training at Niskey Lake. I thanked her and bustled upstairs to collect my children.

During the worship service and the week that followed, I mulled over all the information packed into my conversation with Shawn.

First, that swimming could be spiritual. Not the church pool parties where I learned to swim, where we mixed intimately as a congregation, or even the river baptisms of the Old South. This was something solitary and meditative and completely foreign to me. I couldn't imagine a time that I ever went swimming alone, for exercise or meditation. I couldn't freestyle fifty meters if I tried.

Second, why did Niskey Lake snag in my memory? I had never seen this lake, but the name was familiar.

It was Dr. Darryl Jones, the writer in Rosie's Coffee Cafe who had learned to swim at Morris Brown College who told me proudly that he lived by Niskey

Lake. Unfortunately, like so many of Atlanta's creeks and forests, that name was also burned into my brain from a map of the Atlanta Child Murders. Two teen boys went missing from the area in 1979; the body of one was found in a wooded lot on Niskey Lake Road. And while trying to figure out who dammed Lake Charlotte, I had unearthed newspaper clips about Niskey Lake. It was developed in 1921 "to furnish a mountain resort for busy Atlantans who want to keep active touch with the city's affairs throughout the summer months."

The lake remained a secluded, suburban oasis, inside Atlanta's city limits but outside the perimeter. The fact that Mayor Kasim Reed owned lakefront property on Niskey Lake confirmed that it had become a cultural extension of Cascade Road. It was virtually an all-Black, private swimming hole. Besides the Chattahoochee River, it was one of the only places inside the city limits where you could swim in a semi-natural body of water.

Third, the Y. The Andrew and Walter Young Family YMCA was closer to my house than any public pool. I once visited to check out the indoor pool but never considered joining. The pool was just a drab box with powerful ventilation and no windows, no kiddie pool, no sprinklers or slides. I wanted to trick the boys into thinking swimming was all fun and games, but this was a serious rectangle for serious lessons, training, and competition. But with the right coach, the pool could be a portal.

Just by mentioning these places in one conversation, Shawn had connected the dots along Utoy Creek so that I could see a spectrum of Black swimming in Atlanta—children at John A. White on Cascade, swim team at the Y on Campbellton Road, Masters practice on Niskey Lake. Black swimmers were everywhere, if you knew where to look.

October 16 THE LEGEND OF RIVERBEND

The drive up I-285 at noon ruined my mood. Near SunTrust Park, deep in the wild interstate jumble of I-75 and I-285, I settled on "dispirited." I drove directly from a headache-inducing IEP meeting with Guy's teachers.

I crossed blindly over the Chattahoochee River, then switched back to a smaller, older bridge closer to the water. I passed a massive, multicolored patio restaurant surrounded by an empty parking lot. "The Fiesta Place" was for sale. I sailed past the gated entrance to "Walton on the River" as my GPS bleated, *You have arrived.*

"What coffee shop?" A guard at the entrance joked when I asked. He was prepared with a laminated map of the complex. "Follow little red signs that say Coffee Shop Parking. Park by the 1900 building. It's a four-minute walk down to the river."

I was meeting an engineer in some café by the Chattahoochee River, a location enthusiastically documented by many in my Instagram feed. But instead of a stand-alone coffee shop, I found myself cruising through an apartment complex maze. The promised four-minute walk was lovely, but the feeling of being lost continued, even with the signs. The farther I traveled into the compound, the more I worried that I was trespassing.

I looked for other café patrons toting laptops or iced coffees. Young women in prim spandex traveled to or from a workout. There were kayaks wedged on balconies. I crossed an attractive little stone bridge over a dry creek bed. I crossed paths with a Black man walking his French bulldog. The apartments were sturdy two- and three-story blocks with rough granite walls and columns, well-maintained 1970s buildings. I noted the continuous, unbroken sidewalks and consistent signage, all tastefully tucked into the manicured landscaping.

By the time I made it to the grand three-story clubhouse that housed the coffee shop, I forgot about the river. Then the Chattahoochee was right there, copper and white, astonishing in its breadth. A series of wide, graceful terraces led down to its pebbled banks. Glittering shoals stretched into the horizon. I always forget we have this river in Atlanta.

I followed a sewer line down the wide granite stairway. I was just as fascinated by the sewer line as the swimming pool and the river. I thought about water now with the same frequency as I thought about sex, race, my children. All the time, in fragments, in fear and fascination.

A dozen small groups lounged in Adirondack chairs in the cool shade of the old hardwoods and spindly hemlock trees. I saw Asian, Latino, Black, and White faces gazing out over the water. All the lucky young people who could hang out by the river in the middle of the afternoon. We were all here for the view, no one touching the water.

At the bottom of the stairs, a plastic sandwich board sign stood sentry, reminding me that this was not a public space. "Residents must accompany their guests at all times."

I followed an Indian mom and toddler back up the stairs. I can't guess what language she was speaking to him, but I know the script for yelling at your kids for trying to slide down the banister.

In the coffee shop was the usual milquetoast soundtrack, Real Estate and The Shins. I instantly missed the sound of the river. I watched some developers in khakis meet up as I waited for my cappuccino and my colleague.

■ ■ ■

After my meeting, I wandered into the lobby of the rental center. I almost fell over looking up at the wood-paneled ceiling. A vintage wooden canoe and oars hung in the center of the ceiling's highest peak.

The slim blond guy at the front desk caught me gawking.

"Can I help you?"

"Um, what year was this place built?" I assumed he wouldn't know.

"It was built in the 1960s. When we bought it, it was boarded up." By we, I guess he meant Walton, the management company.

"This is such a stylish building."

"This area was like a sunken pit, like a real swinging lounge," he said, indicating the carpeted shape around his desk. The rest of the floor was a puzzle of large slate tiles. "And there was a huge bar over there. I think the owners were sauced all the time."

What a thing to say. Desks lined the wall. It was hard to picture. A young White man in a baseball cap was now waiting behind me. He had a real question for the management.

"Sauced." I repeated.

He leaned over conspiratorially and said, "It used to be called *Riverbend*." He turned to the renter. I stepped aside, but then I remembered.

"Wait" I interrupted. "Was it . . . famous?"

"Yes," he said, emphatically.

Riverbend was an all-adult, all-singles community that grew into a legendary party scene in the 1970s, in that brief but promiscuous moment after the Pill went mainstream but before AIDS. It spawned a whole river raft party culture that lingered into the eighties. My mother had a big yellow river raft in her basement, and I remember helping haul it down to "the Hooch" while Mom's boyfriend dragged coolers packed with boiled peanuts, PB&Js, and beer. By the 1990s, the water was so polluted you wouldn't dip your toes in the river.

"Wow, I'm at Riverbend," I squealed to no one in particular. I could see the sixties design elements under layers of warm gray paint and cabin-themed art. I started taking photos like a tourist.

I wondered if the patrons of this destination café—the students, the ladies in Lululemon, the stay-at-home moms and dog walkers—would care if they knew that underneath the farmhouse modern decor was a decade of debauchery.

The drive back to East Point was fast. I located and devoured *Atlanta Magazine*'s oral history of Riverbend and the River Ramble, a bawdy raft race that started there and grew into a tradition. These accounts understandably focused on the sex, drugs, and rock-and-roll aspect of the place. The saturated photos featured big-haired blondes spilling out of their bikinis and partygoers on big yellow rafts. But I kept thinking that it was the access to the river that was so remarkable.

In *Atlanta Magazine*'s history, LaRue King, a former Playboy bunny and Riverbend resident said, "You could do rock climbing on the other side of the river. You could swing into the water like Tarzan on this rope swing. It was like having a luxury hotel in the mountains."

Not only was Riverbend reserved for singles, but they were also almost entirely White singles, and Rebel flags show up in grainy photos of those glory days on the River Ramble. Eventually, the all-singles rule was called out for what it was—housing discrimination. The parties came to an end.

I asked my mom if she ever went to Riverbend. "Up at 285," she said. "They had a riverfront park. I remember rafting by, and there was always something going on. It was just some crappy apartments, but they did all this landscaping that made it feel swanky."

These "crappy apartments" were hailed as a pioneering example of landscape architecture and riverfront design. Designed by Richard Vignolo of the San Francisco–based studio Lawrence Halprin and Associates, the site design for the sixty-five-acre complex was included in the archives of the Cultural Landscape Foundation as a notable modernist landscape: "Intent upon preserving the natural beauty of the site, the designers created distinct communities focused on the river, the plateau, and the valley, each providing different views of the river, lakes, streams and created gardens."

The designers knew that the river is what gave the place its ineffable magic. By maximizing views and access to the water, they created a place that still drew people down to the water. To me, that part is wilder than the swingers and keg parties and nude sunbathing. To live next to open water in Atlanta. In the city, swimming, diving, and apparently getting naked in a wild river seems unbelievably romantic now. The Chattahoochee River was once the sexiest place in Atlanta.

October 18 THE BLUEST CREEK

I locked my car in the elementary school parking lot and crossed the street under a low belly of clouds. Down the hill, I could see the primary colors of a swing set and slide under a clutch of oak trees. River Park was a neatly mowed scrap of floodplain.

I walked over to the fenced edge of the park where a tilted yellow sign said DANGER DO NOT PLAY IN CREEK and stared at the strange waters below. The creek was milky turquoise. Slow-moving splotches of white foam drifted along the surface.

I pulled the collar of my shirt up over my nose and mouth.

These were the headwaters of the South River. I saw this Caribbean-blue streak on a satellite view and assumed that Google had tinted the image to indicate water, but this was the real color. It looked like something piped in from Disney World, like it should be cotton candy–scented and swishing to a soundtrack.

The local litter brought me back to East Point—a dumped tire, a red Coca-Cola label on a plastic bottle, the banks bushy with clipped kudzu.

I stalked the perimeter of the fence, occasionally jamming my phone through the chain-link to take photos, all while cussing to myself quietly because the elementary school was right there, the playground was yards away, and kids were no doubt drawn to this toxic funk.

Beyond the fence on both sides of the park was a block of American Small Houses that looked like my own neighborhood. Two Latina women pushed a stroller from the school uphill toward Cleveland Avenue.

A low panic as I watched them disappear. What was this if not an emergency?

I wanted to see this creek because a few days earlier, East Point's director of parks and recreation, Jonathon Penn, had asked me why it was so blue. I told him I was writing about the proposed aquatic center, and he agreed to meet with me. He arrived at the cupcake shop a few minutes late, phone in hand, apologizing.

"That was a conference call," he explained. "We got a grant for a new playground at River Park."

I congratulated him, and we chatted about the planned upgrades at the park, which is named for the South River headwaters that flow through it.

While I picked at a carrot cake cupcake and drank my third coffee of the day, he brought his own Yeti full of water and a plastic container of chickpeas and kale. A lean and energetic Black man, he was a smiling advertisement for the benefits of fitness and good nutrition. Penn knows he looks too young to be the director, so he started by telling me he's been with the department for eleven years, director for the past three. Like me, he had two kids, and we both grew up in Clayton County, but because I'm a few years older and White, our worlds barely overlapped.

He told me about learning to swim at the Rainwood Apartments in Morrow and later taking the swim class at Morehouse College. When he started open water training for triathlons in places like Lake McIntosh in Peachtree City, his wife and mother were terrified for his safety. We talked about the urgency of getting our kids in the water, despite how complicated that can be on the Southside.

Penn explained that East Point needed not only a swimming pool or two but multiple recreation centers. He told me about scheduling events with only one gymnasium in a city of thirty-five thousand people, coordinating with high schools and other public facilities. The Parks Master Plan from 2010 prioritized swimming pools among a long backlog of park improvements. An aquatic center had been in the works for years.

As we debriefed about the combative public meeting, we both shook our heads and shrugged.

"I understand that we need a big, multipurpose rec center," I said. "But with all the parking, and that commercial location, it looks like an LA Fitness. Nobody wants that in their backyard."

"Yeah, but these neighbors. I don't think they understand that this site is going to be developed, eventually," he said. "The owner can sue to change the zoning to commercial, and he'll win. Everything on that strip is commercial."

"So there's not much stopping him from putting, like, a strip mall there anyways?"

"Right. At least this way, the neighborhood gets to provide input, and they end up with something nice for the kids."

So that was what that odd "visual preference survey" was for.

"A swimming pool would be a big deal for East Point. Historic, really," I said. "You can put it in my neighborhood."

He sighed. "I'm optimistic."

Before we left the table, we came back to River Park.

"Do you know what's up with that creek?" he asked, dropping his voice. "The water is bright blue and, like, soapy."

A buzzer went off in my head. I remembered Dr. Jackie Echols's Power-Point showing the headwaters of the South River in East Point. She said that the headwaters start at a Class 1 Hazardous Waste Site, Georgia Environmental Protection Division's worst designation. The soil and groundwater were contaminated with zinc, arsenic, copper, mercury, and lead.

"A guy told me it's from a car wash," said Penn, making a face. "It looks so weird."

There was no car wash in the area. There were some fenced-off wooded areas along the railroad tracks, between the housing projects and the glass factory.

"I don't think it's a car wash," I said. "But I'll find out."

I wanted to figure this out before they refurbished a playground there. To be honest, I was concerned that he turned to me as the expert, and I had no idea either. The creek was a couple miles from my house, and I had never stopped to look.

■ ■ ■

I walked back across Blount Street, following the creek upstream along the side of the school. Behind the fence were rock shoals enrobed in thick whitish gunk. The water was less blue in the shallow places, more tepid gray. I watched the mossy banks for the movement of a frog, snake, or even a bug. Nothing was alive in there.

A maintenance van that said FULTON COUNTY SCHOOLS on the side slowed beside me. A man with bushy black hair leaned out to say, ominously, "It's looked like that for thirty years. As long as I been working here."

No hello, no nothing. The maintenance man knows all. Red button-up with an embroidered name tag: Tom.

I introduced myself as a writer researching pollution in the creek, but he still seemed to think I was a teacher or a parent at the elementary school. It made no sense that anyone else would care. He kept the van creeping along beside me.

"Sure, you could be like a whatshername. Erin Brockovich."

I accepted this as a kind of compliment. Moms radicalized by being moms. "I'll get to the bottom of this," I joked.

He switched off the ignition and joined me by the fence along the backside of the school. He suggested that the hospital up on Cleveland Avenue might be dumping soapy water from their linen service. There's no way, I thought, but I didn't argue. The polyphonic roar of several HVAC units made it hard to talk.

"Maybe this is my ignorance," he started to say but changed course. "Let me ask you something."

I turned to face him. Was he about to ask me on a date?

"Why do you live in East Point? In the past few years, it seems like a lot of yuppies moving to East Point."

Ah, market research, I thought. He must own rental properties.

"Well, uh, I guess, I'm one of them," I said, fumbling. "A yuppie. When we started looking to buy a house, it was like 2005, the peak of the real estate market, and we couldn't afford anything in Atlanta. East Point has all these cute, historic houses. It seemed like a good investment."

He heard the *we*.

"I was looking for a wedding ring."

Awkward laughter. I waved my left hand.

"We like the location. The MARTA train. Jason rides his bike to work," I added. Let me mention my husband a few more times, by name.

I forgot how this looked, this spontaneous conversation in an alley. I thought I was interviewing a local community member about a contaminated creek. In his mind, a decent-looking woman in skinny jeans was eagerly asking him a lot of questions, making eye contact, lubricating the conversation with laughter and anecdotes. What did Erin Brockovich do?

"You couldn't pay me to live here," he said. "Too much crime. Cars get broken into in this parking lot all the time."

I stepped back toward the parking lot, like I'd better be going. The creek was more worrisome than Tom. I thanked him and promised to figure out what's making the water so blue.

"You know where to find me. I'll be here for twenty more months," he shouted, climbing back into his van. "After that, I'm retired."

■ ■ ■

Why was the creek blue? Where was the pollution coming from? Who was responsible for cleaning it up? Was it safe to play at a playground, attend an elementary school, or live in a house next to this crazy-looking stream? And were these dumb questions to ask?

I went home and I emailed everyone I thought would know, including East Point's Water and Sewer Department, the River Park Neighborhood Organization, and Dr. Echols. Educate me, I pleaded.

I cornered a nice guy at church who works for the EPD and asked him what was wrong with the South River headwaters in East Point.

He grew thoughtful, remembering it. "It still looks like that?" he said. Our children threw wooden blocks across a Sunday school classroom. "I visited it years ago. That must be the oddest stream in the state of Georgia."

And then he looked at me, as if I might know, and said, "What's making it so blue?"

Then I did the only thing I know how to do: investigated the history of the site. The past isn't even past and all that.

I researched a path all the way back to the Muscogee (Creek) Nation, the treaty of Indian Springs, the Georgia Land Lotteries, then the railroads, the Battle of Atlanta, Sherman's March to the Sea. Deeper into the sorrowful history of the land, all the treachery and destruction, the siege of a civilian land like a cleansing. Looking for the bottom of the sorrow. There was no bottom.

■ ■ ■

If you studied a satellite image of this area, you'd see two large scruffy patches of green where the South River's headwaters begin. Both of these urban meadows are listed on Georgia EPD's inventory of hazardous sites. The "Tift Site," #10393, named after the last known property owner, Thomas Tift, was designated as a top priority Class I hazardous site in 1995. The EPD's one-pager about it lists all the known contaminants and threats to human health identified in the soil and groundwater. There are double checkmarks next to lead, nickel, silver, arsenic, barium, cadmium, zinc, and more.

Farther along the railroad tracks was the General Chemical site, #10498, listed in 1998. It's a Class V hazardous site, but just as troubling because another headwaters stream begins in this area. It was right next to the cloverleaf of baseball fields of the John D. Milner Athletic Complex. Their parking lot covers the site of the old Randall Street Swimming Pool.

Several industrial relics still line the railroad today—a glass container factory, now shuttered, with its old-school smokestacks, a dystopian-looking recycling plant where giant electromagnetic claws lift mangled cars and wads of scrap metal into a hopper to be mulched, and ChemTrade Logistics, with several towering tanks of God knows what. If you were watching a Little League baseball game at Milner, you might not see beyond the grassy field or know that the field is contaminated.

At the turn of the century, mills and factories lined the railroad tracks, employing thousands of laborers. What were they manufacturing, and what were they dumping in the water? On a Sanborn Fire Insurance map, I found the Old Dominion Guano Company. I thought *guano* meant batshit, but it was one of three massive "fertilizer works" and a cotton waste processor all located on this side of the tracks.

Established in 1883, the Old Dominion was a "sulphuric acid plant, 6,000 tons capacity." A map of the operation marked an "Acid Pit," "Rock Bin," "Acid Chambers," and "Fish Scrap" building. In 1916, Old Dominion products had names like Southern Ammoniated Dissolved Bone Guano, Uncle Remus High Grade Guano, and Maddox's Double Extra High Grade, named for the company director and Maddox Park Pool namesake, Atlanta mayor Robert Maddox. Ads from 1910 promised wages of $1.50 per day at Old Dominion, plus "eating and sleeping accommodations," all accessible by train and streetcar.

Job opportunities like this made East Point the promised land for workers escaping the poverty of rural Georgia, particularly Black sharecroppers. At a time when boll weevil blight and declining crop values made tenant farming increasingly unprofitable, they migrated to the city to work in mills and factories, ironically, producing farming supplies—plows, wagons, and fertilizer. In reaction to the growing population of African American residents, East Point's City Council passed its first residential segregation ordinance in 1912, confining Blacks to the East Washington Road area, a neighborhood within walking distance of and downstream from the foul-smelling, toxic plants that hired them.

A security guard at City Hall, an elderly Black man, once told me he was from "Junglefoot." He explained it was a rude nickname for the Black neighborhood near the fertilizer plants. It sounded like other vulgar names for low-lying, segregated Black districts in Atlanta: Buttermilk Bottom, Darktown, Slabtown, Beaver Slide. Who came up with these insulting names? I doubt it was the residents. The stone church at the heart of the East Washington community was named Neriah Baptist, meaning "lamp of God."

The other half of the Tift Site was occupied by the Elizabeth Cotton Mills, established in 1900 and later bought out and renamed Martel Mills. Eventually, it became the Henry Chanin Cotton Waste Processing Plant. The mill houses along Martel Road were razed with urban renewal grants in the late 1950s and replaced by a public housing project, Martel Homes, in 1963.

Cotton sounds less nasty than vats of guano and sulfuric acid, but textile waste is slow to degrade. According to a 2018 Environmental Site Assessment of the housing authority properties, the landfill "consisted of excess cotton material impacted by various regulated metals and semi-volatile organic compounds (SVOCs), and construction debris." A 1990 EPD memo on "landfill leachate" suggested that this debris was the burned-down "remains" of the fertilizer plant next door.

Leachate is what happens when the rainfall that marinates in the landfill seeps out, carrying all the buried funk with it. The word *leachate* conjured the image of a dark, slimy, sucking creature.

By the 1980s, the mills were obsolete, burned down, or demolished. Randall Street Pool had been filled in with dirt, just like the Spring Avenue Pool, but possibly with some of that contaminated soil from the property next door. I read in a report that the city may have used this "high clay aluminum" to level the playing fields at John D. Milner Park.

In 1984, responding to complaints about a "milky color" in the water, the EPD started inspections of the area behind the glass factory and around the Tift Site. At the same time, Martel Homes became a Southside hub for the "dope-d-game," as immortalized on Goodie Mob's *Soul Food*, that song with the chorus, "What you know about the Dirty South, what you know about the Dirty South?"

He rapped about the "blow traffic" on John Freeman Way, the main artery of Martel Homes. I picture these government scientists trekking back there with their stream sampling kits.

It took another decade to get the Tift Site listed as a hazardous site of the highest order and to track down the former owners who might be responsible.

Ten years later, the EPD picked up the investigation anew. A 2005 memo included the comment: "This has been going on for years and I guess it will take activism and a lawsuit to get something done about it."

■ ■ ■

I found myself doing research to feel productive, a way of "doing something," about this awful reality in my neighborhood. Research as a form of working from home that happens in ten-minute volleys, in historic newspapers, digital archives, historical topographical maps. I perched with a book on the toilet while my kid took a bath, guarding the pages from splashes. Research as an escape on a rainy Saturday.

I read environmental assessments and engineering reports and EPD memos and layered together old maps over many days and nights, accumulating a kind of inner landfill with its own emotional leachate. I dreamed that instead of a railroad line, the city was built on a fault line. I discovered zinc, copper, lead, and cadmium burbling up like lava from a volcano that had been dormant for a hundred years. It was my job to warn everyone about the nearing eruption.

This was around the time I read Toni Morrison's *The Bluest Eye* for the first time. My pile of novels was meant to be a distraction, but when I tried to picture the setting of Lorain, Ohio, after the Depression, the smokestacks along the railroad tracks of East Washington came to mind. The pale blue of the creek was pretty but poisonous.

I went back to the creek a few times in different spots by the school and the projects, just before the rain and right after. I took friends and colleagues with me, to take photos, to poke at the gunk with a stick. I took a reporter, professors, chemistry undergrads, the Altamaha Riverkeeper. Each time, it was a violent jolt to see the nauseatingly blue waters, to recognize their scrap metal odor. I wouldn't bring my children down here. I wouldn't even let them play at the park.

Once, I paced the historic path of the creek by following storm drains across the park. In two low-lying spots by the playground, I kicked the matted lawn clippings aside to find the overgrown drains beneath. As I knelt and pulled the leaves and grass from the drains with my bare hands, I could feel the kids on the playground slowing down, eyeing me from the swings. I laid my ear on the grate and listened for running water. What's down there?

Hours of research and polite emails inured me to the shock, but to witness the creek still flowing, as it flows even now, deaf and dumb on its way to the Atlantic Ocean, brought fresh outrage and a sense of purpose. There was a line of poison threading through my community.

Why were the South River headwaters so blue? An upstream carwash? Hospital laundry suds? An industrial lubricant used in glass manufacturing called Biosol Blue? Crushed glass? Toxic pot likker from a century-old dump?

"The bluish white color is due to the color of precipitates and chemical reactions of colors, for example, copper (pale blue); zinc (white), nickel (blue), lead (white)," explained Dr. Echols. "The whitish film is cotton left over from processing in the 1800s disposed of in onsite lagoons. There has been not enough chemical reaction with the environment to cause the cotton to decay."

One night, I read a bedtime story to Guy that wasn't really a story but a book of trivia called *Our Amazing Planet.* He often brought me an encyclopedia to read, and I would send him back for something lighter, but that night we read about blue Arctic ice. The article explained that the ice itself wasn't blue; light refraction made it look that way.

Maybe the river appeared turquoise in River Park for the same reason water looks blue against the white sands of the Caribbean or in the mandated white bottoms of a swimming pool. The creek was coated in white, so the water looked blue.

A bigger question is why the creek has remained blue for so long. It had been thirty-five years since the first neighborhood complaints made their way into the EPD's files. Dr. Echols told me that the state's Hazardous Waste Trust Fund, which is supposed to help pay for cleanup of these sites, was significantly defunded by the Georgia legislature between 2004 and 2011. A hundred years ago, long before environmental protection legislation, the ruling class in East Point designed a landscape that still operates to isolate these downstream impacts in poor Black neighborhoods.

"It takes a lot of money, data, time. People just get tired," said Dr. Echols. "We get what I call 'river avoidance.' We pretend like it's not there."

The residents of Martel Homes, East Washington, and River Park lived with more urgent threats than the color of the creek. It had always been that way, so it must be normal.

October 23 CALLAWAY POOLS

I drove nearly two hours south to Callaway Gardens this morning to talk to the Georgia Association of Water Professionals about the Flint River. Unlike most Atlanta audiences who have never heard of the Flint, this was one group that knew more about the river than I ever will. These were hydrologists, farmers, engineers, and planners, but none of them, I bet, had spent as much time as I have sneaking around the urban headwaters and plotting their revival.

I hadn't been to Callaway Gardens since I was a Girl Scout, when our troop would spend an annual Saturday at the "beach." I had memories of a big-tent circus, a butterfly conservatory, and a zip line that launched yelping swimmers into the lake. I remembered paddling out to a tall wooden platform, climbing to the top, and waiting my turn to grab the metal handlebars of the zip line. There were picnic pavilions, rocket pops, families biking on hushed trails through the woods. It felt like an amusement park. I don't remember any gardens.

What was this lake, this place? Who were the Callaways, and why did they have so much land? I had no clue.

At the conference center, the tall windows framed a pretty lake nestled in the trees. It could've been the same one I swam in as a child, but it looked different from this side.

The presentation went well. The audience seemed amused, or at least awake. During the Q&A, a scientist from the coastal plain said something encouraging about how even the smallest urban creeks have tremendous ecological and educational value if children have the chance to interact with them. I thought about my girlhood trips to Callaway Gardens, the Cartoogechaye Creek, how they had led, somehow, to me standing at that podium.

Afterward, in the lake-facing lobby, a politician introduced himself, gave me his business card, praised my presentation and "my passion for water." In my head, I objected. It's some other passion that makes me pay attention to water. People maybe. Or justice.

As I followed the patterned carpet back out to the parking lot, Dr. Jackie Echols called. After decades of inaction, it seemed like some changes were coming for the blue creek. We talked about the new playground at River Park, new funding from the state EPD to pay for cleanup activities, and the glass factory upstream that had finally shut down. She was working on a press release from the South River Watershed Alliance. I sat in my car scribbling notes on my new Callaway Resort and Gardens notepad.

Even this parking lot felt familiar, with its rustic split-log fences, sandy pine straw and glossy camellias in the low shade of pine boughs. I remembered walking barefoot through a shady parking lot like this, stepping around pinecones toward the spreading sand of the beach, where I could run into the lukewarm lake.

■ ■ ■

I was far enough away from home that I didn't recognize the anthills. I squashed two sandy mounds as I took photos of the zombie-green water in LaGrange's half-drained public pool. My "passion for water" led to such hazards.

For an outsider like me, it was hard to trace what had happened to the former Callaway pools. I heard that there was a White pool and a Black pool that remained segregated up until the 1990s, somehow, because they were controlled by the Callaway family. How was that possible? While in LaGrange, I wanted to see this anachronism for myself.

Looking for directions to the Callaway pools, I found a nostalgic column from the *LaGrange News* remembering it had been twenty-five years since the Callaway Education Association closed. It didn't say much about the CEA, its history, mission, membership, or its role in upholding racial segregation. It said when the CEA officially closed in 1992, it was the end of an era. The CEA facilities—the swimming pool complex, the library, auditorium, stadium, educational building, and the Ogletree Street Recreation Center—were split up and donated to LaGrange College, the City of LaGrange, and Troup County.

There was only one specific place name in that list—Ogletree Street—and I found it on the map, a short drive from the conference center. I would start there.

Soon I was driving through a neighborhood of small midcentury houses with STACEY ABRAMS FOR GOVERNOR signs in the front yards. I crossed Blue John Creek at the bottom of the hill, then turned onto Ogletree, a quiet residential street with no sidewalks. I parked in front of a sign that said Don Weatherington Sr. Pool, which was next to the Willian J. Griggs Recreation Center. Nothing said "Callaway." Was this the right place?

The pool looked like it hadn't been updated much since it was built in the 1950s. The redbrick pool house was trimmed with dark-green shutters, doors, and iron railings. I admired the stone portico, symmetrical doors to the women's locker room on one side, men's on the other. Stairs led up to what looked like a small apartment above the pool house.

Behind the building was a simple, petal-shaped concrete pool. Enough water had been drained that rounded, Art Deco stairs stood dry and naked in the corners of the shallow end. The deep end held about three feet of murky jade water. It was the color of the water and how it reflected the bare trees that made the place look abandoned. The sky was solid, pearly gray—migraine weather.

I walked around for a while in my trench coat and conference attire, taking photos, unbothered. I saw no one. I stepped on some more anthills.

As I walked over to the rec center, a thin Black woman emerged from an old house across the street carrying a red Solo cup. She was wearing jeans and a fleece jacket, a scarf wrapped around her head. I waved.

"Is this pool open?" I asked. It was an idiotic question. "I mean, was it open? This summer."

"Yes," she said, thinking it over. "But not for very long. When I was a kid, it used to be open all day and all night, for swimming lessons."

Her name was Phyllis, and she grew up swimming in this pool. In fact, she learned to swim in the Ogletree Street pool. Recalling the pool of her youth, she grew so animated, I wondered what she had in the cup.

"We used to have a diving board. It's only six feet deep, but we had one. We didn't need it too deep. It was just for fun."

I asked her about the other public pools, and she gave me directions to the indoor pool, the big one. A right and left, another right, another left, and if I got to the mall, I've gone too far.

"I just walked over here to my mother's house to get some milk," she explained. "That's my mother's house, and my brother lives right over there." She pointed to the little white house across the street and started walking toward it.

It was milk! I asked if she was cooking, and she yelled back to me, "This is for some sugar-frosted flakes."

The Recreation Center next door was not locked. I walked through the quiet, cinder-block hallways lined with trophies and bulletin boards, past a large, colorized portrait of a handsome young man in a suit and horn-rimmed glasses, then another framed black-and-white photo of the same man, older now, speaking to a flock of laughing Black and White schoolchildren. This was William J. Griggs, director of the Ogletree Street Educational Center for Negroes from its founding in 1956. The pool was later renamed for Coach Don Weatherington Sr., who trained a generation of Black swimmers in the community.

I peeked into the gym and found the bathrooms, my official excuse for trespassing. I felt like Goldilocks.

■ ■ ■

I arrived at the Mike Daniel Recreation Center, a big facility directly across from a Kia dealership. A woman's amplified voice floated from one giant parking lot to another, stretching "Mike, line one" into six syllables.

It felt like walking into a mall. No way was this the historic pool I was looking for. Three employees greeted me at the front desk, two Black men and a White woman.

"Can I help you?" she said.

In my trench coat, I must have looked lost.

"I was trying to find the old Callaway pools," I was improvising. "I'm writing about historic swimming pools in the South."

The men stared at me. The woman looked busy.

"They've completely redone the old Callaway pool, and it looks nothing like the original, so it's not worth looking at."

This only made me more curious. I had just visited the Black Callaway pool, and it had not been redone. Did I imagine that the Black men looked away?

"So how old is this building?"

"I couldn't say," she replied.

One guy tried to be helpful. "This recreation center used to be a Lowe's."

"Wow. The home improvement store?" Everything made sense now.

"Originally, yes." He answered proudly. "Feel free to take a look around."

That explained the industrial scale of the place. I followed some signs to the pool, hallways painted with an undersea mural. Through a window, I could see the big indoor pool, like a bright, flooded warehouse. I didn't want to creep in there and distract the water aerobics class in progress. It was as awkward to be fully dressed in front of bathers as it is to be wearing a swimsuit when everyone else is dressed.

The Daniel Center was a brilliant adaptation of a big-box commercial building—easy location; lots of parking; high ceilings; vast, flexible interior—but this was not the pool I was looking for. I was getting hungry and anticipating the long drive back to Atlanta, but I had come this far, so I looked up directions to the LaGrange College Natatorium.

■ ■ ■

The ten-minute drive from the sprawl of Lafayette Parkway to historic downtown LaGrange was like traveling back in time. Across Tanyard Creek, over and under some railroad tracks that divided the city, past blocks of narrow row houses with children on porches and old folks across the street watching them. Brick towers of mills in the distance, hardly any cars, everything still and quiet in the gray, cool afternoon.

I pulled up to the Charles D. Hudson Natatorium and instantly recognized the dark-green trim on bright-red brick, the stone portico. The Callaways liked sturdy symmetry and classical flourishes. It was a copy of Ogletree Street, only this place was far bigger and grander. It reminded me of East Point's generous Spring Avenue Pool for Whites in a prominent location and its smaller version on Randall Street tucked away in the Black neighborhood. Same designer, same materials, reduced scale. It sent a message.

The pool house had been renovated into offices for LaGrange College's athletics department, judging by the coral and teal palette, sometime in the 1990s. Through the rear glass doors, I could see the blue surface of a pool in a courtyard and, behind that, the wide, glass facade of the natatorium. It looked like the original pool had been carved in half. The shallow half of the pool was in the courtyard, the deeper half sheltered indoors.

When a young man in gray sweats found me and asked if I needed help, I had my lines ready.

"I'm researching pools in the South, and I wanted to see this one. I know it's a historic pool, and can you tell me about the Callaway pools?"

He looked about twenty, light hair with a patchy beard, but I was getting bad at guessing ages. I think his name was Ivan. He was delighted to give me a tour of the facility.

"I grew up in the Grange," he said. He went to LaGrange High, went to LaGrange College, learned to swim here, and now worked full-time job as the pool operator.

I marveled that I had walked up to these two pools and instantly found Phyllis and Ivan, two people who grew up swimming there.

I followed him out into the courtyard. I asked him if the Ogletree pool was closed for the summer or closed forever. Why was the water green?

"If I stopped putting chemicals in this pool, it will turn green in a week," he said.

This was news to me. A pool dies fast, or at least, it loses its good looks.

We walked around the indoor pool, its curved wood beams and chlorine smell. Kind of a genius renovation to keep the big trapezoidal footprint of the original pool, which was bigger than a football field, and create two pools for year-round use.

As we walked around the side of the natatorium, Ivan pointed out a bench. "You like old stuff. These look old."

I felt ridiculous, but then I saw that the benches had no reason to be there.

"Hey look," I said. "If you sit on this bench, you're looking at a brick wall. But originally, you were looking at the deep end. At the diving boards."

"My father-in-law told me you had to pass a swimming test to be allowed to use the diving boards. They gave you a little fish patch, and you sewed it on your trunks."

My eyes went to his ring finger. He looked really young to have a father-in-law.

"I could take you to see the dungeon. That place scares me."

He wanted to show me every corner of the place. It was adorable.

"Let's see, you are a stranger. Sounds like a bad idea to go to a dungeon with you."

"There's a big old-time clock down there and all these knobs and switches."

"Okay, let's go."

As we climbed down the stairs to the mechanical cellar, I started thinking about it. Nobody knew I was here, in a boiler room in LaGrange. What was the possibility that this twenty-something athlete will slit my throat and dissolve my body with pool chemicals? But he kept calling me "ma'am." He was probably wondering if I was a threat. Another milestone. Cougar status.

The scariest part about the dungeon was a sign warning of asbestos exposure.

Our tour continued. I finally spotted the dedication plaque: *These facilities and funds for the renovation and additional construction were given to LaGrange College by the Callaway Foundation, Inc., in 1992.* That's when the segregation story came out.

"You're not from around here, so I'll tell you," he said, taking a deep breath. "This was the White pool."

I had already figured this out. Why was it such a big secret?

"And the pool I visited on Ogletree was the Black pool."

"Yeah," he exhaled. "They were owned by the Callaways, and they did not want to deal with integration, so once people started suing, they donated the pools to LaGrange College and the Troup County."

He was sheepish about this, and I felt bad for cornering him. Poor kid was born after 1992 but shouldering the weight of a hundred years of small-town Georgia racial politics.

"It's the same where I live, in East Point," I offered. "There was a White pool and a Black pool before integration. Now there's no pool. At least here people can still go swimming."

■ ■ ■

Driving home along the long vanilla interstate, I called my father to quiz him about his years attending LaGrange College.

"Did you ever go swimming?" I asked.

"Oh yes," he chuckled. "But not in the forbidden pool."

"The Callaway pool?"

"No students were allowed to swim there."

"Who could?"

"Whoever the Callaways wanted. White people. But not LaGrange College students."

I was confused. The pool was part of the college. I needed a chart to understand what facilities were public, private, or institutional.

"That was my freshman year, 1969," he explained. "LaGrange College had just begun admitting Black students. See, the Callaways were Baptist. La-

Grange College was Methodist, so slightly more progressive. Once the college integrated, the Callaways changed the rules so that no LaGrange College students were allowed to use their pool."

"Oh."

"And previously it had been free to students, so a lot of them were very upset."

Not upset about racial discrimination. Upset that the pool was off-limits.

"So, where did you swim?"

"Let's see. . . . We swam in a lake. There was a rock quarry west of there. More natural settings, I guess."

"But no pools."

"Officially, no. Some might have snuck in there for a midnight swim."

Both Dad and Ivan used the term *the Callaways*, but officially, it was the Callaway Educational Association, or CEA, an organization the family founded in 1944 to "provide recreational and educational opportunities for LaGrange, Georgia, youth." What started as a series of enrichment programs for the families of workers in the Callaway Mills—schools, clinics, Little League teams, and music lessons—later expanded to serve the community, specifically, the White community. Card-carrying CEA members could access the library, auditorium, and a swimming pool that far outshined anything provided by the government.

The Callaway family contributed to public facilities, too, like the WPA-funded LaGrange City Pool, which opened in 1935, but the CEA facilities were private, and the organization could control membership. That is how, amazingly, the CEA pool remained segregated up until 1992, when Fuller E. Callaway Jr. died and the CEA was dissolved. The Troup County archives had a collection of photos of the CEA pool on a sunny day in 1990, before the renovation. Every face in the crowd was White. If not for one's little girl's trendy monokini, it could be 1960. This would have been around the time I was swimming with my integrated Girl Scout troop out in the lake at Callaway Gardens.

The shifting rules of the CEA pool fascinated me. It demonstrated how the Callaway pool was a gift to the community but also a tool. Just as city pools could be tools for economic development, this private pool was a useful way to attract and retain employees or even punish them.

In 1919, cotton baron Fuller E. Callaway Sr. said, "We have tickets that entitle the holder admission to the pool. Now, you take a doffer boy, and if he does not behave, we take his swimming ticket away from him, and it has more influence with him than the fear of God."

These privately funded, deeply beloved pools were also a tool to maintain racial segregation. The CEA built the giant swimming pool for Whites in 1946 and a smaller version for Blacks in 1956, right after the *Brown v. Board of Education* struck down segregation. It was a way to buy time, keep Blacks out of the pool, all while advancing an appearance of generosity and public benefit.

By October, I was learning about pools all over the South, hearing the same whispered stories from White people again and again. Segregated pools, abandoned pools, and buried pools were a secret and a shame, but they were everywhere. Confusion around which facilities were public, private, semi-public, or institutional added to the mystery and maintained the status quo of segregation.

Powerful White families like the Callaways were not unique in exercising their influence over the social order. The Warner family in Tuscaloosa, Alabama, wrote checks to build the Queen City Pool in 1943 and the Gulf States Pool for Blacks in 1953. Like Lake Spivey, the Queen City Pool closed rather than admit Black patrons. Today I saw these family names on highways, buildings, plaques, scholarships, and foundations.

The mark of segregation was still visible today. Even when the CEA shut its doors, making lavish donations of its assets to finally desegregate them—better late than never—the White pool went to LaGrange College, a private institution. Twenty-five years later, the Charles D. Hudson natatorium remained somewhat exclusive. Not racially segregated but limited to those affiliated with the college. It was in excellent condition and was active year-round.

On the other side of the tracks, the Ogletree Center pool, donated to Troup County, was half-drained and uncovered and full of algae. The diving board was gone, but the sixty-year-old pool had seen few improvements. Phyllis could tell that the swimming season was too short.

October 24 CATASTROPHIZING

I couldn't sleep. The kids were snoring in bed next to me, their arms and blankies thrown up over their sweaty little faces. Jason was in Chicago; he'd been gone all week. This was the first time he had traveled for work since his heart attack.

Last week, our neighbor across the street was robbed and beaten. In his house. Mr. Howard was seventy-six years old. He was in the hospital, unconscious. If he died, would it be murder? I practiced saying that aloud—my neighbor was murdered. If that was true, what would it mean? Should we move?

That was the same night as the tornado. Hurricane Michael became one of the rare storms that reached inland Georgia as a full-grown Category 2 hurricane, flattening cotton fields, pecan groves, timberlands, and towns across South Georgia. Up here in Atlanta, we sheltered in basements as tornadoes raked the city.

I was fearful of being alone in the house. I lay there thinking of crime in the neighborhood, the abandoned houses on all sides of us, frustrations with Guy's teachers, with Guy himself. All unfair, unreasonable late-night anxiety, a ticker tape with no off switch. OutKast's "Hey Ya" blasted in my head, a track the boys requested on every car ride.

Maybe I need to give up caffeine, or alcohol, I thought. Or take up Prozac.

I looked at online real estate in lieu of porn, something to numb the buzzing.

I rolled over on one side to block the light of my phone as I scrolled in the dark, looking at apartments.

What if we moved to one of those massive new "luxury" apartment complexes in Midtown, near Jason's job? Easy commute, better schools. Everything sparkling new, including a big, blue swimming pool on the roof.

"Outstanding amenities such as a saltwater pool, 24-hour athletic club, cybercafé, gaming room with free Wi-Fi service, foosball, pool table, flat screen TVs and shuffleboard, 24-hour emergency maintenance, 24-hour secure package service, Zip Car rental access and gated parking. Whether you prefer a beautiful pool view or breathtaking city view from your own private balcony . . ."

It sounded like a Disney cruise. Including the price. Rent in one of these two-bedrooms costs from two to three thousand dollars a month.

I scrolled through dozens of these high-rises. The pool was always the precious jewel at the center of the compound. The apartments themselves were like fortifications protecting this inner sanctum of rest and flirtation. Here I discovered a new species of swimming pool, the pool in the sky.

What will these places look like in fifty years? Would they age gracefully like Riverbend, with its masterful landscaping and the eternal Chattahoochee?

I thought about widowhood. Would I change everything? Would I sell the house, simplify? Get rid of all the reminders of our happiness? Move to a maintenance-free apartment with "outstanding amenities"? Could I even afford it as a single mom? Catastrophizing, it's called. Dreaming about the end of the world.

The Mark, Enso, The Cottonwood—fantasy real estate. They all started to look the same.

Eventually, I bored myself to sleep.

■ ■ ■

Our neighbor died a few days later in the hospital. He died alone.

I could hardly think about it, much less talk about it, without short-circuiting.

Around this time, we were watching *Stranger Things,* which was too scary for me but filmed here in East Point. I wanted to see the scenes shot in the neighborhood.

The show's concept of "the Upside Down," a dark parallel universe where malevolent forces reigned, struck me as a metaphor for two Americas. I often sensed that the poor Black people in my neighborhood lived in some kind of Upside Down, which looked the same as my world, only terrible things were possible. Cops were the enemy; violence was to be expected. Car chases, car jackings, overdoses, utilities cut off, evictions, prison time, drowning, a child hit by a car while crossing the street—I glimpsed these emergencies and injustices happening to my Black neighbors but not to me and not to my White neighbors.

Until now. Mr. Howard was White. His death—wait, his murder—felt like a rip in the fabric. As the neighbors gathered on his front lawn and spoke to the police, we knew this attack was somehow related to the Black teenager who was staying with him temporarily, keeping his pit bulls in the backyard, trying to start a lawn care business. This kid had no one else. He was robbed for his lawn mower. Mr. Howard got mixed up in whatever trouble that kid was caught up in. He got pulled into the Upside Down.

How could this parallel universe exist alongside my own? My neighborhood was used as the location for these retro-apocalyptic scenes in *Stranger Things.* On bad days, I wanted to run away, to move somewhere safer.

This neighborhood wasn't safe, but it was real. Little houses lined up like soldiers. I had seen at least three crushed by falling trees. I knew my neighbors, their dogs, the cars in their driveways and the music from their backyards. When the wind shifted, the smell of creosote drifted over from a telephone pole treating facility. The cemetery across from the old public housing complex was green and shady. I knew the hawks and owls that hunted our block.

Safety was a fantasy, like a luxury apartment hovering over Midtown, disconnected from the street and the soil.

It took nearly an hour to bump along Ponce de Leon Avenue from Midtown east to Druid Hills at rush hour in a plodding and steady downpour. I was going to be late for this cocktail party, but rushing was futile. My clients and colleagues, the buttoned-up versions of Atlanta's small world of environmental leaders—the donors and the foundations, sustainability directors, elected officials, and community organizers—were invited to this annual shindig at the Druid Hills Golf Club. We were all alone together on Ponce, in cars, peering at a trail of red taillights through our rain-warped windshields.

The lights of the country club winked behind the trees as a story came on the radio about the day's mass shooting, this one at a bar in Thousand Oaks, California. I vaguely heard the headlines about a "disturbed" former marine as I navigated the potholed road east. Then the tormented voice of a victim's father joined me in the cab of my small truck. He described his last phone call with his son. I punched off the radio.

You raise your children, I thought. You pour everything into the task, more than you ever thought possible. You send them off to kindergarten, to college, to the movies, to be gunned down. Last week, I was the Mystery Reader for Bruno's kindergarten class. Twenty-three chubby faces gazed up at me, rapt or wiggly, dozing off, each one of them unbearably precious, while I thought about Sandy Hook Elementary. They were starting lockdown drills soon, and I was not ready. The windshield wipers were beating back and forth, and suddenly I was weeping in the driver's seat.

Mercifully, the entry gatehouse was unattended. A sign taped to the window pointed me to the parking lot.

This news story settled on top of the traffic, the flooded roads, the sense of being always late, the early darkness, and the day's other bad news to make me cry in a parking lot. In the governor's race, the White Republican candidate declared victory before the votes were counted, including my vote, even as he held the title of secretary of state. How was everyone managing this stress and going to cocktail parties?

I dried my eyes and blew my nose with a stiff napkin from the glove box.

Up the grand staircase to the Druid Hills Country Club, under brassy chandeliers, our name tags were lined up on a table by the entrance to a warmly lit room. A bow-tied bartender was waiting to hand me a glass of cabernet.

I recognized Ted Turner's family by the fireplace. There was the fellow who helped preserve Arabia Mountain. The city's planning commissioner was in a corner, chatting with the director of sustainability. This low-lit room with its bookcases and leather chairs had been a comfortable refuge for thousands of such civilized gatherings, a century of cards games and genial conversations and deals made over whiskey and cigars.

Once I heard the commissioner say that Druid Hills and Olmsted Linear Park and Lullwater Creek were "pure Atlanta." I've always thought Atlanta was a young southern town without a signature architectural style, but the canopied oaks along Ponce de Leon, the mansions with their terra-cotta shingles, carriage houses, and banks of pink and white azaleas did have an iconic plantation vibe. I had spent most of my twenties in black pants and a white shirt, catering parties like this.

Didn't Walker Percy write about a country club in Druid Hills? I read *The Last Gentleman,* or parts of it, in a Southern Literature class years ago. I remembered only the Atlanta scenes and the hero's general feeling of postmodern oppression among a bunch of moneyed southerners. It was a late 1960s novel, so I pictured Burt Lancaster in his tiny swim trunks.

The happiness of the South was very formidable. It was an almost invincible happiness. It defied you to call it anything else. Everyone was in fact happy. The women were beautiful and charming. The men were healthy and successful and funny; they knew how to tell stories. They had everything the North had and more. They had a history, they had a place redolent with memories, they had good conversation, they believed in God and defended the Constitution, and they were getting rich in the bargain. They had the best of victory and defeat. Their happiness was aggressive and irresistible.

Turning to meet the Lullwater Lounge, I clung to my limited knowledge of the club. I asked at least three people if Walker Percy had been a member here, and they had no idea what I was talking about. *Nothing was wrong, but he got worse anyway. The happiness of the South drove him wild with despair.*

The guy who might know was Dr. Mark Berry, the top environmental leader at Georgia Power and an avid reader and paddler. He stood under an oil painting of the English countryside, wearing a bow tie, sipping his drink and talking with someone from a foundation. Unlike nearly everyone else at the Druid Hills Golf Club, both tonight and for a hundred years, he was African American.

I introduced myself and chatted about my work trying to raise awareness about the Flint River in Atlanta.

"I've been here three years," he told me. "I've never been anyplace that is so disconnected from its water. If you asked someone on the street to name five rivers in Georgia, any rivers, they couldn't do it."

He was right. I could name a dozen rivers, but how many had I touched? Just the Chattahoochee and Flint. A lifetime in Georgia, and that was it.

"Is it because we're a water-rich state?" I said, thinking aloud. Do we take it for granted?

"Not necessarily. We don't have groundwater. It's all surface . . . it's at the pleasure of the rains. When it rains, it's plentiful."

I told him that I had become obsessed with the Flint River because I grew up in suburbia, feeling like I was from nowhere. Without defining natural features, my home had no identity.

"If you're from Clayton County," I said, "it's all about *Gone with the Wind*. Tara on the Flint River. Which is fiction."

"The rivers are like fictional characters."

I laughed and drained my wine.

It hit me that someone had recently given me an illustrated children's book about the Flint River, with a blue-haired, White-skinned, broad-chested river god on the cover that reminded me of Captain Planet. I found this cheesy but useful, especially for kids.

In some ways, it was natural to personify the river, as a way of naming and knowing an ancient and powerful life force. I felt the same presence around a particular old sycamore in my neighborhood and the pair of hawks that perched there at sunrise every morning, like I should pay my respects. Every time I looked down a storm drain or under a bridge to see the Flint, I felt a little rush of recognition. Hello, old friend. Our river deities probably revealed more about our personalities than the river itself. What happens when we outgrow our superhero mascots?

We traded book recommendations. I pulled Janisse Ray's *Drifting into Darien* out of my purse, a travelogue about Ray's epic paddle down the Altamaha River from Middle Georgia to the coast. Even though I had never seen the Altamaha, I now felt as though I knew it intimately. We need a dozen more river books like this, I told Dr. Berry. So the rivers are no longer fictional.

He scribbled down the title in his journal.

Later that weekend, probably at 3:00 a.m., with a flashlight in bed, I finished the book. The river was the main character In the story, a character with a Muscogee name, and it no longer felt fictional to me. The river journey led Ray past Georgia Power's Plant Hatch, a nuclear power plant that she implicates as the cause of her mother's death from cancer. It is a gut-scraping chapter, raw with the pain of her loss, the whole community's loss, and the sharp fact that there is no "clean" way to sustain our insatiable need for more energy. As I read, "Pull the plug. Shut down the plant," all I could think was how I had just recommended this book to a VP of Georgia Power. If the Altamaha is our hero in this story, Plant Hatch is clearly one of the villains.

The golf club gathering wound down with handshakes and dinner plans, and I slipped over to a ballroom window to look over the golf course. There had to be a swimming pool somewhere. It was raining again, and sodium lights washed the tidy grounds in an orange glow. A young woman confronted me with a polite, "Can I help you?"

Sheepishly, I told her I was just looking for the pool.

"Are you a member?"

"No, no. I don't want to go swimming or anything. I just wanted to see it."

"Of course," she said, as if this were a perfectly normal request. Maybe I could pass for a prospective club member in my business casual skirt and blouse. "It's right over here. It's covered for the season."

She led me down a hallway and out to a tiled courtyard. The wide pool with its telltale diving board lay a few steps below, sleeping under its tarp. Rain dripped from the pergolas; wind nudged puddles along the deck. Umbrellas and white lawn chairs were neatly folded and stacked against a wall.

She told me that the pool was built in 1914 as she pulled her cardigan around her body. I wanted to interview her about this pool, what she saw there, where she swam, but I felt bad for making her walk out in this miserable weather for reasons I could hardly begin to explain.

November 20 BELOVED COMMUNITY

On our third visit to the MLK Aquatic Center, I got it.

At five in the afternoon, with the sun sinking behind the downtown skyline, the cavernous natatorium glimmered like the inside of a kaleidoscope. The big cinder-block wall was aflame with the pool's reflected light. Each cannonball rained gold doubloons on the swimmers.

Anticipating the daily glare, the lifeguard wore sunglasses. With her shaved head and serious expression, she looked like an Egyptian goddess enthroned on a golden lifeguard stand.

Previously, we had visited this pool on gray summer days with clouds pressing down on the city. That's what indoor pools are for—rainy swim sessions. Today the late-fall light was cold and sharp. The tall narrow windows were filled with the yellow fringe of a sugar maple shimmying against the blue sky. I showed another lifeguard, a woman in a pink turban.

"It looks just like a painting!" she smiled. "That's why I love this one."

The other indoor pools—Rosel Fann, Adamsville, Washington Park—had no windows, no other children. They looked like warehouses compared to this jewel box.

"Are you from around here?" she asked me. "Did you go to the old natatorium?"

I confessed that I did not.

"It had windows like this," she said, more to herself. "It was full of light."

The musical shouts of children bounced across the water.

For the first time, I understood why the MLK pool was beloved. The light had not changed.

December 10   UPSTREAM

Always driving, this time in our little pickup truck to Marietta, weighed down with the sandbags and aluminum poles of a ten-by-twenty-foot white rental tent.

On Friday afternoon, Jason and I worked in the freezing rain to hoist this tent up in our backyard. On Sunday, we wrestled it to the ground. In between, we crammed most of our friends and family under the tent with twinkly lights, space heaters, Christmas albums, and a low table covered with berries, wine, cheese, cider, and Christmas cookies.

Every year, we hosted a Christmas party to celebrate Jason's birthday. Because our house was so small, we relied on a couple firepits in the backyard to accommodate the crowd. Somehow, in all the years of winter birthday parties, it had never rained like this. Once it even snowed on his birthday—a couple inches of decorative Georgia snow that would melt in the morning—but we still managed to host a cheery gathering in the backyard. This year, the forecast never wavered from 100 percent chance of rain all weekend, so I rented a tent.

As I made my way to Suburban Rentals, thirty miles across town, I sorted through all the merry and embarrassing scenes of the party. It had grown into a kind of annual wedding-scale bacchanal, complete with homemade invitations, over-the-top decorations, custom CDs, Mom's catering, and instead of wedding cake, a bûche de Noël with birthday candles. We were the Clark and Ellen Griswold of East Point.

On party day, I jumped out of bed early—after a bad night of sleep, running through the party prep list in my head—and sprinted until the last crushed cranberry was swabbed off the hardwood floor at midnight. In the rush to prepare, I snacked on stolen olives and cherries and gingersnaps from the trays as I sealed them in plastic wrap. I drank coffee until noon, when the growler shop opened, then sampled party beverages for the rest of the afternoon—a hot wassail and rum, a pumpkin-spiced cider, bottles of beer that I sipped and set down and lost forever.

The gathered guests represented a cross section of our life—colleagues in tacky sweaters chatting with our high school friends, our neighbors sorting through albums with our siblings, dozens of children weaving underfoot, how tall they had grown. I couldn't believe they all ventured out in this cold and tumbling rain, but perhaps a heart attack inspired one to feast with renewed vigor. Under the tent, Jason held court, describing how he had twisted his ankle stapling C9s on the roof and had to borrow a set of crutches.

It was stressful to be the hostess but fun to remember the night. Once the party was in full swing, the votives lit and Bing Crosby crooning, I became tipsy on the laughter of my guests. It made me dizzy and self-conscious, having all these people perched on my sofa, edging through my kitchen to the buffet, taking turns with the sole toilet in our tiny house. It made me think about who Jason and I are as individuals and as a couple, all the choices that had led, repeatedly, to this annual tradition and what I would be doing tonight if Jason hadn't survived for another birthday.

Driving back to return the tent, alone, under a dismal sky of ragged clouds, I looked for the river. It had become a kind of driving game for me, like cow poker or spotting license plates. As the road descended, I scanned for storm drains at the bottom of the hill. I cut off a Tercel and they honked at me, tailed me all the way from Riverside Drive to Heard's Ferry Road. Sorry, I practiced for the confrontation. I was just looking for the Chattahoochee River.

Past the older ranch estates left between the newer mini castles. Here was what looked like a late 1970s modernist cathedral, there a sprawling Grecian compound with shitty inflatable Christmas decorations deflated on the marshy lawn. At this hour, the traffic was all landscaping trucks, maintenance vans, service workers attending to the riverside estates of North Fulton County.

The street names all included a Ferry, Mill, Ford, Bridge—vestiges of a riverine worldview. The city was called Sandy Springs—surely there was a spring somewhere. Winding downhill, where Johnson's Ferry used to be, stood a creamy new seven-lane bridge.

I detoured to the Chattahoochee River National Recreation Area so I could really see the river, hear its thunder after a weekend of rain. A tasteful, putty-colored sign built to National Park Service standards said INTERSTATE NORTH, COCHRAN SHOALS UNIT. In an odd reversal of our historic naming convention, the park was named after the road.

For a Monday morning, the parking lot was busy. SUVs, all some variation of silver, white, and black, blended in with the winter landscape. A group of gray-haired men with walking sticks prepared for a hike. A brightly dressed cyclist lifted a bike off a roof rack. Two White women in visors crunched purposefully along the trail. Not bad for a drizzly forty-one-degree morning.

They knew where to find their river—upstream of the city and its polluted runoff. It was like the dynamic of city "heights" and "bottoms" on a larger scale. Suddenly, I understood that cities must be defined by an upstream and downstream side of town, subtle benefits for one side and consequences for the other. I warmed myself on my envy of the Northside.

The swollen river ripping southward looked brown and brutal. The silvery forest stood submerged at its edgeless banks. I shivered as I walked past historic markers and stately dedication plaques, a row of shiny bike-share bikes and picnic tables. A jogger in fluorescent yellow passed me on the trail.

The river's roar was amplified under I-285, where whitecaps flipped and foamed. One spot looked like a little beach—some boulders and logs arranged around a gentle edge. At the Cartoogechaye, this would be a dent in the river cane where the pasturing cows entered the creek. Could it be a public swimming hole?

I took a few photos and turned back. It was too cold, and the day's work still lay ahead of me.

In the distance, beside a figure walking a couple terriers, a white truck rolled toward me. Why was someone driving on the trail, ruining the view?

A National Park Service ranger in a green uniform emerged. A fit young White man with a military buzz cut and gray stubble, brass name tag on his chest. I waved to him.

"Do people swim here?" I asked.

"Today?"

"No, no. Just in general. I've been trying to find a swimming hole in the city."

He explained that the NRA was forty-eight miles of river from Buford Dam to Peachtree Creek, with ten thousand acres of river park access on the Northside.

"People swim in it all the time. In the summer, you put in over there. People tube in it." He pointed to a half-moon-shaped pier on the eastern shore, with stairs descending into the river.

I wrote on my hand. *Sandy Point, Bull Sluice, Aker's Mill.* My palm was papery from a month of spruce-scented hand soap. I fell in love, briefly, with this fetching man in uniform for indulging my questions about where to swim.

"Be careful in the summer," he started, and here I thought he would say something about bacteria or drowning risk. "Because of all the drunken college kids. Go early in the morning. Go before noon. . . . Hey another thing—"

My heart leaped.

"If it looks like chocolate milk, don't swim in it," he said. "Like right now. The *E. coli* levels are through the roof."

■ ■ ■

I can do this anytime. Create a scene. Find the water. Fall in love. Make something out of my useless suburban, soccer mom commute. Make art out of garbage.

More and more, I realize that I feel compelled to write out of shock, to work through my own unease about race and class.

I do this because it rescues me.

Somewhere on I-75 South, before Moore's Mill Road (another river relic), I passed a sad little sign that said Chattahoochee River Watershed. A stock illustration of a river. A green-and-blue blur. I squinted through my windshield for some hint of water and saw only a big metal freeway wall and the Atlanta skyline in the distance. Some G-DOT worker had jammed that signpost in the ground to meet some requirement for public watershed education. It was so small, almost missed it.

The Atlanta History Center's Kenan Research Library had a lot of rules.

First, you needed to register for an official researcher card, which you obtained by answering a few multiple-choice questions about yourself and the purpose of your visit. Then you had to leave your purse, laptop, and even your favorite sketchbook and pens in a little locker. All notes must be made with little pencils on the provided baby-blue scraps of paper.

In the reading room, all movement was hushed and methodical. One couldn't just chase their research whims through the stacks, pawing at the shelves. You had to request materials in writing using the designated form. The librarians pulled materials once an hour, on the hour. Then you waited.

One must resist touching the golden, nine-foot-tall, hand-rendered 1870s Atlanta map on the wall.

The first time I visited the Kenan Research Library, looking for information about an obscure East Point philanthropist named John J. Eagan, I was annoyed by all these rules.

When I finally received my requested boxes, opened the first Eagan file, and lifted out a crumbling leather ledger from the 1890s, I understood. My chest tightened as I studied these primary sources, brittle property deeds and diaries. Eagan's calligraphy on formal correspondence and loose pencilwork prayers in his diaries. I could hardly believe I was entrusted with his century-old papers. What if I cried on them?

At the table next to me, a white-gloved student gazed at a Confederate soldier's letter through a magnifying glass.

The Kenan Research Center was not set up for spontaneous research browsing. It was not a great place to take two little boys during the gray days leading up to Christmas. But when Guy's low-grade fever meant we had to cancel our indoor pool playdate, I thought maybe if I called ahead and requested the plat maps in advance, I could swing by for just an hour and the kids would sit quietly and the whole bleak, drizzly day wouldn't feel like such a waste.

"Stay right here," I whispered, parking my children in two stiff armchairs by the librarian's desk with their iPads. "Don't touch anything."

I waited for the "yes ma'am" in response. Bruno was already folded criss-crossed into the seat and wearing his headphones. With one finger, he slid a cartoon sandwich into the mouth of a cartoon monster. Guy curled up on his side, head on the armrest, and let his glossy eyelids close. The Tylenol he had chewed in the car reached its target. I tucked my raincoat around him and kissed his forehead to reassure myself and anyone observing that he wasn't contagious. The only sound was the hum of the overhead light, quiet researchers breathing in the background.

The librarian and I worked together to move a wide, flat box of laminated plat maps from a rolling cart onto a table. These were large hand-drawn maps of the subdivisions created by surveyors for turn-of-the-century developers like Eagan, Candler, and Inman. Some of them looked like negatives, white print on blue. "Egan Heights Subdivision of F. B. Phillips' Property," one read, "Lot of Land situated in Land Lot No. 133, Fulton County, Georgia."

Each map detailed a subdivision. I have always heard the word *subdivision* used to describe a specific kind of private suburban pod. It meant uniform houses built and sold together with an aspirational name in gold on the entry gate. Nice subdivisions had a central private swimming pool and tennis court with a clubhouse. Luxury subdivisions were connected to private lakes and golf courses.

Flipping through the stack of plats for Atlanta's oldest neighborhoods and cherished parks—Inman Park, Adair Park, Candler Park—reminded me that these, too, were subdivisions. Just pieces of land carved up into streets, alleys, and rows of uniform lots marketed for sale together. Somehow this neutral surveyor's term *subdivision* had become the default word for an exclusive, private space. But Atlanta's first subdivisions were anchored by common greenspaces.

My neighborhood, Semmes Park, lacked any unifying park or branded entryway, so I never thought of myself as living in a subdivision. But mixed in with all the other plats, I spotted the avenues near my block: Semmes, Spring, Lester, Forrest. I stopped and studied the 1880 layout. Here was the lot where East Point's swimming pool used to be. The curlicue letters of "Cold Springs 'Cue Club" straddled a squiggle so faint you could mistake it for the scrape of a fingernail on the blueprint. It was labeled simply "Branch."

I had never heard of the 'Cue Club, but I should've known Spring Ave. was named after a natural spring. Hey kids, I wanted to whisper, I found our pool! Better yet, I found our spring!

My sons were blessedly stationary for once—Guy sleeping, mouth open; Bruno glued to his tablet.

I snapped a few photos of the map and replaced it in its archival box.

Then, hoisting the sleeping seven-year-old into my arms, I nudged his brother out to the parking lot.

I felt inspired finally, at the bleak end of this long and soggy year, to find out what was underneath East Point's swimming pool.

■ ■ ■

The Cold Springs 'Cue Club was more like an event facility than a membership organization. The "'Cue Grounds" in East Point were operated by club president Harry C. Stockdell, "Illustrious Potentate" of the Yaarab Shriners and "one of the best-known insurance men in the South." For twenty years, the 'Cue Club hosted thousands of guests at traditional outdoor barbecues under long wooden pavilions in a shady meadow next to a spring known as "Cold Spring" that originated from downtown East Point.

All this was a few blocks from my house.

The earliest shindig to garner local press coverage was in 1895, when the mayor of Atlanta entertained the mayor of Philadelphia and a delegation escorting the Liberty Bell to the Cotton States Exposition. As a gesture of post–Civil War unity, the Atlantans offered their Yankee guests southern hospitality in the form of a barbecue featuring "pig, lamb, kid, chicken, Brunswick stew, tomatoes, onions, sweet peppers, potatoes, green corn, watermelons, etc. Also, paregoric and other cordials and refreshments from the big spring."

There's a grainy black-and-white photo of Mr. Stockdell and the 'Cue Club crew in the *Pictorial History of East Point* book. Six burly White men in flat caps, bowler hats, and top hats frown under their thick mustaches. A thin Black man in a Panama hat stands over a cast-iron cauldron in a white apron. According to historian Samuel Norris Thompson, "His aides were the best that could be had." Old Uncle Jack McElroy or Old Andy Lee posed with a wooden spoon the size of a small oar. "They knew their business," he wrote. "Their Brunswick Stew was canned and sold all over the United States."

Once I started reading stories about the parties at the 'Cue Grounds, it was hard to stop. I found articles about barbecues for 500 to 700 people, conventions of bankers, librarians, grocerymen, Shriners, "wheelman" (bicyclists), the entire Georgia legislature, House and Senate ("one of the most enjoyable features of the session"); and the 1911 Saengerfest, featuring a 250-man German choir. How funny to imagine this quiet little patch of lawn down the street from my house was once the destination for crowds of conventioneers and dignitaries. This went on for decades! Can a place be haunted by celebration, just as it can be marked by tragedy?

After Stockdell's sudden death in 1912, the barbecues continued for a few years. Eventually, the pavilions went quiet.

In 1931, when East Point's City Council debated a proposal to build its first municipal swimming pool on the site of the Cold Springs 'Cue Grounds, it's possible that many councilmen held memories of outdoor frivolity on the site. This was a chance to bring back the good old days. It wasn't hard to imagine the land dedicated to public leisure once again. On June 17, 1931, the day they voted to approve funding for the pool, the high was eighty-six degrees, the South was in drought, and there was no air-conditioning.

It only took one year to build the park. Memorial Park was dedicated the next May, featuring "a swimming pool, tennis courts, and a clear, cold spring." For the next few years, opening day of the swimming season meant a photo opportunity with pale-skinned Russell High School girls frolicking in dark bathing suits. The bespectacled chairman of the Park Committee clutched a few bashful-looking teenagers on his lap.

It occurred to me that most of the houses on my block were constructed around 1940, when the pool was a major attraction. The land was subdivided and sold in 1925, but the pool, in a way, is the reason my house was built. My neighborhood could have been marketed as a swim and tennis community. The pool was there because of the 'Cue Club, and the club was there because of Cold Springs. The springs were what had put the place on the map.

The springs were what made the place valuable for the Honorable L. J. Hill, who operated the Hilldale Dairy Farm on the land before the 'Cue Club. It was a huge operation stretching out on both sides of the railroad, including an immense, two-story barn that could hold a hundred milk cows, all supplied by the spring. East Point historian Ina Hemperley Short wrote, "The water from the spring was channeled out in the troughs which had been used by the dairyman to cool the milk." Beyond free water, the spring offered free refrigeration and a rudimentary sewer.

L. J. Hill was scrawled across land lots 156 and 133 on the wall map at the Atlanta History Center. Hill bought the property from a Mr. Edwards. Edwards bought it from someone named Allen, who acquired the land around

1874 and cleared the timber. Fifty years before Allen, this was Creek territory.

The railroad was on East Point's city seal, but the springs were the reason why the trains stopped here in the first place. Free water is why the city grew here. In 1933, Thompson wrote: "There is no healthier city in the United States than East Point. We stand high and dry, some twenty feet above Atlanta, as the rain which falls on East Point runs to three different rivers: on the east to the Ocmulgee and Flint, and west to the Chattahoochee River, and we can't help but stay clean. We would be healthy without the Artesian wells, as we have a firm, red subsoil that will turn water like a slate roof, and our wells could not possibly become contaminated with filth of any kind. Many citizens have kept their wells, regardless of our Artesian water and water connections, and use well water in summer, curtailing their ice bills."

I tried to track how the springs went from public to private, then back to public ownership as a pool, but it was not simply one or the other. Even when it was a private dairy farm, the public had some access to the water. Thompson wrote: "We pupils would go in twos after the water that we got from the springs. . . . Prof. Parker got permission to open a way from the schoolhouse to the Allen or Edwards Spring, as it was called and later the Cold Spring, afterwards developed by the Cold Spring 'Cue Club. This spring had a long wooden spout that ran under the hill and the water poured out through the same." And even when it was part of a private "club," the springs were marketed as a wholesome destination in Victorian Atlanta. The Cold Springs 'Cue Club brought national prominence to a growing suburb, and the whole city benefited from opening the springs to the public.

Of course, this was a time when "the public" was strictly defined as White citizens. It was inconceivable that East Point's Black residents could help themselves to the wooden trough at the Hilldale Dairy Farm or attend Saengerfest at the 'Cue Grounds. Since 1912, East Point's landscape was segregated by law, and city council minutes include restrictions on their access to the springs and swimming holes. "Mr. W. H. Caldwell protested 'against the Negroes having picnics at Nabell Springs, stating that same was a nuisance'; on vote, Clerk was instructed to issue no more Permits for same."

The club, the city, the pool, and ultimately my house could all be traced back to that spring. I couldn't help feeling dismayed that the reason for all this development was invisible at the dead end of Spring Avenue, hidden in a pipe underground.

December 27 BIG-BOX POOL

Packing to leave for the beach. The trip is my Christmas present.

Meg texts: Merry Christmas! Can't wait for Tybee.

Yesterday I spent all morning dismantling the Christmas tree, re-boxing the decorations. Two thin young men in full elf suits tossed the shriveled fir into the bed of their pickup truck. It made me feel old, tipping them.

The boys were already nuts. Ten minutes with Legos, ten with colored pencils, ten with light sabers.

Boxes and bags of toys stacked in their room, and they were bored.

I texted Tripp's dad about a playdate. He lived in Lilburn, a suburb on the northwest side of Atlanta. That's how I found the Bethesda Park Aquatic Center. We made a spontaneous expedition to the exurbs to meet Bruno's best friend at a giant pool.

We arrived at the sprawling site with its giant parking lot.

A dim natural light filtered through the rainclouds. Only a few high light fixtures, warehouse fluorescents, showed us the blood under our skin. The boys' lips looked violet. Infrared vein finder. Bruno socked me with a soggy ball when I wasn't looking, and it left a magenta splotch on my chest.

Newish, vast. The biggest pool we've seen since the Derda Rec Center in Colorado. It gives me some hope that the suburbs, at least, have the land and tax base and the will to create an entirely new kind of public swimming experience.

■ ■ ■

Later that night, falling asleep, Jason and I spoke in the dark.

"Are you gonna do the Polar Bear Plunge with me?" The weather forecast was warm, I told him. For January.

"I lost my nitroglycerine again. It's probably in the laundry."

"Come on."

"Nope. No risk-taking this year."

Was he kidding? Was it even safe to plunge in a freezing ocean if you just had a heart attack?

On the weather radar, a snot-green smudge across the East Coast. The backyard was a swamp. The sump pump in the basement fired up every few minutes, waking me up.

At Christmas, my family called it "Jason's incident." I knew it was life-changing. I just didn't know yet how it would change our life.

December 29 RACISM WITH NO RACISTS

It never gets old. Driving and descending. Back to Tybee Island, another year older, for New Year's Eve.

"Is this the coastal plain?" Second-grade geography lessons shining from the back seat.

We talked about the Fall Line in Macon. The churning Ocmulgee River down there, all the rivers high and getting higher. License plates from cold places zipped past us—Michigan, Illinois, Ontario, New York, Connecticut.

Then I-16 East. Jason coughing and driving. Kids on their iPads. I got a Lucia Berlin book for Christmas, and the bright-yellow cover nearly emanated a tropical fragrance and heat. I read and reread her stories, tried to untangle her memoir and imagination. The shortest fragments read like a photograph pressed between pages, her children fixed in moments of boyhood. Dear Lucia, patron saint of mom writers, falling asleep on her typewriter, scribbling brilliance between distractions and emergencies.

Then the first sighting of palm trees and Spanish moss woke us up as we sailed into downtown Savannah. The Talmadge Bridge, named for a segregationist, faded in the fog. Quick glimpse of tourists wandering through historic downtown before we zoomed out to the long, singular causeway to Tybee Island. Limitless marsh on the right, ocean to the left. Sometimes erased by high tides, the causeway out to Tybee was unbelievably tenuous.

We rolled up to the Southern Cross, and our friends came out to help us unload.

"It's been quiet," said Meg.

"We can help with that," I joked.

Jason took the boys straight to the hot tub.

In the narrow kitchen, I unloaded chocolate milk for the kids and Fat Tire for me, tins of Christmas candy and bourbon. Meg and I chatted about momlife, health, moods, and anxiety dreams. We didn't see each other very much throughout the year, but we had these intense check-ins every New Year's Eve that had become very influential for my own annual resolutions. She confessed that last year, following Trump's election, she was depressed and buying boxed wine.

I felt a little self-conscious about the amount of beer I was plunking into the fridge door. I was looking forward to the leftover Christmas ciders. I wanted Meg to tell me what to do.

This irritable, headache trigger, tightrope of days at the end of the year. This waking up in the middle of the night with a bad song blasting in my head, fruitlessly running through a list of regrets about the day, drafting to-do lists for dumb shit that didn't matter. Was this anxiety a normal reaction to the too-muchness of motherhood and an unbearable political climate? Or was it perimenopause?

Or was it this project? I had been looking for water all year, uncovering hidden swimming pools, thinking about access to swimming, questioning who was allowed to enjoy water and where. I was feeling less safe in a place called the Southern Cross, more unstable in my body and my segregated world. But somehow this seemed preferable to being numb and sheltered. This was real.

"What you are doing is extraordinary," said Julia Pearce, one of the few Black residents on Tybee Island. This was the first thing she said to me, and I nearly burst into tears. Chris Garbett, who advocated for the Tybee Island Community Pool, told me to talk to Julia if I wanted to understand racism on the island.

"It's a part of what we have to do to dismantle racism and White supremacy," said Pearce. "Our country was based on it, founded on it. But many pretend it doesn't exist."

By erasing the pools, cities participated in this pretending and the effects were devastating. "Young Black people drown here every year because they do not have access to water training," said Pearce. "It is Recreational Apartheid."

A registered nurse and Spelman alum, Pearce had moved to Tybee in 1997. When she married a White man and longtime island resident in 2000, she told me their wedding was "the most integrated occasion in the history of Tybee Island." The mayor toasted the couple at their reception and thanked them, saying their marriage "opened up our island."

In the decades since, Pearce raised her family and established the Tybee MLK Human Rights Organization. They created Tybee's first Martin Luther King Jr. Day parade and program and promoted year-round actions to honor Juneteenth, the Savannah Beach Wade-Ins, and Indigenous Peoples' Day. In her campaigns for city council and eventually mayor, she advocated for public schools, transportation, and pools on Tybee Island. The failure of the referendum to build a community pool on the island was a perfect example of how racism functions quietly in private, with clear and tangible results in public.

"The volunteer committee was mostly women," explained Pearce. "They worked hard, did everything they were supposed to do; they had a location, site plan, cost analysis, and code regulations."

She told me about a White resident who had voiced his opposition in the days leading up to the referendum vote.

"He got on his bicycle, like a witch with a bullhorn, and went all over the island saying, 'No Pool! It will destroy the island!' Peddling fear. As he passed our house, I yelled, 'You're a racist!' He ain't pay me no doggone mind."

I interrupted her story, asked how he claimed a swimming pool would destroy anything.

"He didn't have to explain *how* it would destroy the island. It was a dog whistle. They were not confused. That's that code talk. Trust me, they know the code; they made the code. They pretend like we got racism with no racists."

This description made me want to jump up and down. This was gaslighting, this prevailing insistence that the pools were sited, constructed, designed, policed, funded, and defunded, then drained, demolished, and erased because of a hundred reasons but that race had nothing to do with it.

Later it rained. Fat drops from the eaves hit the outdoor light fixtures like steel drums. We huddled on the porch and watched the storm sweep over the island.

"What if the highway floods?" we muttered. It's happened a few times and not just during hurricanes. A full moon or a "king tide" will flood the only road on and off Tybee Island. The place felt temporary, on the verge of tremendous change.

The rebel flag was still on the house at the end of 2018, but the property was for sale. A couple months later, new owners would make some upgrades. They painted the dark pine paneling white, tore out some walls, and renamed the house "Beach Therapy."

December 31 BEACH FOG

Sixty-one degrees and a fog advisory. Had I ever seen a beach like this, smothered with clouds? The ocean soundscape sealed behind a wall of fog?

We walked to the Back River. Tiny waves lapped. The boys chased the sound of the surf around the southern tip of the island. I squinted to see veiled jetties, seagulls, fishermen, my children scampering into the white distance.

What is a beach without an ocean view? The oceanfront hotels, the piers, the water tower, a giant golf ball on a tee, all vanished. There was something democratic about the way the fog blanketed the island.

Tiny people were out in the fog, feeling their way to the water's edge. I could hear them calling out to each other.

I stopped trying to convince the boys to stay out of the water. Followed their neon shirts, one orange, one yellow. Splashing without shivering, they never seemed to feel the chill.

All day it felt like morning. The dim sky shifted to bright gray, then dimmed again.

The Polar Plunge was tomorrow, New Year's Day. The forecast was seventy-four degrees at noon, and I was hoping to ring in 2019 with full immersion, not just the scalding, waist-deep splash I had managed in the freezing waves at the beginning of the year. Thousands of people would gather on the beach, then run, crashing into the ocean. I didn't want to do it alone. I didn't want to miss it. Without Jason, the story was all wrong.

That afternoon, we took the kids to a playground encircled by creeks to let them run around before the early sunset. Scrolling my phone, I caught a stray news item: 2018 was the wettest year in Georgia since 1948: seventy inches of rainfall—the most in my lifetime and my parents' too. There was a drought only two years ago, but now Atlanta's reservoirs were at full pool, the creeks flexing, the ground saturated.

A blue heron paused in the reeds beyond the playground. Was that fresh water or salt? Creek, river, marsh, ocean. The water resisted categories and forms. This island a liminal space by the sea.

The fog cleared by evening. I bobbed in the hot tub with the children, savored the pink edges of a sunset behind the palm trees, starved for color at the end of a gray year. Looking up at the house on stilts, I measured the storm surge that will cover the ground floor. The PRESERVE AUTHENTIC TYBEE sign ripped away and floating on waves. This hundred-year-old house, so solid, would topple. Just running scenarios, the way any responsible mother should.

Julia Pearce talked about the push and pull of the sea. Back in 1997, she fled an abusive husband in Atlanta and drove to Tybee Island in the middle of the night. As she grabbed her young children and put them in the car, they asked, *Where we going, Mama?* She told them, *To the beach.*

"I knew the water helped me," she explained. "I would spend all day at the beach after I dropped the kids off at school. Just sitting there, from eight in the morning to four in the afternoon."

"Being a nurse, I know we are made up of water. When we get to the water, we feel a kinship. You come to the ocean to heal. The water draws you."

Even in the cold, the fog, in the darkest depths of December, the ocean had the effect on me too.

"Most people don't want to live at the ocean because they understand that one day, all that water is going to come out that pocket, and there ain't nothing you can do about it. They want to visit and then go back where it's safe. But people who live at the ocean are not stable people. They're comfortable with that possibility. The moon pulls on the water. You have a lot of emotions about living near the ocean."

■ ■ ■

We made soup for dinner, beans and kale and butternut squash. Jason sat at the big dining room table wearing his new reading glasses, hunched over a thousand-piece puzzle. Meg toasted s'mores in the oven, a marvelous trick.

I tucked the kids in bed by nine o'clock, then dozed off with Lucia Berlin in my lap. The next thing I remember was Jason's silhouette in the doorway. My phone said eleven forty-five.

"Should we wake the boys for the countdown?"

"Of course," I mumbled, pretending like I wasn't asleep.

We carried them, sleepy-eyed and bundled in their fleece blankets, out to Eighteenth Street. The air was balmy and warm, the island wide awake. Thumping trap music from cruising cars, tinny shouts and noisemakers from porches and dark yards. More people in the streets than cars.

Jason moved easily through the crowd with Guy in his arms. Bruno wrapped his arms and legs around me.

"Wait for me," I called. "I want to kiss you at midnight."

We followed streams of people marching toward the sea to watch the fireworks.

On a distant balcony, some revelers made a heroic ruckus with cheap plastic horns. We followed a man in a sequined jacket and a man in a tiara. They embraced, kissed in the street. This made me smile, a good omen.

We found our way toward the same pier we saw this morning in the fog when it looked like the edge of the world. Clusters of people dotted the sand below. I couldn't make out their conversations over the stereo rumble of dark waves crashing in from the east and south.

Two minutes to go, and the crowd gazed northward toward the big pier. The boys sat perched on the handrails of the boardwalk; Jason and I wrapped our arms around them. For a moment before the fireworks streaked the sky, we could see whole constellations overhead. I saw the winking lights of container ships on the horizon. The sailors were with us in the countdown, waiting for our signal to kiss.

ACKNOWLEDGMENTS

I am indebted to friends, family, colleagues, neighbors, and strangers, named and unnamed, who ended up in this book just by sharing their lives with me. Thank you to everyone who invited me to go swimming over the last few years, met me at pools, suggested secret swimming holes, told me about the ghost pools in their towns, and shared their swimming stories.

This includes Meg Watson, Eve Rogers, Johnathon and Jessica Kelso, Natalie Chanin, Martha Kimes, Karyn Lu, Keith Huff, LaShawn Green, Michelle Rawlings, Dr. Darryl Jones, Jonathon Penn, Tania Wismer, Jamie Vernon, Nicole Calix, Linda Radcliffe, Tia Blandenburg, Wesley Bolden, the late Charles Strickland of the East Point Historical Society, and my late grandparents, Frederick and Ruth Slagle. Thank you for allowing me to share your words and stories here.

I am especially grateful to Dr. Jacqueline Royster and her family for helping me understand the story of Carolyn Harmon's death.

I have been fortunate to work with colleagues who have taught me so much, including Ryan Gravel, Dr. Jackie Echols, Michael Halicki, Dr. Mark Berry, J. Drew Lanham, Ben Sutton, Darryl Haddock, Dr. Yomi Noibi, and everyone at the Atlanta Watershed Learning Network. Extra special thanks to the Finding the Flint visionaries—Stacy Funderburke, Shannon Lee, Ben Emanuel, Jenny Hoffner, Katherine Zitsch, Katherine Atteberry, Danny Johnson, Tasha Hall Garrison, R. J. Gipaya, and Gordon Rogers—for encouragement and insight through years of book writing and river investigations.

Thank you to the Hambidge Center for Creative Arts and Sciences for a fellowship in 2017, during which I learned how to stop multitasking and immerse myself in this project. Many pages of this book were written during subsequent getaways at Hambidge, at Jodi Mansbach's magical mountain house in North Georgia, at Jess Bernhardt and Tareq Al Salaita's home in Monte-zuma, and in my mom's kitchen in Sewanee, Tennessee.

Thank you to Dr. Brennan Collins and Floyd Hall for inviting me to present this research publicly for the first time as lectures at Georgia State University and Pop-Up Zine, respectively. Thank you to Kirstie Tepper, Julia Brock, and Teresa Bramlette Reeves of Selvage Collective for inviting me to Tuscaloosa to create *Swimming Together* and *An Evening at the Pool*. Thank you to Anne Archer Dennington and Flux Projects for expanding the concept into *Ghost Pools* in East Point for an entire summer. Rebekka Kuntschik, Ann Hill-Bond, Julia Hill, Santiago Páramo, Christopher Swain, Ballethnic Dance Company, Kathy Dingler, and the East Point Historical Society made the installation and experience far richer and more beautiful. Because of *Ghost Pools*, I was able to connect with Chief Corey Thornton, Jim Grayson, Chris Garbett, and Julia Pearce, who provided stunning insights on swimming pools and the persistence of segregation. I am grateful for the scholarship of Jeff Wiltse, who helped me situate Atlanta's pools within national trends, and local historians Herman "Skip" Mason Jr. and Lisa Shannon-Flagg, who taught me about my own backyard.

Thank you to the editors and readers who made these pages smarter and kinder, including Dr. Carolyn Finney, Emma Calabrese, Ed Southern, Myra Oviatt, Adam P. Newman, Heather Bird Harris, and Elizabeth Gratch. Thank you to Jenny Keegan and LSU Press for seeking out this manuscript and transforming it, finally, into a book. Merci à Virginie Drujon-Kippelen, Kyle Tibbs Jones, and The Bitter Southerner team for documenting and publishing my creek-finding adventures. And thank you, Rachael Maddux and Abby Greenbaum, for holding me close through the odyssey of parenting and publishing.

While I was away somewhere working on this project, Jayne Slagle, Jesse and Gayle Slagle, and Myra and Rob Oviatt were helping Jason with carpools and homework and bedtime stories back home. Thank you to all the Slagles, Oviatts, and Palmers for the practical support, love, and faith that makes my writing possible. Dear Jason, Guy, and Bruno, thank you for all the family trips and cannonballs and moments I want to capture in words and hold onto forever.

NOTES

INTRODUCTION: July 2017 WE NEED A POOL

5   working-class white communities abandoned public spaces: Kevin M. Kruse, *White Flight: Atlanta and the Making of Modern Conservatism* (Princeton, NJ: Princeton University Press, 2005).

6   a national wave of suburbanization: Jeff Wiltse, *Contested Waters: A Social History of Swimming Pools in America* (Chapel Hill: University of North Carolina Press, 2007).

7   In 2017, a study of swimming ability: T. Layne, C. Irwin, J. Pharr, and R. Irwin, "Factors Impacting Swimming Participation and Competence: A Qualitative Report," *International Journal of Aquatic Research and Education* 12, no. 4 (2017), https://doi.org/10.25035/IJARE .12.04.10.
    scenes of violence and protest were mostly avoided: "Negroes Swimming at All City Pools," *Atlanta Constitution*, June 14, 1963.

January 1 THE SOUTHERN CROSS

15 first labeled as Weelaunee: "Map of the State of Georgia, Prepared from Actual Surveys and other Documents, for Eleazer Early, by Daniel Sturges," Savannah, GA, 1818, Columbus State University Archives and Special Collections, https://digitalarchives.columbusstate .edu/items/show/34.
    It's on the 1822 survey: Francis Lee Utley and Marion R. Hemperley, eds., *Placenames of Georgia: Essays of John H. Goff* (Athens: University of Georgia Press, 1975), 216.
    they called I-285 the "Circumferential Expressway": Metropolitan Planning Commission, "Up Ahead: A Regional Land Use Plan for Metropolitan Atlanta," Atlanta, February 1952.

17 In 1960, eleven Black students were arrested: "Tybee Seizes 11 Negroes in Wade-In," *Atlanta Constitution*, August 18, 1960, 1.

January 8 BIG-BOX POOL

20 The South Cobb Aquatic Center was built in 2002: Steve D. Hendrix, "Let's Go Sliding," *Recreation & Parks in Georgia*, Fall 2007.

21   This concept of replacing traditional public pools: *City of St. Charles, Missouri, Citywide Aquatic Facilities Master Plan*, May 2015.

January 24 GATED BEACH

25   the brainchild of Walter Spivey: Elizabeth Hulsey Marshall, *A Unique Partnership: Walter and Emilie Spivey* (Morrow, GA: Walter and Emilie Spivey Foundation, 1991), https://www.scribd.com/doc/234538370/a-unique-partnership-rev-7-19-14?secret_password=JwQSJyzVdIZ5dUIJD6Hl#.

glitchy old films about Lake Spivey: Lake Spivey Civic Association, *Atlanta's Fabulous Playground*, directed by Jerry Brown, a Provence Production, https://www.youtube.com/watch?v=e96L_4Il2cM, posted on December 7, 2013.

March 2 BLANK RIVER

37   By 2004, all the landfills were closed and capped: Georgia Environmental Protection Division, Solid Waste Division, "Landfills Post Closure 2016," https://epd.georgia.gov/sites/epd.georgia.gov/files/Landfills_Post-Closure_062816.xlsx.

When the Atlanta Housing Authority demolished the last of its housing projects: Donna Kimura, "Atlanta Says Farewell to Last Large Public Housing Building," *Affordable Housing Finance, January 1, 2009*, https://www.housingfinance.com/news/atlanta-says-farewell-to-last-large-public-housing-building.

38   The "lakes" were formed by pits quarried by the South River Brick Company: Kate Sweeney, "History in the Trees: A Tour of the Doll's Head Trail," WABE, October 3, 2014, https://www.wabe.org/history-trees-tour-doll-s-head-trail.

March 17 LAST DAYS OF THE NATURE CENTER

43   Didn't a child recently drown there: Alexis Stevens, "5-Year-Old Camper's Drowning Death Prompts Nature Center to Close," *Atlanta Journal-Constitution, July 25, 2017*, https://www.ajc.com/news/crime--law/nature-center-where-year-old-drowned-closed-until-further-notice/cmRGav4xhCRsQSAeJfdl8L.

44   a feel-good interview piece from January: "Meet Terri Clark of Cochran Mill Nature Center in South Fulton County," *VoyageATL*, January 20, 2017, https://voyageatl.com/interview/meet-terri-clark-of-cochran-mill-nature-center-in-south-fulton-county.

April 4 THE TYBEE PEOPLE

48   voters defeated a referendum to build it: Andrew James, "Tybee Island Referendum Project Dividing Community," *WSAV*, October 26, 2015, https://www.wsav.com/news/tybee-island-referendum-project-dividing-community.

49   Opponents said the ocean is a perfectly suitable source of salt water: "Tybee's Contro-

versial Pool Referendum Decided," WJCL, November 3, 2015, https://www.wjcl.com/article /tybee-s-controversial-pool-referendum-decided/938619#.

published an editorial in the *Savannah Morning News* in favor of the community pool: Christ Garbett, "Tybee Pool Would Provide Alternative to Hazardous Beach," *Savannah Morning News,* October 19, 2015, https://www.savannahnow.com/story/opinion/letters /2015/10/20/letters-editor-tuesday/13612122007.

dismissive treatment by local merchants and residents: "Editor's Note: Tybee Mayor Says Orange Crush Not about Race," Connect Savannah, April 8, 2015, https://www.connectsa vannah.com/savannah/editors-note-tybee-mayor-says-orange-crush-not-about-race/Con tent?oid=2602926.

April 15 **URBAN BAPTISM**

54   The city of Griffin had no public swimming pool: "Black Citizens of Griffin Want Pools Reopened," WSB-TV, April 4, 1969, http://dlg.galileo.usg.edu/news/id:wsbn55993.

April 20 **THE LAKE AND THE LANDFILL**

56   a kind of heat map of forests around the city: Center for GIS at Georgia Tech (CGIS), *Urban Tree Canopy Assessment,* 2015, http://geospatial.gatech.edu/TreesAtlanta.

57   In 1993, when Waste Management applied for a permit to expand: Kimberly H. Byrd, "'Enough Is Enough,' Landfill Foes Say," *Atlanta Constitution,* January 28, 1999; Ben Smith, "Landfill Protestors Warn Officeholders," *Atlanta Constitution,* April 9, 2002; Eric Stirgus, "Landfill Foes Plan Monday Rally at Capitol," *Atlanta Constitution,* April 4, 2002; Eric Stirgus, "Landfills Protested Today: South DeKalb Claims Discrimination," *Atlanta Constitution,* April 8, 2002; Eric Stirgus, "Officials: Shut Landfill in '04," *Atlanta Constitution,* May 13, 2003; Hal Lamar, "Residents Rally against Live Oak Extension," *Atlanta Voice,* November 15, 2003.

58   I had to dig into the city's planning documents: Atlanta Bureau of Parks and Recreation, *Annual Report,* 1975; Planning Atlanta, Planning Publications Collection, Georgia State University Library; Atlanta Regional Commission, "Areawide Outdoor Recreation Planning in the Atlanta Region: Proposed Nature Preserves. Status Report and Update," 1979; Planning Atlanta Planning Publications Collection, Georgia State University Library. Jay Lawrence, "Atlanta Putting Emphasis on Open Space for Parks," *Atlanta Constitution,* March 17, 1977; Barry King, "Atlanta Decides to Construct Own Campsites," *Atlanta Constitution,* June 8, 1979.

59   In 1986, the city scrapped the entire project: Nehl Horton, "City Accepts Bid on Lake Charlotte Land, but Loses $145,756 with the Decision." *Atlanta Constitution,* May 1, 1986.
"I wish I hadn't seen the body," said Jackson: Brenda Mooney, "Slain Youngster Had Been Told to Be Careful," *Atlanta Constitution,* November 4, 1980.
A twenty-seven-year-old lawyer: Tony Cooper, "Lawyer's Body Found in S.E. Atlanta Lake," *Atlanta Constitution,* September 29, 1981.
Lischkoff combined the Lake Charlotte parcel: Nehl Horton, "Beverly Hills Residents Applaud Zoning Denial," *Atlanta Constitution,* February 20, 1986.

61   Structures dotted the road here in 1928: "Atlanta 1927–30 Topographic Maps with Open
      Street Map Overlay," Emory Center for Digital Scholarship (ECDS), http://disc.library.emory
      .edu/atlanta1928topo.
      Dr. R. F. Ingram came up several times: "Dr. R. F. Ingram, Candidate for Council from Sec-
      ond Ward," *Atlanta Georgian and News,* September 21, 1908, https://gahistoricnewspapers
      .galileo.usg.edu/lccn/sn89053728/1908-09-21/ed-1/seq-14/print/image_632×817_from
      _2144,81_to_4260,2813 (presented online by the Digital Library of Georgia).
      Miss Charlotte Sage, a wealthy, well-documented Ansley Park debutante: "Miss Charlotte
      Sage to Make Debut at Reception on Dec. 22," *Atlanta Constitution,* September 27, 1936;
      "Miss Charlotte Sage Weds Mr. McKnight at Church," *Atlanta Constitution,* November 18,
      1948; "McKnights Off to Trinidad," *Atlanta Constitution,* March 28, 1950; "Mrs. Charlotte S.
      McKnight Dies; Funeral to Be Today," *Atlanta Constitution,* March 14, 1956.
62   archaeologists in the late 1970s made a heroic effort: *Soapstone Ridge: Its Environment and
      Land Use,* DeKalb County, Georgia Department of Planning, Planning Atlanta, Planning
      Publications Collection, Georgia State University Library; "Metro Scenes: DeKalb. Indian
      Relics," *Atlanta Constitution,* May 9, 1984.

April 22 HOTEL POOL

65   Just standing near the rippling water made you feel light and hopeful: Wallace J. Nichols,
      Blue Mind: The Surprising Science That Shows How Being Near, In, On, or Under Water
      Can Make You Happier, Healthier, More Connected and Better at What You Do, foreword
      by Céline Cousteau (New York: Little, Brown, [2014]).

May 16 STORMWATER

69   The *Atlanta Constitution* reported that late Friday night: Susan Laccetti, "College Park
      Flood Victim Still Missing," *Atlanta Journal-Constitution,* September 7, 1992.
      In one article, the water was waist-deep, in another, shin-high: Barbara Ann Moore, "Ten-
      ants Feared Hard Rains," *Atlanta Constitution,* September 24, 1992.
70   volunteers found her jacket downstream: "Volunteers Search, but Woman Not Found," *At-
      lanta Constitution,* September 20, 1992.
71   Harmon was, "by her conduct, the proximate cause of her own drowning": Barbara Ann
      Moore, "Ruling: Woman's Death Her Own Fault," *Atlanta Constitution,* October 6, 1994.
75   Who always settled in the Bottom: Ujijji Davis, "The Bottom: The Emergence and Erasure
      of Black American Urban Landscapes," Avery Review 34 (October 2018), https://www.avery
      review.com/issues/34/the-bottom.

May 20 PFDS

78   I loved that he brought paddleboat rentals to Piedmont Park: Ken Willis, "Non-Swimmer
      Father Saves Son, Drowns," *Atlanta Constitution,* July 11, 1977, 1.

79   two more children, ages five and seven, drowned at Dancing Waters: Scott Marshall, "Drownings Mystify Officials," *Atlanta Constitution*, August 5, 1993, 288.

My classmate's mother sued Dancing Waters: Ralph Ellis, "Mom Sues Dancing Waters over Son's Drowning Death," *Atlanta Constitution*, August 4, 1994, 387.

80   The CDC found that "the fatal unintentional drowning rate": Julie Gilchrist, Jeffrey J. Sacks, and Christine M. Branche, "Self-Reported Swimming Ability in U.S. Adults, 1994," *Public Health Reports* 115, nos. 2–3 (2000): 110–11.

Grizzard wrote a preachy opinion piece: Lewis Grizzard, "No Excuses," *Atlanta Constitution*, July 12, 1977, 27.

81   In news footage that shocked the nation: Anne Schindler, "Family of Infamous 'Swim-In' Protester Visit Site of Acid Attack," *First Coast News*, June 1, 2023, https://www.firstcoastnews .com/article/news/local/family-of-infamous-swim-in-protester-visit-site-acid-attack/77 -661fd836-d709-4f2b-86f9-9655eb36f2a9.

rather than comply with court-ordered integration, officials in Greenville: Judith Bainbridge, "Lawsuit Leads to Closure of Cleveland Park Pool, Skating Rink," *Greenville News*, June 7, 2017, https://www.greenvilleonline.com/story/news/local/greenville-roots/2017/06 /07/cleveland-park-swimming-pool-greenville-sc/376008001; J. Drew Lanham, "Swimming with Seals," *Bitter Southerner*, June 18, 2020.

Some of Greenville's seals ended up in Atlanta: "Mayor Hurls Out First Ball for 6 Sea Lions— Bears Late," *Atlanta Constitution*, August 24, 1961.

May 26   SHINY NEW NATATORIUM

85   Mayor Reed said, "We don't lose assets with the name Martin Luther King on them": Ernie Suggs, "New King Pool to Open Next Year in Atlanta," *Atlanta Journal-Constitution*, July 15, 2016.

87   For a generation of Atlantans, the pool was a legendary proving ground: Molly Samuel, "MLK Pool on Atlanta's List of Infrastructure Bond Projects," *WABE*, March 13, 2015.

May 27   ORANGE PARK

90   The park, with its granite walls and massive oak trees: Oakland City Historic District Nomination to the National Register of Historic Places, prepared by the Oakland City Neighborhood Association, February 2003, https://npgallery.nps.gov/NRHP/GetAsset/c897486c -5413-4e69-9f73-14ac2ee7dc6f.

92   Jane Jacobs said that a neighborhood park is a "creature of its surroundings": Jane Jacobs, *The Death and Life of Great American Cities* (New York: Random House, 1961). 98.

93   The city renamed Oakland City Park the Rev. James Orange Park in 2011: Jeremiah McWilliams, "Oakland City Park Re-Dedicated in Honor of James Edward Orange," *Atlanta Journal-Constitution*, October 30, 2011.

"Creating places where young people enjoy safe and fun recreational activities": "Twice as Many Pools Will Open in Summer 2010 vs. 2009," Mayor's Office of Communications, City of Atlanta, May 26, 2010.

At the park's rededication in July 2015, Mayor Reed said, "Rev. James Orange Park was abandoned": David Pendered, "Atlanta's New Bike Officer Led Effort to Redevelop Rev. James Orange Park," *SaportaReport*, October 8, 2015, https://saportareport.com/atlantas-new-bike -officer-led-effort-to-redevelop-rev-james-orange-park.

94   where the economic problems ran much deeper: Dan Whisenhunt, "Gunfire Causes Early Closure of Pools in the City of Atlanta," *Decaturish.com*, June 14, 2016, https://decaturish .com/2016/06/confusion-surrounds-early-closure-of-pools-in-the-city-of-atlanta.

May 28   WATER BALLET

95   Freestyle skateboarding was born out of the decaying swimming pools: Matt Calkins, "Pool Skating Evolved from 1970s Drought," *San Diego Union-Tribune, June 13, 2015*, https:// www.sandiegouniontribune.com/sdut-clash-at-clairemont-tony-hawk-pro-skateboarding -2015jun13-story.html.
Funded by the WPA, it opened in 1936 and lasted until the early 1980s: Ben Sisario. "It's Been Quite a Pool Party, but the Days Grow Short," *New York Times,* August 1, 2008.

97   a dance performance to be staged in an empty pool in Atlanta: Jasen Johns. "Glo Atlanta in Maddox Park," September 25, 2012, https://www.youtube.com/watch?v=0L4wjxUAluY.

99   maps of the racial makeup of Atlanta illustrated with census block data: Matthew Bloch, Shan Carter, and Alan McLean, "Mapping America: Every City, Every Block," *New York Times,* December 2010, https://www.nytimes.com/projects/census/2010/explorer.html.

101   In 2010, a master plan for Maddox Park and vicinity: MACTEC Engineering and Consulting, Inc., with Perkins+Will and Grice and Associates, "Atlanta BeltLine Master Plan Subarea 10: Boone/Hollowell, Appendix 4: Maddox Park Master Plan," December 6, 2010.

May 31   POOL PLANS

109   I spotted them in a photo from opening day in June 1974: "Swimming and Squirting," *Atlanta Constitution,* June 11, 1974, 12.
opposition from white neighbors: "Whites Oppose Grant Park Pool," *Atlanta Constitution,* October 14, 1970, 33.
In 1960, the city drained the lake and filled it with dirt: Advertisement for Bids, *Atlanta Constitution,* April 5, 1960, 24.

June 21   SWIMMING IN EAST POINT

116   The city's original pool had been closed for years: "E. Point Children Cool in College Park's Pool," *Atlanta Constitution,* June 20, 1952.

117   In 1953, the city solicited bids for two new pools: "East Point Council Gets Bids for Two New Pools," *Atlanta Constitution,* June 17, 1953.
Lillian Smith broke down exactly how segregated spaces: Lillian Smith, *Killers of the Dream* (New York: W. W. Norton, 1949). 95.

118   According to the *Atlanta Daily World,* these citizens purchased the land: Photo Standalone
      2, Members of the East Point Community Civic Club, *Atlanta Daily World,* June 15, 1954, 1.
      It ought to make me flinch: Nell Irvin Painter, "Why 'White' Should Be Capitalized, Too,"
      Washington Post, July 22, 2020, https://www.washingtonpost.com/opinions/2020/07/22/why
      -white-should-be-capitalized; Ann Thúy Nguyễn and Maya Pendleton, "Recognizing Race in
      Language: Why We Capitalize 'Black' and 'White,'" Center for the Study of Social Policy,
      March 23, 2020, https://cssp.org/2020/03/recognizing-race-in-language-why-we-capitalize
      -black-and-white; Eve L. Ewing, "I'm a Black Scholar Who Studies Race. Here's Why I Capital-
      ize 'White,'" *ZORA,* July 2, 2020, https://medium.com/zora/im-a-black-scholar-who-studies
      -race-here-s-why-i-capitalize-white-f94883aa2dd3.

119   A few weeks later, the Randall Street Pool was formally dedicated: Alice Holmes Wash-
      ington, "Dedication Services Set for E. Point Swimming Pool," *Atlanta Daily World,* June 12,
      1954.
      In 1956, the Parks Department organized the first annual Water Show: "Water Show and
      Beauty Parade at East Point," *Atlanta Daily World,* June 30, 1956, 3.
      there were "Dive-In" movies every night of the week: Harriette Schreiber, "Dive-In Movies
      Are Big Splash in East Point," *Atlanta Constitution,* July, 23 1956, 14.

120   swim instructors with the American Red Cross: Ted Lippman, "Official Suspended in Racial
      Incident," *Atlanta Constitution,* August 28, 1959; "White Women Barred from Future Negro
      Pool Demonstrations," *Atlanta Daily World,* October 4, 1959, 2; Eddie Barker, "It All Began
      15 Months Ago When a 9-Yr.-Old Boy Drowned," *Atlanta Constitution,* January 11, 1961, 5;
      "Vandals Dye East Point Pool Yellow," *Atlanta Constitution,* August 13, 1962.
      The Spring Avenue Pool admitted four Black swimmers: Bill Shipp, "2 More Negroes Barred
      by Maddox," *Atlanta Constitution,* July 7, 1964, 1.

121   Lester Maddox, segregationist firebrand who published editorial rants: "Pickrick Says: In-
      tegrated Pools?" *Atlanta Constitution,* September 1, 1962, 8.
      Between 1950 and 1970, suburban development fueled many innovations: Jeff Wiltse, *Con-
      tested Waters: A Social History of Swimming Pools in America* (Chapel Hill: University of North
      Carolina Press, 2007).
      A newspaper covered the formal summer opening of Lakeside: "Supper at Club Opening,"
      Atlanta Constitution, June 21, 1960, 18.

123   "City officials can only speculate as to why the referendum failed": Jim Greene, "A Restless
      Reminder," *Atlanta Constitution,* June 28, 1984.

124   There are two histories of East Point: *East Point Pictorial History* (Dallas: Taylor Publishing
      Company, 1982).

125   Hilliard commissioned Herman "Skip" Mason: Herman Mason Jr., *East Point,* Black Amer-
      ica Series (Charleston, SC: Arcadia, 2001).
      Mayor Patsy Jo Hilliard, East Point's first African American mayor: "East Point Game
      Changers: Patsy Jo Hilliard," EPTV, East Point City Government, February 28, 2020, https://
      www.youtube.com/watch?v=1ijwzlKga58.

126   In 1953, construction crews were surprised to discover: "Covered and Uncovered," *Atlanta
      Constitution,* July 29, 1953.

July 6 NATURAL BODIES

134 "the Malaria line": Arthur Ben Chitty, "Sewanee: Then and Now," *Tennessee Historical Quarterly* 38, no. 4 (Winter 1979).

136 the influential 1977 book: Christopher Alexander, Sara Ishikawa, and Murray Silverstein, *A Pattern Language: Towns, Buildings, Construction* (New York: Oxford University Press, 1977).

July 22 DISADVANTAGED YOUTH

158 Jeff Wiltse's book *Contested Waters* explained that what I was seeing was part of a trend: Jeff Wiltse, *Contested Waters: A Social History of Swimming Pools in America* (Chapel Hill: University of North Carolina Press, 2007).

159 the *Atlanta Voice* quoted a twelve-year-old swimmer: "Splash! New Pool Is Open in Anderson Park," *Atlanta Voice,* June 21, 1970, 1.

July 28 DEMAND GOODS

163 There was a quote in the Piedmont Park Conservancy's book: Darlene Roth and Jeff Kemph, eds., *Piedmont Park: Celebrating Atlanta's Common Ground* (Athens: Hill Street Press, in association with the Piedmont Park Conservatory, 2003).

August 4 THE SWIMMER

164 On top of the rain, the defeat of the locked pool, the end of summer malaise: John Cheever, *The Stories of John Cheever* (New York: Knopf Publishing Group, 1978).

August 5 CARTOOGECHAYE

167 No one ever used the term *land rich, cash poor:* Sarah Mock, "The Fallacy of Being 'Land Rich, Cash Poor' in Farming," *Medium,* May 27, 2020.

168 But they weren't abolitionists either: John C. Inscoe, *Mountain Masters: Slavery and the Sectional Crisis in Western North Carolina* (Knoxville: University of Tennessee Press, 1989).

169 "the first permanent white settler in Macon County": "Jacob Siler," Find a Grave, https://www.findagrave.com/memorial/57049704/jacob-siler.

August 11 RESCUES

171 Originally, this pool was built for White Atlantans: "$8,000 Improvements Set for Adams Park in '53," *Atlanta Constitution,* March 25, 1953.
after Cascade Heights was annexed into the city limits: Atlanta Department of Budget and Planning, "Annexation Map of Atlanta," 1954, Planning Atlanta City Planning Maps Collection, Georgia State University Library.
In 1979, the pool was repaired at great expense: Carole Ashkinaze, "City Speeding Repairs on Three Closed Pools," *Atlanta Journal and Constitution,* June 23, 1979.

By the 1990s, decades of deferred repairs to sewer infrastructure: Na'Taki Osborne Jelks, "Sewage in Our Backyards: The Politics of Race, Class, and Water in Atlanta, Georgia," *Projections* (Journal of the MIT Department of Urban Studies and Planning) 8 (January 2008).

August 24 SURF SAN FRANCISCO

178 The hotel pool was one of only two swimming pools in country on the historic registry: "Work of Art in Swimming Pool Gives Motel Owner a Deep Dip into Law," *Los Angeles Times*, May 10, 1990.

September 16 DENVER ENVY

193 Later I read about the Rocky Flats Nuclear Weapons facility: Kristen Iversen, *Full Body Burden: Growing Up in the Nuclear Shadow of Rocky Flats* (New York: Crown Publishers, 2012). the U.S. Fish and Wildlife Service made the controversial decision: Kieran Nicholson, "Nuclear Whiplash: Rocky Flats National Wildlife Refuge Opening Delayed, Then Reversed. Opens Saturday as Planned," *Denver Post*, September 14, 2018.

October 16 THE LEGEND OF RIVERBEND

208 oral history of Riverbend and the River Ramble: Charles Bethea, "Hoochie Koo! An Oral History of Riverbend, Atlanta's Most Notorious Singles Complex," *Atlanta Magazine*, November 2009.

October 18 THE BLUEST CREEK

211 The Parks Master Plan from 2010 prioritized swimming pools: Pond & Company, *City of East Point Parks and Recreation 10 Year Master Plan Update, 2011–2020* (East Point, GA: Pond & Company, 2010), 13.

215 Job opportunities like this made East Point the promised land: Lisa Shannon-Flagg, "'A Little Bit of Heaven': The Inception, Climax and Transformation of the East Washington Community in East Point, Georgia," (master's thesis, Georgia State University, 2008).

217 This was around the time I read Toni Morrison's *The Bluest Eye:* Toni Morrison, *The Bluest Eye* (New York: Vintage International, 1970).

October 23 CALLAWAY POOLS

220 a nostalgic column from the *LaGrange News:* Julia Dyar, "Memoried Glances: Callaway Education Association Closure End of Era," *LaGrange News*, June 23, 2017.

226 officially, it was the Callaway Educational Association: From the description of Callaway Educational Association records, [ca. 1920–92], (Troup County Archive), WorldCat record ID: 38727958, Social Networks and Archival Context (SNAC), https://snaccooperative.org/ark:/99166/w6j44ww3.

how the Callaway pool was a gift to the community but also a tool: Scott Smith, *Legacy: The Secret History of Proto-Fascism in America's Greatest Little City* (N.p.: CreateSpace, 2011).

November 7 FICTIONAL CHARACTERS

232   Didn't Walker Percy write about a country club in Druid Hills: Walker Percy, *The Last Gentleman* (New York: Farrar, Straus and Giroux, 1966).

233   We traded book recommendations: Janisse Ray, *Drifting into Darien: A Personal and Natural History of the Altamaha River* (Athens: University of Georgia Press, 2013).

December 15 COLD SPRINGS

242   According to historian Samuel Norris Thompson: Samuel N. Thompson, *A Historical Sketch of Pioneer Days* (East Point, GA: East Point Historical Society, 1984).

243   East Point historian Ina Hemperley Short wrote: Ina Hemperley Short, *As I Remember It* (East Point, GA: East Point Historical Society, 1987).

December 29 RACISM WITH NO RACISTS

247   I got a Lucia Berlin book for Christmas: Lucia Berlin, *Welcome Home: A Memoir with Selected Photographs and Letters* (New York: Farrar, Straus and Giroux, 2018).